The Westering Experience
in American Literature:

Bicentennial Essays

edited by Merrill Lewis
and L. L. Lee

Bureau for Faculty Research
Western Washington University
Bellingham, Washington

Acknowledgments

Frank Sadler's "The Frontier in Jack Spicer's 'Billy the Kid'" and Richard Cole's "North American Primer" appear in <u>Concerning Poetry</u>, Vol. 9, No. 2. Martin Bucco's "The East-West Theme in Dreiser's <u>An American Tragedy</u>" appears in <u>Western American Literature</u>, November, 1977.

PS
169
W4
W4

Copyright © 1977 by Merrill Lewis and L. L. Lee
Library of Congress Catalog Card Number 77-080814
International Standard Book Number 0-930216-01-6
Published by the Bureau for Faculty Research
Western Washington University
Printed in the United States of America

For

the Western Literature Association
and
J. Golden Taylor
first editor of Western American Literature
and Executive Secretary of the Western Literature Association

TABLE OF CONTENTS

vi

Preface

The idea for this collection of essays on the westering experience in American literature had its inception in the Fall of 1975 just as the nation was preparing to mark its two-hundredth birthday. Our object was not an unusual one: to collect some of the best and most representative criticisms of the bicentennial year in order to commemorate that occasion and to celebrate the activity of literary criticism itself. To demonstrate, in other words, that the well-being of the profession was interdependent with the intellectual well-being, intellectual awareness, of the country, and that occasions for celebrations and examinations were appropriate for both.

Most of the essays developed from papers read at the Eleventh Annual Conference of the Western Literature Association, hosted by the city of Bellingham and Western Washington University. Bellingham has its symbolism for the book, not just because it is nearly as far west--and north--as one can go in the forty-eight contiguous states. We are also next door to Canada and Canada too has its place in this book. Moreover, Bellingham is in an area richly endowed with place names given it by the English explorer, Captain George Vancouver: Whidbey (Island), Puget (Sound), (Mount) Rainier, (Port) Townsend, Georgia (Strait), etc. They are intermingled with earlier names from the age of Spanish exploration such as the Strait of Juan de Fuca (who may have been a Greek)--and with Indian names that remind us that the region had a history that antedates the age of European discovery.

There are names that link the region to the legends as well as to the history of the westering experience. Deception Pass was the name given to what was initially thought to be a large river flowing from the east--perhaps the outlet of the fabled Northwest Passage, the very aim of some of the first who explored the west side of the Atlantic. And appropriately, but also ironically, the town itself was named for Sir William Bellingham, Knight: "controller of the storekeeper's accounts of his Majesty's Navy," and provisioner of Vancouver's expedition, according to historian Edmond S. Meany. Bellingham, of course, never saw the place.

Beyond the constraints imposed by the theme, we expected the book to be shaped, as it was, by the collective nature of the enterprise. However, where we discovered lacunae following the initial screening of manuscripts, we solicited additional articles in order to fill them. There are still lacunae, some of them explained later. But there is a kind of over-view of American literature, extending from William Byrd II to Richard Hugo and offering both a broad geographic representation and a representation of types.

II

Innumerable critics have addressed themselves to the westering theme in eighteenth and nineteenth century American literature since Henry Nash Smith published his seminal _Virgin Land: The American West as Symbol and Myth_ in 1950. Most critics who in this volume write of that earlier literature do so selectively and with an eye towards arguing with and modifying what they perceive are the accepted critical opinions of that literature. In short, they are revisionist in spirit and conception. The fact that many of the essays examine the work of twentieth-century writers may indicate that the critics feel that there is little more to say about the westering theme in the work of such writers as Cooper, or Whitman, or Twain. But it may also suggest that many critics are more intrigued in the 1970s with the continuing interest in the western experience by modern writers--although the historical frontier is long since closed, its meaning is still alive. (We should add that, as for the treatment of the westering experience in the several _regions_ of the West, where any of these essays touch upon these experiences, none seriously modify the critical views of John T. Flanagan on the literature of the mid-West; of J. Frank Dobie on the life and literature of the Southwest; or of Franklin Walker on writing in California.)

Several essays do reflect the current interest in ethnic literature and ethnic experience. Jack Davis' essay, "W. Gilmore Simms' 'Oakatibbe' and the Failure of the Westering Imagination" is the most obvious example, showing as it does that the revisionist critic of the 1970s may interpret western writing more as rhetoric than as fiction--instructive rather than pleasureable, a venerable position to take which shows that revisionists may share something of "high seriousness" with Victorian critics. Carlota Cárdenas de Dwyer's essay explores the relationship between Chicano literature and the literature of the westering experience. So much new work is being done here (our own university publishes _The Journal of Ethnic Studies_) that our examples are mere tokens.

We had, too, originally intended to include several essays exploring the image of women and the work of women writers. But in this case the response to our request for papers was so overwhelming that we decided to collect these essays in a separate volume, _Women, Women Writers, and the West_, a book which will be published by the Whitston Publishing Company in 1978. Our most regretable lacuna is in articles that analyze the black treatment of the westering experience, say in the works of Ishmael Reed that make use of the motif.

The "discovery" of women and women writers and the "rediscovery" of the Indian in connection with the frontier experience are motivated by intellectual and social forces outside the westering experience itself. With two hundred years of history since the founding of the nation and well over two hundred years of literary treatment of the westering experience, there is much that ought to invite revision. While no one critic seems to directly use Harold Simonson's recent book, _The Closed Frontier: Studies in Literary Tragedy_, as a point of departure, still many writers and critics alike are preoccupied with the belief that the westering experience can no longer be seen with the innocent eyes that Americans seem to have seen it in the era of expansion. And so the spirit of revision is fed as much by changing perspectives as by the discovery of neglected writers or themes.

The critical spirit in these essays is still closer to Henry Nash Smith's than to Richard Slotkin's Regeneration Through Violence. But like Smith (whose book was certainly revisionist in its day) the writers of these essays do not see the significance of the westering experience in Turnerian terms as did, for example, Dorothy Dondore, Lucy Lockwood Hazard, or Percy H. Boynton, writing in 1926, 1927, and 1931 respectively. The shifting critical mood can be captured in the writers as well as in the critics: compare, say, Bishop George Berkeley's 1752 "Verses on the prospect of planting the arts and learning in America" with Richard Hugo's "Port Townsend, 1974." (Hugo's poem is discussed by William Lockwood in his essay on Hugo in this volume.)

III

Beyond revisionism, several other important implications emerge from the essays. The Prologue by Max Westbrook, the Epilogue by John Ditsky, and the three essays by Don Walker, Jack Brenner, and Richard Harrison show the complexities and largeness of the subject from a critical as well as a thematic perspective. Westbrook and Ditsky deliberately relate the subject of westering to the major streams of American thought and literature and build cases that should help remove any lingering doubts that westering is more than a regional and therefore provincial concern. Harrison compares and contrasts the treatment of the theme in Canadian and American writing by noting some basic contrasts in culture values. His essay leads to the essays in "Comparative Visions" which analyze the work of a few of the many Canadian writers who have explored the westering experience. While historians have been working with the study of comparative frontiers for some time, we think this is the first time studies of Canadian and American writers have been collected in such a book. But westering is North American, American, not just the experience of the United States.

The essays by Walker and Brenner mark a distinctive moment in western literary criticism. For years most literary historians and critics assumed that the imaginative writer and the historian were competing for the same territory. But historians began pointing out the disparity between fact and fiction, between myth and reality, in order to dissociate authentic historical study from fanciful make-believe. Walker, however, ends his essay by concluding that historians have given us less of the real cowboy than perhaps fiction writers have--in the sense that the writers of fiction have realized or made real their subject. In the sense that Walker refers to the "reality" of the writer, it is a creative act of the imagination, not an accident of history. And so he restates the case for fiction made by Henry James in "The Art of Fiction." Both wish to defend the imaginative construction called fiction or poetry: James in defense of the novel, Walker in defense of the western story. Then, as if

3

picking up the problem where Walker leaves it, Brenner argues persuasively that the reality of the western story is also a matter of style. The western writer not only creates a fictional world, related to but separate from historical reality, he creates a perception of things, an angle of vision that is unique. The style is the message? Not quite, but almost.

These two essays make the case not so much for the separation of history and fiction as they make the case that western fiction does not dumbly depend upon history for its power or pleasure. Fiction is not pseudo-history. Where fiction is historical, history cannot give it validity. Walker's method of reading literature should also be contrasted with Westbrook's, since the two kinds of criticism they practice are the two best available today. As Westbrook says elsewhere (in "The Ontological Critic"): "Theory is the study of essentials, not the study of characteristics." While he certainly does not ignore the reading of the individual poem or story, Westbrook's work is always concerned with essences--with the archetypal patterns. Walker, on the other hand, habitually works with cases, both real and hypothetical, and with those characteristics, Walker pursues the conscious possibilities of art; Westbrook pursues the unconscious possibilities. Walker's critical principles always allow him to discover writing that fails; Westbrook's principles allow him to identify writing that misses.

The examples of Brenner, Harrison, and Ditsky demonstrate, however, that there are other significant views of western criticism and western literature. The existence of their work in this collection gives readers one of the best and most representative collections of western literary criticism since the publication of Interpretive Approaches to Western American Literature (Idaho State University Press, 1972).

The other seventeen papers show, on the other hand, that more typically the critical act is the confrontation of a critic and a writer, or, that is, a reader and a text or texts. Generally the essay begins with a fresh explication and ends with some re-identification of the writer's peculiar genius and a re-affirmation of the writer's power to capture our imaginations.

IV

But in almost every case, the critic also feels compelled to address some subject other than the writer's work--a subject that lies behind it or embedded within it. And that is the westering experience itself. The journey to the West is after all an image behind the American experience, or, rather, the American dream. The dream did not involve simply the West itself, it must be remembered, but the movement towards something called the West--a movement in the direction of the West. The dream was to reach that West sometime and there to find out what the movement was all about: in Eden we can look back at time and explain it.

By the American dream, we mean the European-American dream, largely. And so, whatever else they propose to be and do, the essays in this volume are also examinations of the American dream, in much if not all of its

4

multiplicity, including possible endings of it, certainly of counter-dreams.

V

Ideas may lead somewhere, but the idea for this collection would have lead nowhere if the contributors themselves had not helped us to realize it. We also, though, must thank James W. Davis, Dean of the College of Arts and Sciences of Western Washington University, who gave financial support to the Conference and to the costs of editing this book; and to Jane Clark, Director of the WWU Bureau for Faculty Research, who enabled us to publish the results. Between them they have maintained the tradition of Bellingham as a generous "controller of the storekeeper's accounts" and "provisioner" for the venture.

Two students have given much time and intelligence to the volume. Debbie Daniels helped collect and prepare the manuscripts for publication, and Rob Stothart read proofs. We also want to thank Tom Lyon, editor of Western American Literature, and Richard Keller, editor of Heritage of Kansas: A Journal of the Great Plains, for their editorial good will.

Finally, our dedication marks the debt we owe the Western Literature Association and J. Golden Taylor, Executive Secretary of the Association and first editor of Western American Literature. The Association and Professor Taylor have contributed immeasurably to the intellectual atmosphere that made the venture possible.

Merrill Lewis
L. L. Lee
Western Washington University

PROLOGUE

MOUNTAIN HOME: THE HERO IN THE AMERICAN WEST

by Max Westbrook

Revolution is a dangerous thing and should not be undertaken lightly, even when the cause is just. The revolution may fail, driving the established government to harsh reactions in the name of loyalty and security. If virtue does triumph on the battlefield, the cause may be lost in the political struggles that follow. The new government could be worse than the old. The human price may put to shame a small gain in justice. Even if all goes well and the price is accommodated by political grace, the terrifying implication of revolution is that human beings are above the law, that all are invited to rebel when they disapprove the existing government.

Being fully aware of the odds against military success and the probability that rebellion would lead to endless war, many of the leaders in Colonial America were reluctant. Benjamin Franklin was in England for 16 years working for peace, and he worked so hard that he lost, for a time, his good standing with the people he represented. And the Continental Congress itself, in the midst of fire and patriotism, appointed a peace commission as late as 1775.[1]

Against all odds, the dangerous game was won. The enemy was superior in numbers, wealth, weapons, and training; but we won. And the high moral risk did not lead to a terrifying sequence of civil wars. Thus we Americans, 200 years later, like to tell the story again, to celebrate the story, and--most of all--to see the achievement repeated in specific events; for this shows that what we admire about the birth of our nation is not merely a worship of the past but is, rather, a moral achievement that has become part of our national character. We like to hear stories of local rebellion against tyranny, stories which confirm once more that human beings can go beyond the existing form or face of law and achieve the real law of a higher justice.

One way to tell this story is to write of the hero in the American West. The characteristic themes of the American West are not exclusive property, of course. The spirit of Westering can be found in the East, the South, Canada, Australia, and, I suppose, all over the world. It's the same with the hero, who comes in staggering varieties, who is always changing, and who is usually a fascinating and puzzling combination of the local and the universal. Thus I am not making any claims that are supposed to be exhaustive or inclusive or exclusive. I am concerned with a tracer, a pattern, a connection between one type of Western American hero and the story of the American Revolution. Briefly stated, this pattern is a devotion to values that are beyond the law, located, somehow, in nature. In the West, a typical source is the hero's experience with original creation; and political justice may be thematic or ancillary rather than ontological. Still, the connections are too clear and strong to be accidental.

9

Essentially, the **Declaration** of Independence is based on the assertion that civil rights are unalienable, but according to whom, by what evidence? Thomas Jefferson said that civil rights reside in nature, a claim not grounded in fact, in a coherent philosophy, or in nature. [2] Later, scholars began to study a problem that is central to the Constitution: the will of the people is said to be the ultimate authority; but it is clear that a majority vote requiring--for example--segregation by race would not make segregation right or constitutional. What, then, is the source, the rationale for the act of rebellion and for the Bill of Rights?

One direction among partial explanations, I feel, is that the Constitution appeals to a higher truth (which cannot be reduced to law) as the rationale for a lesser law (which can be written down). Clearly, Jefferson and the Deists had something like this in mind when they appealed to nature as the source of civil rights. They were talking, in their 18th century language of reason and practicality, about God. Clearly, from Jonathan Edwards to Ralph Waldo Emerson, many of our early leaders were seeking a truth beyond words. That problem of the intellect--like our paradoxical love of law and bandits--is well known; but what does this have to do with theories of the hero in the American West?

Both the history and the literature of the American West warn against what I'm doing. Repeatedly, the West is the place where people are purged of theories and restored to the healthy exercise of practical action, or else. Granting the importance of this emphasis, the challenge is to understand a devotion to practicality; for, certainly, it is not a simple-minded devotion. Note, for example, the end of Jack Schaefer's most famous novel, Shane. Marian Starrett says that Shane is "not gone. He's here, in this place, in this place he gave us. He's all around us and in us, and he always will be." Bobby, in an afterword, says that his "mother was right. He [Shane] was there. He was there in our place and in us. Whenever I needed him, he was there. I could close my eyes and he would be with me and I would see him plain and hear again that gentle voice." [3] I don't see Shane as the Jesus-Militant, but the Biblical style and the appeal to higher values are clear; and they cannot be dismissed on the grounds that the story is seen through the glory-filled eyes of a little boy. Bobby is older now, writing after the event; and his experience, the style, and Marian's testimony all suggest that the higher values associated with Shane are not to be discounted as the illusions of a child.

Or what would most people think if you told them that the Virginian--the number one he-man cowboy hero of the Protestant Ethic version of the American West--killed his villain as the mystic instrument of a higher justice, was a nudist, and--before he became a hard-driving business man--a pantheist? Here is the description of the climactic shoot-out:

> A wind seemed to blow his sleeve off his arm, and he replied to it, and saw Trampas pitch forward. He saw Trampas raise his arm from the ground and fall again, and lie there this time, still. A little smoke was rising from the pistol on the ground, and he looked at his own, and saw the smoke flowing upward out of it. [4]

You have to read carefully to see that the Virginian's gun has fired twice, although our practical man of action merely sees Trampas rise and fall, as if he himself had nothing to do with it, but were merely an instrument. A moment later, when the Virginian examines Trampas, he says, "Both of mine hit," which means that, as he consciously watched Trampas rise, his mystic pistol aimed and fired.

It is this same All-American hero who has long had a special place in the mountains, a secret island. Upon arriving there alone, he recalls, he "would ford to the sheltered circle of his camp-ground, throw off the saddle and blanket from the horse's hot, wet back, throw his own clothes off, and, shouting, spring upon the horse bare, and with a rope for a bridle, cross with him to the promised pasture." This time, having come to the island with his new bride, the Virginian reveals some of his inner thoughts: "'Often when I have camped here, it has made me want to become the ground, become the water, become the trees, mix with the whole thing. Not know myself from it. Never unmix again.'"[5]

And the Virginian, remember, is a man who has been with prostitutes and who is calmly efficient on the range, in a tense barroom confrontation, and in business. Now it is not my intention to make fun of the character or the novel, or to suggest that the Virginian is a doctrinaire mystic, nudist, or pantheist. The Virginian is devoted to the practical values of the Protestant Ethic, and the most significant instance of his appealing to a higher law is his attempt to justify the lynching of cattle rustlers. But the fact remains that the source of the Virginian's practical values is a covert belief in higher values--associated with nature and with the spiritual -- which are quite different from the clear code which guides his everyday life.

If we recall that decadence is defined in The Virginian as the disassociation of merit and rank, some interesting implications are suggested.[6] Democracy calls for equal opportunity and earned wealth, but the rationale of equality is believed covertly or is expressed in some very impractical language in the formal moment of the Constitution. The Virginian, who embodies so well the American myth of practical success, celebrates his inner beliefs when no one is watching or when alone with his new bride at a sacred place and time. Possible connections with the theme of nostalgia are also interesting. Granted, nostalgia for a primal West that is now ended is an important theme in Western American literature; but that may not be the whole story. Nostalgia, after all, does not fuel a people to energy, celebration, or repetition. And the Westward movement was forward-moving, forward looking, clearly a part of the initial plan of American democracy. In this context, nostalgia might have a relation to the original creation (the source of unalienable rights) and thus include but go beyond the more personalized stage of history associated with the literal frontier.

In terms of the hero, the most reliable sign of connections such as these seems to be the mountain. Some of the heroes I have in mind are actual mountaineers. Most are not. But all of them have at least a metaphorical home in the mountains, that is, a home elsewhere, removed from society and close to

11

the gods. They have a home there in the sense that something happened which made them different. In the ancient and classical tradition of heroes, they have had a second birth, or an experience which changed them, and they can never be the same again. Basically, this hero has seen God, or had a vision, or experienced the original creation. Nature, afterwards, is not a symbol of God. Nature is God's personal and immediate hand alive and at work.

The experience I wish to describe, metaphorically, as the mountain home is not accurately designated as mystic or sentimental, as psychic or nostalgic. A longing to see God's creation again is not the same as nostalgia for a former time in history. The hero has seen some part of reality itself, not as a theory about reality but as a personal confrontation with the ultimate. Wakan is an Indian word for this special experience.[7] Another appropriate term is figura, the concrete instance in which the real and the actual are one and are available to sight and perhaps to touch. The experience of the mountain home, of the original creation, goes beyond the categories of the ordinary eye but carries its own conviction. For those who have not had such an experience, explanations tend to arouse impatience.

Many Western American heroes, in fact, operate in a time and place alien to the sacred moment; but if the culture is friendly, there is a striking sign of the nature of the mountain experience: the categories of the intellect become united. What, for example, would you call John G. Neihardt's Black Elk Speaks? The book will hold up quite well if you read it as literary art or history, religion or philosophy; and the same applies to the mythology of ancient Athens. A story about the gods, for the Athenean believer, was art, history, religion, and philosophy . . . all in one. The separation came later, after civilization lost the sense of the original creation, the sense of living in God's personal world.

In Athens, in the time of Beowulf, in the time of the American Indian, people lived in a world different in kind from the world of today. People had a sense of having been made by God and placed on a land made by God. Consider Beowulf. If Grendel is busy at slaughter, on a regular schedule, why do the guards go to sleep? How do you account for the strange manner of Grendel's coming, his emergence into the mead hall in the way that a monster comes to you in a dream? Hrothgar and his troops, it is clear, are guilty of moral negligence; and if you live in God's immediate world evil is not sociological, not something you can stop by the good management of guard duty. Evil, rather, is personal, direct, immediate, as much intrinsic as extrinsic. In the same way, a tree, to the American Indian, was not a thing of nature, that is, a symbol of an intellectual abstraction; it was God's tree. Chief Weninock described it this way:

> God created the Indian country and. . . He put the Indians on
> it. . . . God created fish in this river and put deer in the
> mountains and made laws through which has come the increase
> of fish and game. Then the Creator gave us Indians life; we
> walked, and as soon as we saw the game and fish we knew they
> were made for us. . . . I was not brought from a foreign coun-
> try and did not come here. I was put here by the Creator.[8]

The Indian, remember, had no Sunday and said he needed none; for he walked, each day, on God's world. And this is what he meant when he used dead wood for his fires and apologized to the deer before shooting it.

For such people, a story about what happened (history) was the story of religion (God) and also truth (philosophy) and at the same time a drama of the concrete universal (literature). As Western Civilization grew, this immediate sense of God's hand began to dull and fade before the constant presence of streets, buildings, institutions, bureaucracy, committees, representatives, intermediaries, processes, of kings and priests and motor cars. Man became a social creature, that is, born of society, touching society instead of God's earth, no longer exercising the senses by touching the naked flesh to the original creation. God became second-hand, symbolic, alive only for a set time, in a certain building, on a fixed day.

Numerous characteristics of the hero suggest the connection I am trying to establish, the comparable dependence of the American Constitution and the Western hero on a sense of the original creation; but five of these strike me as having a special interest and importance.

First, the type of hero I have in mind is both abstracted and alert. This is an unusual combination, an apparent contradiction. But Cain Hammett, the hero of Manfred's Riders of Judgment, is first seen riding down from the mountains, lost in thought, feeling poetic and philosophical about this high land he loves; and yet he is instantly alert to danger. It is the same with Dick Summers in A. B. Guthrie, Jr.'s The Way West. Summers gazes off into the distance, longing for the mountain life he had known at an earlier time; and yet he is instantly alert to danger. Shane too gazes at the mountains, as if to gather strength there, like some demi-god born of mixed parentage; and yet he praises Bobby for being alert and is almost preternaturally alert himself. The Virginian is also capable of withdrawing into deep thought, and yet seeing, at the same time, everything that goes on around him. Maria, in Frank Waters' People of the Valley, shares this and other qualities with the hero I am talking about; she is often removed from her followers, even contemptuously removed, but she sees more than anyone. Art Bridges, in Walter Clark's The Track of the Cat, has lost the ability to "come and go" between these two conditions, and the loss gets him killed. Among American Indian heroes, the combination of being both abstracted and alert is so recurrent that it could almost be called a character- istic of the race.

The implication is that abstraction and alertness are in allegiance, that one somehow helps the other. But how can abstraction be a source of alert- ness? Jefferson's appeal, it is now appropriate to recall, was not to a rational theory but to the thing itself, to nature, to reality, to values felt to reside in nature. Now an abstracted contemplation of a theory does militate against alertness to the actual world; but if you are lost in thought about that which is Wakan, about a land you see as having been made by God, then the appearance of abstraction may simply be alertness to the actual world, that is, a type of alertness more profound than the usual. When the Western hero reads signs, he is reading also the higher reality, for he lives in a world in which religion

13

and philosophy, literature and history are all one. To examine God's tree is to examine God. As the center falls apart, when the nation's hoop is broken, this becomes difficult to do (which is Art Bridges' problem) and, finally, impossible to do. And so it is that there comes, from time to time, a person who still has that original sense of unity; and this person therefore has the capacity to become a hero or heroine, but not the capacity to become domestic--in most cases--for the sacred experience has doomed the hero to a home elsewhere.

The second characteristic reveals in a more obvious way the national relevance of the Western hero. Again, the case is mixed, but that's a strength to the story, not a weakness. The Western hero with an allegiance to a metaphorical mountain home often finds himself acting above the law for what he believes to be a just cause. Examples vary from Vardis Fisher's Sam Minard, in Mountain Man, to Eugene Manlove Rhodes' Paso Por Aqui. Sam is more characteristic in his deep love of the original creation, but Ross McEwen is more characteristic in that he becomes an exception to the law because of his total and immediate selflessness. Another strain is represented by Shane's reluctance to take up his pistol again. Shane allows himself to be insulted, delays until Ernie Wright has been killed, and even then does not return to the warrior role until it is clear that Joe Starrett is determined to face Wilson in a gun fight. In other variations, Cain Hammett is reluctant to the point of culpability and even death; the Virginian consults church and state, his girl and his own conscience, and clearly would prefer to avoid violence; Dick Summers is restrained to the point of lethargy; and Maria, though her words are often sharp enough to draw blood, refuses the climactic confrontation and settles for a compromise.

The causes of restraint, obviously, include human decency, common sense, and the realization that violence as a policy is impractical. But the personality of the Western hero includes other dimensions. The hero of mythic powers, for example, knows that superior strength must be exercised with extreme caution. This is perhaps most obvious in the case of Shane, who is a gentle and celibate lover, but who is capable of calling up and putting to use a prowess that is frightening to behold. Ross McEwen is domesticated and lacks the sacred touch, but the appeal of his story is to a higher law which justifies breaking the lesser or codified law. In addition, Rhodes makes it clear that obedience to the codified law, in this instance, would be associated with the decadence of civilization's finery.

The third characteristic is that the personality which results from mountain values is often characterized by a presence, a bearing that is immediately recognized. This is clear when Dick Summers tells Tolty the mule-trader to "take it easy," when Flood and Hames confront the illegal trail-cutters in Andy Adams' The Log of a Cowboy, [10] and when the Virginian appears before anyone except a fool. Shane, of course, as the mythic version of the mountain hero, appears with a presence that brings fear; and Maria's followers often stand aside in awe, afraid even to speak to her. From the domestic to the more purely mythic or sacred, the connection is that those who have touched the original are different, and their difference can be recognized. You can make a fool of a man who has a second or third hand notion of what is right, just as you can talk political flim-flam and have it carry weight with people who have a second-hand knowledge of natural rights. But when you confront the hero who is in league with the original creation, the puncturing of falsity is brief and certain.

The fourth characteristic is one that is common in religion and in primal cultures: the Western hero often has an unusual capacity to listen. In a practical sense, you have a better chance to survive in a desert or mountain if you are quiet rather than talkative, but everything depends on the type of world you are listening to. Little Bear, in Jack Schaefer's The Canyon, is fascinated when he discovers a sleeping badger. Badgers, he knows, have "many powers and strong medicine." They are "wise" and should be approached with respect. Little Bear waits until the badger awakens, and then he says, "'Oh badger, speak to me.'" Schaefer is working with the skill of a con man, just here, and I mean that as a compliment. Note the expectations of the reader and how they are played with. Surely the reader is prepared for one of two reactions: the badger will speak, in some fashion, in which case, for most, the story is unrealistic; or the badger will run away, in which case, for most readers, the story is probably a realistic study of a superstitious Indian who doesn't know that badgers can't talk. Now the next sentence, after Little Bear says "Speak to me," is this: "It jumped from the stone and was gone." So the reader can relax, knowing that he is in his own familiar world and not wasting his time. And the next lines confirm this reaction: Little Bear thinks a long time and concludes that "He had been wrong. A man should not speak to a badger." A reader who lacks a sense of the sacred world is now content, and also hooked, for Schaefer has set him up for the sting: "A man should not speak to a badger," Little Bear decides, because "It knew what was in his mind without his speaking. He should wait for it to speak."[11]

Exactly. You do not use the intellect to initiate contact with God's world. You shut your mouth and you listen and then, with a good soul and a little luck, some part of God's world may speak to you. Always, the practical side is there, receiving its due: if you listen, you have a better chance to hear the onrush of a Spring flood, the sound of game you are hunting, the small possible noise of an enemy waiting in the bush. But for the hero with a sense of original creation, the practical and the sacred are not in conflict. They are one, as Manfred shows with such high good humor in Manly-Hearted Woman; and they are one in such wholesome community that the objects and officers or original creation--helper, badger, sign--can have a poor batting average without jeopardy to faith.

The fifth characteristic of the hero of the mountain home is that his school is unaccommodated nature, but the lesson is a sophisticated morality of the type represented by the American Constitution and the Bill of Rights. Sam Minard wages bloody war on an entire nation, but he sees in the face of a young Indian a lesson in brotherhood that would satisfy Immanuel Kant. Hugh Glass crawls on the earth, planning revenge, and learns about forgiveness. Little Bear--probably with the aid of a detachment caused by his physique and his family circumstances--learns that it is wrong to kill for sport. Maria, as a child, has acquired wisdom; but she "never suspected it was philosophy. She only

15

thought that she was learning about goats."[12] Of course, there is no guarantee, as we see in Guthrie's The Big Sky. The majority, in fact, can walk in the original creation and not learn much of anything at all. But the hero--Dick Summers, the Virginian, and the rest--can learn humanistic values from the original source.

One type of Western hero, then, derives his personality from a sense of the original creation and does so in a way that is relevant to the founding of the nation. Included in this paradigmatic story is a very poignant problem which is also relevant to the nation: if you have seen God at work, you have seen something of the truth, but what do you do about it? On the national level, the problem shapes up this way: this eminently practical and anti-intellectual nation is guided by a philosophical document. Our national character features know-how, action, work, evidence, results, and a clear preference for John Wayne. Such a people would seem to want a practical constitution, a how-to-do-it list of laws of specific detail, which, in fact, is the nature of the state constitutions I have seen. The national constitution, however, is a splendid statement of political principles. On the Western frontier, the problem may be represented by Sam Minard, Little Bear, Dick Summers, Cain Hammett, the Virginian, Shane, and others who saw the truth of God by some natural means but were then forced--in spite of their splendid abilities--to compromise or to defeat. Black Elk, of course, is the most poignant example. His vision was not a child's dream, an Indian imagination running wild and lost in savage superstitions. Black Elk, to put it bluntly, saw the truth. His rebirth, his home in the mountain, was so close to God and God's truth that, as a mere human being, he was incapacitated from action. Black Elk asked, repeatedly, What should I do? How should I use my vision? How can I restore the nation's hoop?[13]

Like Sam Minard, he cannot forget the symphony of God in which he has lived. Dick Summers cannot adjust down from God's glorious mountain world to the merely social world of human beings. Shane cannot become a homesteader but, like Black Elk, is doomed to use his power in the aid of a few individuals. And, in variations on a paradigm, Maria and the Virginian--for something like opposite reasons--learn to compromise.

Perhaps the chief importance of this American and Western hero is that he does perform one of the essential tasks of the classical hero: in having touched the original creation, the hero reminds the best of sociological people --Lige Evans, Joe Starrett--that the spiritual values most of us accept on faith do enjoy, after all, a physical existence as the energy of the world and as the potential energy of our own depressed lives. And perhaps the chief relevance of this story to our own dark day is that Black Elk is not alone. We have all read the Constitution, a merely political vision, granted, but nonetheless a very fine political vision. Most of us know something about a religion and have been moved. Most of us have touched at least a second-hand nature. But what do we do?[14]

If one essential American hero is the person who can go beyond the codified law to a higher law, in repetition of the original revolution, then perhaps we know the real damage of Richard Nixon's perfidy. A crook merely violates the codified law; but American leaders need to exercise authority with restraint, and if they decide that circumstances warrant an appeal to higher law--Lincoln's Emancipation Proclamation, for example--they have to be right, or the nation suffers.

It is equally important to remember that Maria liked to stand on the sidelines, offering her frightful silence, an occasional and fierce oracle, but refusing to get out in front and say "Follow me, my children." Dick Summers too stood on the edges, supporting Lige Evans but refusing to take the lead himself. Even Shane waited as long as he could for the homesteaders to do it themselves and, when forced to get out front, did his job and left immediately. The story is clear, and those of us who blame our leaders for national failures in civil rights, Vietnam, and Watergate must remember that our leaders won their offices by appealing to us in the name of segregation, the non-right to smoke marijuana, and the need to get the communists. Perhaps we need to remember, most of all, that Lige Evans could tell the difference between Tadlock and Dick Summers; Joe Starrett knew the difference between Fletcher and Shane. American democracy, in terms of the mountain home, is a story of paradigms in tension: the rights of the individual, the necessity of working together, the mythic rationale of original creation, and the occasional hero who may remind us once again that virtue, in a democracy, is voluntary.

University of Texas - Austin

NOTES

[1] See, for example, Samuel Eliot Morison, The Oxford History of the American People (New York: Oxford University Press), 1965, pp. 210, 218, 270-71.

[2] Jefferson appealed to an innate moral sense, utilitarianism, natural rights, and ethical relativism. He did not develop a philosophy which could house such diversity.

[3] Jack Schaefer, Shane, chapters 15 and 16.

[4] Owen Wister, The Virginian, chapter 35.

[5] Ibid., chapter 36.

[6] Ibid., chapter 13.

[7] See, for example, Sword, through J. R. Walker, "Oglala Metaphysics," in Dennis Tedlock and Barbara Tedlock, editors, Teachings from the American Earth (New York: Liveright), 1975, pp. 205-07.

[8] T. C. McLuhan, compiler, Touch the Earth: A Self-Portrait of Indian Existence (New York: Promontory Press), 1971, p. 10.

[9] Ibid., p. 15

[10] A. B. Guthrie, Jr., The Way West, chapter two; Andy Adams, The Log of a Cowboy, chapter seven.

[11] Jack Schaefer, The Canyon, chapter three.

[12] Frank Waters, People of the Valley, chapter two.

[13]It should be noted that before the white man came, the Indian with a vision was expected to act and did act. See, for example, Tedlock and Tedlock, p. 150.

[14]The recurrence of this theme in traditional American literature is widespread, but see, especially, Herman Melville's concept of the "Divine Inert" in Moby Dick, chapter XXXIII.

Richard Cole

North American Primer

Ted and Nick are friends
Waiting on an Adirondack shore
For the secret call of Lone Eagle.
The boys have grown up together,

Silhouetted against the grandest
Mohican sunset you ever saw,
A comfort of red and yellow ink
Blazing across the full page illustration.

Admittedly they are patient,
Gazing at a distant squiggle of pine
And casually hold a yachting pose
Imported from an ideal England

Of lean jaws, an aquiline nose
And the sloe velvet eyes of a Gibson girl.
Yet they bear a warrior's heritage
Earned beside their cunning instructor,

Lone Eagle, trapper and sometime scout
Who has taught them his tribal wisdom,
The long myths, the words for legend,
The tale of Edward, nervous wolf-child,

Who roamed aloud in the forests
Until he was captured and died;
Has taught them wilderness skills as well,
Setting snares, preserving the game,

Or fashioning a willow whistle,
Bark delicately tapped loose
And sloughed from the heartwood
To wake them out of an Autumn vigil.

And he will teach them in time
What he knows of the future with words
So grave, so musically simple,
As if the forests went on forever,

As if they were Indians listening
To whatever a man could find to say
As he watches the falling peace of evening
Brighten the page of a boy's new world.

CRITICAL
PERSPECTIVES

WHO IS GOING TO RIDE POINT ?

by Don D. Walker

Old cattleman: "I know you can get those cows to Abilene, but goddamnit that's not where we want to go."

Nobody, so far as I know, has ever tried to get all of the Westerns of the world into one library. For the bibliographer and book collector it would be a formidable task indeed. There is first of all the matter of breed. Somehow the powers that be never got around to telling Calliope or whoever runs the Western show exactly what the conformation ought to be. And if there is an ideal Western up there in Plato's place, it seems to have, from down here at least, a dozen different shapes and sizes. Some will say The Prairie is a Western; some will say it isn't. Some will say The Last Picture Show is a Western; some will say it isn't. An old rancher friend of mine, his eyes and mind conditioned by fifty years of Herefords, studies a Limousin standing wheat yellow among the sagebrush. "I'm not sure," he finally says, "whether that's a beef cow or some other thing that just happens to eat grass."

Then there is the matter of numbers. For well over a century Westerns have been coming out of the publishers' chutes in undiminished regularity. If it is a mixed bunch, it adds up nevertheless to an impressive statistical figure. Borrowing an easy rough way of counting from Shanghai Pierce, one might sing out, "Just an even million." It would be hyperbole of course, and even the greenhorn bibliographers are likely to say, "Seems a bit high," but there is a symbolic rightness in it. Give or take a few thousand, the final tally is clearly over there on the bigger side.

However, as the poet who sold only one copy of his collected works observed, numbers don't really matter. It's literature, not paper, we're talking about. So the question narrows: how many of all this bunch of books are literature, not merely Westerns but Western literature ? If we cut out the good stuff, will we have enough to fill a stack or two ?

Again the critics will cuss and chew. Let's keep Andy Adams and Gene Rhodes, and leave out Owen Wister, who was after all only an Eastern dude. Owen may have been a friend of Henry James, but he sure as hell didn't know much about taking care of cows. Let's leave out The Log of a Cowboy and put in The Virginian. Wister may not have known much about cows, but at least he could tell a novel from a neck yoke. Let's keep North of 36. Anybody, even Miss Tasie, who comes from Texas and owns all those cows, has got to be as genuine as a hand-made boot. But let's not put in The Drovers. Even with all those cows and self-reliant men and impending tragedy, what does it have to do with getting the herd to Abilene or Dodge ?

23

What survives this regional shoot-out among critics is further decimated, if not wholly wiped out, by the judgments of national scholars and editors. In any standard anthology of American literature, how many selections can be said to come from Western literature?[1] In any standard department of English in an American university, how many of the following writers are regarded as important, if not major, American literary artists: Wister, Adams, Rhodes, Harvey Fergusson, Paul Horgan, Thomas Hornsby Ferril, Walter Clark, A. B. Guthrie, and Frederick Manfred? And if some of the works of some of these writers win a silent respect, if not a place on a reading list, a vast accumulation of Westerns still seems to litter our cultural home land. Beyond providing entertainment, escape, a macho fantasy, perhaps an index to popular myths and dreams, in the wisdom of the higher critics these many books hold little worth. At best they are a part of popular culture; at worst they are a paper garbage.

To the Western writer and scholar, the word comes harshly. He believes that some of the higher critics may be Eastern snobs, but he knows too, in his own critical honesty, that Western literature truly does not yet deserve to loom large in classic American letters. His own list of the good, if not great, will be longer than the lists, if any, descending from the Eastern seminaries of learning; but even his own list will be short. For he knows that the proportion of distinguished to undistinguished remains small indeed.

He hears some of the wise ones say that the trouble lies in the West itself, that the materials themselves are deficient in possible greatness. Cowboys are dumb, cows are dumber, and women don't even belong there. No society, no traditions, no history except the chasing and being chased by Indians. It all amounts to a game which we all played out in our childhood. It is of course very clever to put it this way, and we snigger inwardly at our seriousness. And yet the Western writer and scholar does not really believe these wise ones. He knows that the West itself is not to blame. The failure is ours, not the land's. In spite of a century and a half of exploring, trail building, and mapping the unknown canyons of a thousand hills, we have not yet found the certain literary way.

What is it, in our deepest convictions, that we seek to do? Where is it, as literary artists, that we seek to go? One kind of simple answer sometimes given is that the Western writer seeks to tell the truth about the West. Another is that he wishes to tell the real story of the West. The real story will of course be a truthful story. The magical word, in what sometimes seems a magical land, has become reality. The scholar observes that "the image violates reality,"[2] and we feel that a critical blow has left us a lifeless literary body. For however pretty they may be, images that violate reality are valueless as plastic butterflies.[3]

Thus, like so many before us in other lands and times, we are on a quest for Truth and Reality. How shall we find them on the prairies, the deserts, and the mountains of the West? And, to use an old Western metaphor, who among us is going to ride point?

Since the West in Western has usually been regarded as the historical **West,** one persistent definition of reality has been the historian's: the way things actually were. For three-quarters of a century, eminent men of the literary saddle have been insisting that Western literature, whether history or fiction, should tell us how it actually was along the beaver streams and across the ranges of the American West. Webb, Dobie, DeVoto, Hutchinson, and Dale, they have ridden well. They have shown a Western self-assurance in the way they have sat their saddles. As any literary pilgrim might well say, how can we get lost when these men are leading the way?

Lifelong, dedicated students of the West, they have believed they have known its realities. As historians, they have sought to present these realities in their accounts of the fur and the cattle trades. As literary critics, they have measured literary worth with these same realities. "In many cases," wrote Edward Everett Dale, imaginative writers "have had little conception of the real conditions of ranch life."[4] A history like Fifty Years on the Owl Hoot Trail "gives to the reader a more authentic understanding of ranch life and the social history of the American frontier than he is likely ever to get from fiction or so-called 'Westerns.'"[5] Unlike the cowboys of popular Westerns, J. Frank Dobie's cow people were, he claimed, "out of reality."[6] The praise for Andy Adams and Gene Rhodes echoes around the camp. Adams knew how it actually was on the long trail northward; Rhodes knew how it actually was on the ranges of New Mexico.[7] No need for talk about style and form and theme when so much Western truth is there for the taking.

So let us for a time suppose that the historian is right, that a literature needs to start with a real, an authentic understanding of range life. Let us follow the historian to the way things actually were. As believers in the literary potential of the cowboy, we are eager to set out to discover his reality. Putting aside all dreams and false romantic notions, we are earnestly waiting to confront the truth, to see and smell and taste the facts of cowboy life.

Unfortunately we soon discover that the historian rides a curiously timid and self-contained point. If we had supposed that historical actuality is back there, hard, open, demanding to dictate its own reality and that the historian would show us how we must give ourselves to it, we have been misled. For in the name of a history of the way things really were, we are actually tip-toeing across the grasslands. Is that a historical realist up front in the saddle?

Consider two instances of this reticence on the range. In the early 1880s, after miles of barbed wire had begun to end the so-called freedom of the ranges, fence cutting disputes, even little wars, broke out. Stern warnings appeared on fences both legal and illegal. The historian, to learn the nature of these warnings, has invariably gone to one source, a report by George W. Fairfield printed in the U.S. House Executive Documents. "Upon their fences," wrote Fairfield, "they have posted at intervals notices as follows: 'The son of a bitch who opens the fence had better look out for his scalp.'"[8] This was 1885, but an official government document had boldly led us right up to the fence itself.

Then came the historians, who said, there is the fence, but don't look too close-ly at it. Writing in the <u>American Historical Review</u>, Frederick L. Paxson made the notice read: "The . . . who opens the fence had better look out for his scalp."[9] Louis Pelzer bowdlerized its reality to "Notices were posted fre-quently bearing vile, canine names and warning anyone opening the fence to 'look out for his scalp.'"[10] In dealing with another historical situation, Carl Coke Rister alluded to the same canine epithet and avoided it with tortured ele-gance: "The etiquette of prairie life . . . absolutely forbade the use of a cer-tain form of malediction, which, while calling down divine punishment on the person addressed, cast an unwarrantable imputation on the character of his mother."[11]

The literary traveler in the West knows of course that historical realism does not require the blunt naming of every Western epithet and malediction. Still the historian's circumlocutions betray a curious timidity. In this instance he cannot really present the intensity of the historical moment without being ful-ly explicit. William Dean Howells put limits upon American literary realism because he was concerned about the delicate sensibilities of the young ladies who were reading the new novels. But cow history, one supposes, has had a different audience: A few cattlemen are interested in history; a few professors are interested in the history of cows and cowboys. If these are the readers, what are we worrying about? Cattlemen have heard the epithets without undue shock. Can it be the professors whom we are protecting?

Consider another bit of historical realism. A standard complaint about the cowboy in fiction is that he does almost no cow work. The real cowboy, we are told, was different. "The keynote of . . . [his] existence," wrote Philip Ashton Rollins, "was hard work."[12] "What cowboys did best and most," said Gene Rhodes, "was to work the cattle."[13] Dobie hoped he was writing of cow people "true to life and occupation," the occupation of course being cow work.[14]

One might suppose, then, that the historians, grasping the whole of real-ity, would have presented the whole of a cowboy's work. An abundance of writ-ing details the work of the "picturesque" or "interesting" or "colorful" round-ups (the adjectives are the historians', not the poets'), but in most of this his-tory we are left with a curious, almost miraculous transformation. Thousands of little bulls are dragged to the branding fire, to be turned loose as thousands of little steers. What strange work has happened? As readers we have not been allowed to see behind the gentle veil of dust and smoke. Theodore Roosevelt, in an early account, rendered the scene in this way: "The ropers, spurring and checking the fierce little horses, drag the calves up so quickly that a dozen men can hardly hold them; the men with the irons, blackened with soot, run to and fro; the calf-wrestlers, grimy with blood, dust, and sweat, work like beavers; while with the voice of a stentor the tallyman shouts out the number and sex of each calf."[15] Roosevelt, as everyone knows, did not object to blood, but he wasn't much for explaining its presence. Still perhaps we can excuse him; cow history was almost certainly genteel in his day. However, by the 1920s a less taboo-dominated culture was emerging; clinical details were beginning to show up in all sorts of literary texts. Why not in histories of the cowboy? In Rollins'

The <u>Cowboy</u>, the unbranded animals "were not only branded, but also treated to such surgery, if any, as might be necessary."[16] In Douglas Branch's <u>The Cowboy</u> and His <u>Interpreters</u>, the bellowing of the cows is "matched by the raucous shouts and the fervid swearing of men running about stripped to the waist and smeared with blood and dust, branding-iron and knife in hand."[17] In Raine and Barnes' <u>Cattle</u>, "the dogie is stretched taut, and a red-hot iron applied. The acrid smell of burning hair and flesh arises. Ears are slit. The calf struggles to its feet, shakes itself, and runs blatting to the mother."[18] So we have knives, surgery, slit ears. That seems to cover it, except that we still don't really know how those thousand little bulls became a thousand little steers.

One further instance needs to be added, this in a work by an English observer published in 1882. One might put it aside as a shorthorn note with the peculiarities of British usage were it not for the fact that a distinguished Western historian insisted that the Englishman's "accounts are faithful mirrors of the West."[19] So far as I know, it is the only version of this bit of cowboy work in which the cowboy starts with a steer and ends up with a bull. "Equally easily is the strong steer thrown, for in the hands of the trained cowboy the lariat is a dangerous tool. The loop about the neck, or over one or both hind legs, about the body, or over one foreleg . . . and the powerful bull lies prostrate and helpless on the ground . . . ."[20]

Let us, however, put aside epithets and surgery. If there is a genteel timidity here, perhaps the critic makes too much of it. It is only because the historian has sometimes seemed to claim a monopoly on reality, insisting that he has the facts of cowboy life while fiction is blurred and soft with romanticism, that the literary critic so doggedly works this ground. So let us allow the historian-critic his own way to what is important in cowboy life.

The cowboys of popular Westerns, wrote Dobie, "have never known humanity, sucking calves, before-daylight freshness, evening shadows."[21] In another context he complained about the neglect of screwworms. "Cattlemen," he observed, "have probably lost a thousand times more cattle to screwworms than to cow thieves, but cow thieves have received a thousand times as much attention. You will look in vain through range autobiographies for a consideration of screwworms."[22] You will look in vain too, he might have added, in the cowboy novel. And there is yet more to cowboy work. By the late 1880s, wrote Ernest Osgood, "mowing machines, hay rakes, and ditching tools became as important a part of ranch equipment as the chuck wagon, the lariat, and the branding iron."[23] Thus the real historical cowboy may turn out to be a working hand who divided his time between mowing hay, fighting screwworms, and looking after sucking calves.[24]

If this proves to be the historical reality of the cowboy, no one will deny its minor importance in the total social history of the West. If this is indeed the way things actually were, we are perhaps content as historians.[25] The trail may have been worth traveling. But when as literary students we have been led to this reality, have we arrived where we need to go? Is imaging this reality of the cowboy's work what the art of the novel is really about? Or have we not perhaps been letting the wrong bunch ride point?

However, before we dismiss the historians, we should ask another sort of question. Lest we easily conclude that they have done their different job well, lest we too quickly separate literature from history, we should finally ask: is this what the <u>art</u> of history is really about? One supposes that the reality of the cowboy includes the reality of his person as well as the authentic facts of his saddles, halters, the nudge and bunt of sucking calves, and methods of fighting screwworms. The historians have accused the fictionists of dealing in unreal, romanticized types, in idealized mythic figures; but have their own historical abstractions provided a better model? Does a thickly detailed, solidly documented account of how a cowboy brands a steer truly hold the <u>human</u> reality of the cowboy himself? If, as Marc Bloch said, history is finally about human consciousness, how much history can we find in most histories of the cattle trade?

We should nevertheless remind ourselves of an important if elementary distinction: that between historical cowboy reality as it may be discovered in a particular time and place and human reality as we hope to perceive it in all times and places. Even if we can find and present the historical cowboy person, we should not confuse that person with the imagined person of fiction. The latter interests us as novelists not because he works with cows but because, to put it simply, he is human, because his special cowboy predicaments, historical and imagined, permit dramatization of significant human situations. There are what we might call cowboy problems and there are what we ought to call human problems. A cowboy may be caught up in both, but certain of his problems should interest only the historian of the cattle trade or the expert in ranch management. To illustrate: a cow has been attacked by roundworms. A cowboy armed with a medigun loaded with thiabendazole paste must shoot her in an unmentionable part of her anatomy. This is what I would call a cowboy problem. A crisis has developed in frontier relationships. A cowboy armed with a sixgun loaded with cartridges must kill or be killed. This is what I would call a human problem. To repeat, the treatment of roundworms, like the treatment of screwworms, deserves a place in range historiography, but one doubts that it belongs in most cowboy novels.[26] The shootout, on the other hand, if well imagined can be fraught with human meanings and might therefore have an integral place in a good many cowboy novels. It need not be historical. Whether suggested by history or not, its important features must still be created. A chance to depend on history does not diminish in any way the novelist's responsibility to imagine his subject.

<u>The responsibility to imagine his subject</u>. Here is the nub of our problem. We cannot blame the West; we cannot blame the shallowness of our historical research. We can only blame our unwillingness or our incapacity to assume the responsibility of becoming writers in the ultimate sense of being makers of important fictive worlds. By responsibility I have in mind less the earnest enthusiasm of Frank Norris than the total artistic commitment of Henry James. And by <u>subject</u> I mean also what James meant. When James praised Wister's <u>The Virginian</u> for the way the author had conceived his subject, he may have overvalued Wister a bit in friendly admiration; but he was nevertheless closer

to the literary truth than was DeVoto. At least James knew what it means to conceive a novel.

Let us look finally at a classically Western incident in a little-known novel.

> Ike Anderson's mind and nerves and muscles were always light-ning-like in the instantaneous rapidity of their action. The eye could scarce have followed the movement by which the revolver leaped to a level from his right-hand scabbard. He had forgotten, in his moment of study, that with this six-shooter he had fired once at the whiskey barrel, once at the glass of straws, once at the negro's heel, twice at the floor, and once at the broomstick. The click on the empty shell was heard clearly at the hotel bar, distinctly ahead of the double re-port that followed. For such was the sharpness of this man's mental and muscular action, he had dropped the empty revolver from his right hand and drawn the other with his left hand in time to meet the fire of the sheriff.
>
> The left arm of the sheriff dropped. The whole body of Ike Anderson, shot low through the trunk, as was the sheriff's invariable custom, melted down and sank into a sitting posture, leaning against the edge of the stoop. The sheriff with a leap sprang behind the fallen man, not firing again. Ike Anderson, with a black film now come upon his eyes, raised his revolver and fired once, twice, three times, four times, five times, tapping the space in front of him regularly and carefully with his fire.[27]

Do we have reality here? I think it safe to say that we do not have his-torical reality. Although the fictional cattle town here was perhaps suggested by Ellsworth, Kansas, we cannot document the episode from the historical sources. It does indeed violate the historical reality presented by Robert R. Dykstra in his study of Ellsworth and other cattle towns. The whole corporate reality, to use Dykstra's term, so important to the social historian is missing.

But, to repeat, do we have reality? Let us try coming to an answer in another way. We cannot, I think, make a final critical judgment here with only a piece of violent action torn out of the context of the novel. Certain bits of language seem melodramatic on the face of it: _lightning-like_ and _the_ _sheriff_ _with_ _a_ _leap_ _sprang_, but such bits, like the two whole paragraphs, must be un-derstood within the fabric of the entire novel. For only in relation to the whole context of the novel can we determine the adequacy of motivation, the accept-able pace of violent narrative, the rightness or wrongness of the story's reso-lution. It does no good to hunt for sources, to hope for answers by way of foot-notes.

Judging the shooting of Ike Anderson within the context of the novel in which it occurs, I confess at last that I am not satisfied. The subject of the novel has not been imagined fully. The novel leaves too much out. The characters are thinly defined; the narration of their predicaments is merely a telling of surface, an easy arrangement of the expected. But note that these reservations, these doubts, are literary reservations and doubts. They have nothing to do with history. The historian cannot here lead us to the better novel we wish the novelist had written.

So let us put another bunch of riders at point. Let DeVoto and Dobie and others ride off into the sunset of critical memory. They spoke to us with a fierce commitment to things Western--we honor them for that--but let us now look to other leaders. The literary art of the West needs all of the craft and sophistication and philosophical seriousness it can muster. I do not know that we can ask old Henry James to put on his chaps--Douglas Branch will now be turning in his grave--but we can nevertheless hope for a Western writer-critic of equally high literary knowledge to show us the way.

University of Utah

NOTES

[1]In contrast one can easily design a national anthology of Australian literature in which what might be called the Australian "West" would have considerable prominence. With no gestures of special goodwill to regions, it might include, for example, the outback poetry and fiction of Henry Lawson, a droving play by Louis Esson, Douglas Stewart's bushranger play Ned Kelly, perhaps even selections from the novels of Patrick White.

[2]The words here are those of Robert Dykstra, The Cattle Towns (New York: Alfred A. Knopf, 1971), p. 123, but they epitomize a judgment frequently made by other historian-critics. Dykstra at this point is commenting on the traditional image of the town marshal as a quick-drawing gunman whose actions seem to have little relationship to civil structures of law and order.

[3]Or cardboard grasshoppers.

[4]The Range Cattle Industry (Norman: University of Oklahoma Press, 1930), p. xv.

[5]Introduction to Harry E. Chrisman, Fifty Years on the Owl Hoot Trail (Chicago: Sage Books, 1969), p. xvi.

[6]Cow People (Boston: Little, Brown and Co., 1964), p. vii.

[7]As DeVoto said, in Rhodes' fiction, "Water in barrels at a cook wagon stinks as water does stink when carried fifty miles and left under the desert sun." "The Novelist of the Cattle Kingdom," introduction to May Davison Rhodes, The Hired Man on Horseback (Boston: Houghton Mifflin Co., 1938), p. xxvi.

[8]House Ex. Doc. 119, pt. 2, p. 2, 48 Cong.

[9]"The Cow Country," American Historical Review, XXII (October, 1916) p. 72.

[10] The Cattlemen's Frontier (Glendale: Arthur Clark Co., 1936), p. 178.

[11] Southern Plainsmen (Norman: University of Oklahoma Press, 1938), p. 128.

[12] The Cowboy (New York: Ballantine Books, 1973), p. 214.

[13] "The Cowboy: His Cause and Cure," The Sunny Slopes of Long Ago, ed. by Wilson Hudson and Allen Maxwell (Dallas: Southern Methodist University Press, 1964), p. 219.

[14] Cow People, p. ix.

[15] Ranch Life and the Hunting Trail (New York: Charles Scribner's Sons, 1906), p. 99. First published in 1888.

[16] The Cowboy, p. 214.

[17] The Cowboy and His Interpreters, p. 61.

[18] Cattle, Cowboys and Rangers (original title Cattle) (New York: Grosset & Dunlap, 1930), p. 301.

[19] Pelzer, The Cattlemen's Frontier, p. 231.

[20] William Baillie-Grohman, Camps in the Rockies (London, 1882), p. 343.

[21] Cow People, p. ix.

[22] "Captain Cook's Place Among Reminiscencers of the West," James H. Cook, Fifty Years on the Old Frontier (Norman: University of Oklahoma Press, 1954), p. viii.

[23] The Day of the Cattleman (Minneapolis, Minn: University of Minnesota Press, 1929), p. 229.

[24] It should be clear that this is a critical extrapolation, not a serious historical proposition.

[25] I am not supposing that all historians will believe that an ultimate cowboy reality has been historiographically worked out. There is obviously more to historical reality than a few hard facts piled around a point in time. Nevertheless, this sketch (burlesque?) of method and philosophy provides, I believe, a valid contrast with what the novelist ought to be doing and thinking.

[26] This is not to say that cow medicine has no place in the novel. If the herd is threatened by disease, heroic measures may be necessary to save it. If it is not saved, there may be tragic human consequences. But this is quite different from saying that in defining the cowboy in his work we need to have a close delineation of his skill with a livestock syringe.

[27] Emerson Hough, The Girl at the Halfway House (New York: D. Appleton, 1900), pp. 244-245.

IMAGINING THE WEST

by Jack Brenner

Western fiction, Wallace Stegner has observed, is rarely approached by critics "from the near, or literary side. They mount it from the right...and ride it hard as myth, as folklore, as a part of the history of ideas...."[1] In Stegner's view this state of criticism came about naturally, since the bulk of Western fiction, a virtual Pike's Peak of books by now, seems to offer little for the critic to weigh or evaluate. Standard hack Westerns, shaped by the large and easy simplicities of fiction--adventure, physical danger, a masculine code, a romantic landscape--appear to be more concerned with fitting into a mythic formula than with fictional invention, and critics have generally treated the novels in that light. In the years since Stegner made his remark a number of critical studies of Western fiction have been published,[2] and the variety of their approaches and concerns would seem to modify Stegner's point. Yet all of these studies bear out, in a general way, his contention: they press fiction into the service of supposedly "larger" arguments. Novels are made to perform as historical documents, as mythic expressions, even as yardsticks of cultural maturity or the lack of it. But seldom is the fiction treated as fiction, as something that, in Richard Poirier's phrase, we could ask to be "compelled and compelling about its own inventions."[3]

The tendency of critics to look beyond, and not at, fiction written about the American West seems to be connected to the pressures put upon the literary West from what I will call "custodial attitudes." Something in Western experience and fiction, and in our attitudes toward what the West means, introduces more than the usual confusion into a hard and confusing question: the relationship of literature to life. So often what should be a critical or fictional problem--that is, the managing or describing of words and how they act--is translated into another kind of problem, one that obscures distinctions between what is "real" and what is fictive. Moreover, when critics gallop off in search of their mythic or sociological hobby-horses, overleaping the fiction as fiction, the experience of reading itself is ignored, lost, or mislaid. As a result, those descriptions of the contouring of self worked on any reader by any book, descriptions I regard as crucial to criticism, are most often sparse and perfunctory.

The roots of my argument here are to be found, as I suppose is always the case, in my own experience. I grew up in the dry West, and my earliest memories are tied to dryness, space, wind, the land. The Dust Bowl winds that drifted dust through my early years still moan, and not just in memory, for even now the sound of wind fills me with the bleak, fugitive unease that a rattling window or stovepipe brought to me as a child. Other sounds too have that power to erase years and locate home: the joy held in a meadowlark's song, the fine, unhurtful ache carried in a mourning dove's call, softly rounded by distance. My point in mentioning these sounds, always associated for me with the sere sweep of sandhill grasslands, is not to reminisce nor to claim special credentials, but to say something of how my roots have branched into the view of Western fiction I express here.

When I began to fumble toward writing fiction about my West, I was sure I knew exactly what had to be done. If I could render the clean burst of golden aspen against grey granite, or bring the huge and sullen power of a plains hailstorm to the page, I should have accomplished everything. The land and its harsh weathers were my subjects: the pouncing blizzards, the heavy sun, the constant lack of rain. Surely nothing could be more moving or dramatic or frightening or wonderful than what was <u>there</u>. One had only to find words. People did not present a problem either. They acted as they had to in that space, in those weathers, and acting as they had to was their distinction. A horseman caught in a punishing hailstorm would do as my grandfather did--crawl beneath the horse and try to keep the animal from stepping on him. Or a pregnant woman, snowbound, would deliver her own baby. Women and men, of course, acted as they had to in clearly defined ways: during an invasion of grasshoppers, as sudden as a hailstorm, the men spread nicotine-soaked sawdust and fixed holes in the screens, while the women tried to protect their gardens and swept the pests out of their kitchens.

And since natural facts were the texts--in a dry summer, a cloudbank coming up in the west was conned with almost Talmudic care--I began to feel, as most Westerners seem to feel, that I had been born too late. If natural facts were the world, both in life and in fiction, then the more natural the better. To have seen the sandhills when my great-grandfather homesteaded there in 1882! Then, I heard in story after story, the grass was belly-high to a horse, with random patches that were even lusher and higher, flags that marked where hide-hunters had left rotting carcasses of the Republican River buffalo herd, more than fifteen years before. And if I yearned to see the land as it was when my great-grandfather moved across it, piling buffalo bones into his wagon in order to support his family in a dry year, then to think of it as it was before he came was even more compelling. Insofar as the physical and natural facts of my world pulled my interest, then, I was pushed to imagine that world as it had been. For me as for many Westerners, the world most real was the vanished world. I did not, probably could not then, see the paradox I was committed to: that I had, through an imaginative act essentially fictional, created a world more "real" than the one I lived in.

I recount this not to parade my youthful naivete, though of course I was naive, but rather to say that what I will press here is in some sense a journal of the arguments I have held with myself. This may account for the pressure-- undue pressure, I'm sure some readers will feel--exerted on arguments when the ostensible debate is with Vardis Fisher or some other Western spokesman. I could not disagree with Fisher and others as I have unless I once had a deep need to believe their words. I grew into that need, as many Westerners have,

33

and do not regard that as a lamentable fact; yet what many have offered me in fiction and criticism and history as a way of regarding myself and a part of the world I care about seems sparse, thin, in need of something more. Some of my attempt to see my way round that "more" is recorded here.

My own experience exhibits, in small ways, the special obstacles to fictional performance posed by the West as a literary subject. I find, for example, my nostalgia for a "purer" natural world reflected in the tendency of Western fiction to "amputate the present," in Wallace Stegner's term. In Western fiction nostalgia is the underwater boulder that sculpts and carves the flow of fictional current; yet I think that the nostalgic impulse is also a constricting force, a dam. Just so with the other two great concerns of Western fiction, the need to merge with and to be purified by the land, and the ideal of masculinity associated with that merging. These three concerns, as they intertwine and affect the others, are the vital impulses, the very heart's blood, of Western fiction. Yet if they are the forces that drive Western experience into language, they are also the reason for Western fiction disclaiming its authority. For Western fiction, generally, is a fiction concerned to show that fiction should be distrusted. This distrust is not of the sort we are becoming familiar with in the fiction of Thomas Pynchon and John Barth and others, in which plot is replaced with plotting, sometimes paranoid, and in which we are shown that suspending our disbelief in favor of one fiction over another is a mug's game. It is, rather, a distrust which stems from assumptions having to do with the primacy of "fact." The stories in Barth's <u>Lost</u> <u>in</u> <u>the</u> <u>Funhouse</u> treat us as though we were students in Barth's classes in Creative Writing, explaining busily the way they go about their business, asking us to see that the illusion a story might induce is, after all, only a fiction among fictions. But Western fiction invites a distrust toward itself of a different order: basic to most Western fiction is the implication that coherence and meaning in language is authorized by facts outside the maker of language. When I felt that my only task was to reproduce the icy swipe of hail's scythe I was participating in that conviction, and the conviction led me to disclaim my role as a craftsman, a maker of language. What is one to make of fiction that is based on the belief that silence is more natural than speaking, that "imagination" is inferior to "fact"? In the West the name of "artist" carries a special dubiety, and to see something of this we can look to some critical arguments about Western fiction.

II

An old, bitter Western complaint is that some powerful and mysterious "Eastern Literary Establishment" works in deliberate complicity to ignore Western writing. However well-founded or defensive the complaint, we can surely say that Westerns have not often been the subject of serious critical inquiry. One reason for this, of course, is that Westerns are a "popular" and "lowbrow" form. Critics who hold themselves responsible for measuring fiction against "the best that has been thought and said" have seemed often to cast themselves as embattled frontiersmen pushing back the limits of dark ignorance,

34

defending the civilized territory against rampant barbarity out there. Westerns, in that view of things, will be not only dreck, but dangerous dreck, since they are assumed to assault and blunt the civilized capacity for finer delicacies. The argument about "taste cultures" burns brightly just now, and readers are invited to go elsewhere for a discussion of it;[4] for my purposes here it is enough to observe that cultural custodianship of fiction prejudges, rules certain forms of expression outside of that worthy to consider. It is not my intention to claim that Westerns should be welcomed into the guarded circle of great literature-- though I do want to say in passing that there is more of fictional interest in even hack westerns than we have yet been able to describe--but only to point out that here is a case in which fiction is judged without being observed.

This form of custodianship must have its effects on the West as a literary subject. Even though serious Western writers seem to pride themselves on their isolation, they do not write in a vacuum. Known or felt criticism is a part of the shaping force of the fiction itself, and certainly a writer's knowledge that his very material may well place him below the salt will have an effect on the final shape of the work. But it is striking that the Western complaint about Eastern disdain carries its own custodial values, ones that can scoot us past the fiction itself as quickly and efficiently as dismissive Eastern attitudes are supposed to do. We can see something of this in a speech delivered by Vardis Fisher to the Western Literature Association in 1967, on the occasion of his being honored as a distinguished Western writer:

> Wallace Stegner is reported to have said recently that he is sick and tired of reading about Jewish moms. I suspect that Western writers have about as much interest in Jewish moms and the tiresome trivia of Jewish family life as most Jewish book reviewers have in our magnificent mountains, rivers, valleys and forests, or in the fact that this western part of our country is by far the most remarkable physical wonderland in the world. Those people back there, choking on their poisons, bathing in stinking water, and listening day and night to the infernal din of what Wolfe called their ant-swarms, can no more be expected to like our country and our books about it than I, to speak only for myself, can like the proliferating lunacies of their cities, the robotized togetherness of their feverish lives, and their dull, inbred, and over-praised books.[5]

However we take Fisher's statement--as provincial anti-semitism, as disgust with the twentieth century, as authentic Western sentiment--we can see in it some of the difficulties that plague our fictional understanding of the West. But Fisher's position is not unique, and rather than discussing his contentions alone, I should like to show how his general convictions and attitudes inform Edson Lee's study From West to East.[6] Lee's central argument holds that experience in the West was singular, and therefore should have sired a new, authentic Western voice:

The condition of life in the West, particularly in the nineteenth century, was a unique thing, and there really was something to be learned by sitting there "naked and ignorant as a savage"....But, to the degree this study indicates, the East refused the reality of the West, and the Western writers themselves concurred in the East's wish to treat romantically the concepts of freedom and individuality in the West. It is a consistent trend in the writers considered here, from Lewis and Clark to DeVoto, to accept the ideology, or at least the tastes, of the East. The firsthand experience was consistently altered to some lesser thing (p. 159).

So Lee maintains that genteel and romantic notions of language and life, imported from the East, distorted "honest" fiction, by which he seems to mean fiction that would report the experience as it happened. Because "firsthand experience" is for him the sine qua non of successful fiction, he can make such judgments as these:

Twain's coyote in Roughing It is "so far abstracted from nature iself that it is in no sense real..." (p. 108).

Willa Cather "chose the rosy tints of romanticism...and idyll or a pastoral...that hasn't the strength or the vigor or the reality of the history itself....She had come, by 1913, to write from the point of view of the East, substituting artifice for truth" (p. 135).

"Little Big Man is a product of what Berger has read, not of what he has seen and experienced. No one pretends it is literature" (p. 157).

Lee's statements, almost empty of any recognition of the real powers or limitations of fiction, show that the writer who is attempting to imagine the West need not look to New York publishing offices to be misapprehended. By Lee's standards, neither Hamlet nor Don Quixote could be regarded as literature, and very few other books either. Lee wants real toads in real gardens, seen and experienced by the writer, then carried full-blown in all their "reality" to the page. But in arguing that "genteel" language is artificial, while reportorial language is "real," Lee confuses the realms of experience and language. Different forms of language call forth their own responses, of course, but that is not to say that a word naming a physical object is more "real" than one which names something less concrete. Both are words, words cannot be the experience itself, and fiction is made of words.

Under these boggy notions of "artifice" and "reality" in fiction, then, resides Lee's basic conviction that any imaginative shaping is dishonest, unreal, "Eastern." Lee's custodial attitude is toward a Western history that he assumes to be more "real" than fiction could ever be. But Lee himself could not have experienced the historical moments that he wants to rescue from fictional distortion; he could have known that history only through words and pictures and the power of his own imagination. So in his own terms the "real" history he wants reflected in the fiction is a fiction itself—it is a construct of words. Lee's critical act, then, is to claim that the story he has in his head does not jibe with the story told by his writers. Such is the ground upon which he stands to condemn the writers for capitulating to an "Eastern point of view," scoring them for substituting artifice for reality.

In the face of such convictions, one needs to repeat a simple truth: the fictional West is a world of words, as all fictional worlds are. Those words, with their arrangements, echoes, meanings, and resonances, provide us with our experience. We sit in a chair, turn pages, become caught or tired or amused or bored. But the experience of the fiction is not the experience itself, and never can be. It may matter a great deal to my reading of Clark's The Track of the Cat if I have, like Curt Bridges in the novel, hunted across the mountains in a snowstorm, but the hunting itself and my reading about it are of different orders of experience. Moreover, my knowledge of the historical West is deeply an invention, fictional in its quality; what I know of the fur traders I know through reading and talk and pictures that my imagination has shaped into a "fact." I don't mean by this that I am a prisoner of my language, since without it I would know nothing of Jim Bridger, but only that for all of us, including Edson Lee, the West of 1825 is a West of words.

That simple home truth seems hard to keep before us when the subject is Western fiction. No one seriously asks if Bellow writes about a "real" Chicago or whether Hemingway got the facts straight in the retreat from Caporetto. Yet, from one quarter at least, such questions are regularly put to Western fiction, and the intent of the questions seems to go beyond a fuzzy or partial understanding of literary realism. That intent is to judge the fiction by the quality (or supposed quality) of the experience that the fiction represents. "To write as 'Gene [Eugene Manlove Rhodes] wrote one would have to live as 'Gene lived, and I know of no writer in this country, at Breadloaf or elsewhere, that has the guts to do that even if there was left a place to live that way,"[7] Walter Prescott Webb has said about a writer who, many Westerners have claimed, was unjustly ignored by Eastern tastemakers. One could observe that Webb was a historian with a regional axe to grind and let it go at that, but Webb speaks for others too, and in a way that shows how Western attitudes might shackle the fictional imagination. In Webb's statement we can see that Rhodes earns his spurs as writer through the facts of his life: he knew the man who shot Billy the Kid, could saddle a horse, knew about mining, was familiar with deserts and mountains. The facts of his life, not the fiction he made of them, are crucial.

This fierce insistence upon the authenticity of experience and the allied distrust of the distorting power of fiction stems, in part, from the fact that the West was frozen into legend and stereotype—that is, the fictions became "real" —almost before it was settled. Because of that, caring Westerners have perhaps more reasons for feeling prickly about the literary reflection of their area than do other regionalists. It could be true that the mention of Buffalo Bill carries special ironies to the Westerner that even a myth-ridden Southerner might not have access to. Yet there is something altogether striking in the pressure put on "cheap" formula fiction by Westerners. Why are the hacks held responsible for ruining something of inestimable grandeur? Why are they charged so bitterly with cheapening the dream? The question gains force when we see that the literary history of the West has much in common with other Western historical experience, which is to say that perhaps the central fact of all Western history is exploitation. Those who have worked the Comstock of the dime-novels or mined the latest TV Bonanza have behaved as many early hide-hunters and prospectors behaved: get it and get out. So it is hard to see why those who have hacked out books rather than gold, who have gone over old ground rather than breaking out sod, have been elected to bear such bitter blame. The ghost towns of the mining West, so lovingly memorialized by Western historians, are tangible monuments to the same spirit that produces formula Westerns, though I have not often seen the connection noted.

That anomaly can perhaps lead us to grasp something of the way in which custodial attitudes have charged Western fiction with being both more and less important than it should be. Westerners have invested fiction with powers and strengths that it cannot have, robbed it of its legitimate functions in other ways. In part this skewing occurs because the Western landscape has been thoroughly mythologized. In the congeries of mythological uses the West has been put to, one potent, common conviction stands out: that the West was and always will be the Other Place, the Territory that Makes a Difference, the Newest of New Worlds. Fisher and Lee and Webb express in their own ways the idea that experience in the West differs radically from other American experience. Part of the energy of Fisher's diatribe against "those people," awash in triviality and pollutants and not able to understand the "physical wonderland," can be charted as his rage against the fact that Western experience, supposed to be regenerative, is being ignored. I don't think the bitterness of his statement can be understood otherwise. The West as the Territory Ahead, where cocoons of old larval existence would be shucked off and bright butterfly life released, is an old and familiar conception, of course, and not held only by Vardis Fisher. But perhaps the very age and familiarity of the myth makes us overlook one of the most important consequences: the effect the myth has on expectations toward language. Stated simply, the myth of open spaces and wilderness holds that older "social" forms will be disrupted by the new experience; in Frederick Jackson Turner's borrowed phrase, the frontier experience would "break the cake of custom." Lee's conviction that Western experience should have broken "Eastern" forms of fiction is therefore good Turnerian doctrine. If the frontier experience produced a new kind of American, it should have produced a new literature. Yet the myth itself carries defeat for that hope: since the West was regarded as that place where "natural" experience rather than social "artificial" life was encountered, language itself was suspect. It has always been a core feeling in Western fiction and even in Western experience that the man who is on speaking terms with a mountain needn't speak, that that ultimate Westerner who

38

knows "natural" laws will have no need for "artificial" language. This is part of what Leslie Fiedler means when he says that our essential experience with the West is with the Indian, for whom the New World is the Old, and it begins to explain why taciturnity has been invested with such moral weight in the Western mythos.

But even though we seem to cherish the West for being that "place" where language is out of place, in fact what has aroused the most energy in Western fiction are purely literary questions, questions having to do with the proper form of language: naming, gesture, style. The concern ranges from the bristly guarding of honor that names can besmirch--"When you call me that, smile" --to the insider's need not "to talk it away" to the deeply felt need to name without naming those mergings of the spirit with the Other that so much of the fiction is at pains to convey. In one sense, this attitude is only the old dilemma of "realistic" prose restated: to speak without seeming to speak, to be literary without allowing the reader to realize that he is in a fictive world. Yet there seems to be added pressure on the question in Western fiction, for the problem is not regarded as a literary matter, finally, but as a question of "reality." Thus (pace Lee), literary strategies other than the one that corresponds to someone's notion of reality are "artificial"--even though the "realistic" strategy is fully as literary, and therefore as "artificial," as any other deployment of words.

As an illustration of the point, I want to look to a passage from Hondo,[8] one of fifty-odd novels written by a man who calls himself Louis L'Amour. Hondo, we are told, is "a big man....There was no softness in him. His toughness was ingrained and deep, without cruelty, yet quick, hard, and dangerous. Whatever wells of gentleness might lie within him were guarded and deep" (p. 1). That description is followed by an exchange between Hondo and a woman who has been abandoned on her ranch by a no-good husband. Hondo has mentioned that he once lived with the Indians and was married to an Indian woman, who died. "I'm sorry," the woman says, "I didn't mean to bring up an unhappy memory."

> He turned, letting the horse stand. He pushed his hat back on his head and considered her remark. 'I don't remember anything unhappy about Destarte.'
> 'Destarte! How musical! What does it mean?'
> 'You can't say it except in Mescalero. It means morning, but that isn't what it means either. Indian words are more than just that. They also mean the feel and the sound of the name. It means like Crack of Dawn, the first bronze light that makes the buttes stand out against the grey desert. It means the first sound you hear of a brook curling over some rocks--some trout jumping and a beaver crooning....It means like you get up in the first light and you and her go out of the wickiup; where it smells smoky and private and just you and her, and kind of safe with just the two of you there, and you stand outside and smell the first bite of the wind

coming down from the high divide and promising the first snowfall. Well, you just can't say what it means in English. Anyway, that was her name. Destarte.'

Rather amazed, Angie stared at him. 'Why, that's poetry!'
'Huh? Didn't mean to go gabbing....' (p. 36)

The passage is clumsy, inauthentic, "literary" in the worst possible way, yet the way it strains against itself discovers the problem of language I have been trying to describe. Hondo must both speak and somehow deny himself language; or perhaps he has to deny the language because he can use it. "Huh? Didn't mean to go gabbing." He tells us he can't say it in English, though of course he does say it, and his words, liberated by alien speech, linger and caress those images of softness he supposedly has no language to name. These contortions coil out from L'Amour's need to keep Hondo before us as a real man, one as "hard as the desert," and since a touchstone of hack Western fiction is that "soft" or "poetic" language is feminine, the real issue here is the sexual propriety of words. And L'Amour goes to really extraordinary lengths to qualify the "poetry"; we have to know that Hondo is not a womanish dude gushing over sunrise, snared by beauty into forgetting the savage Darwinian claws of his world. The internal strains of the passage let us see that a sense of beauty, unless tempered by endurance and pain and sweeping space, is artificial, "Eastern," womanish. Style is of absolutely central concern, for the avoidance of womanish words is crucial unless Hondo, in saying them, can disclaim them too. "Style is the man": not often have cojones swung such a ponderous weight on that phrase.

I feel sure that Fisher, Lee and Webb--and here again I elect them to represent Western attitudes held by many others--would be united in their scorn of the passage. They would regard it as another irritating example of the phony cardboard literary West sired by Eastern ignorance out of Hollywood greed. Yet it is exactly my point that their critical stance puts fiction in the same contorted, straining, having-it-both-ways dilemma that L'Amour displays so awkwardly in Hondo's speech. As each of them believes that Western experience is unique, they are forced to believe in a "reality" which measures fiction as "artificial"; and insofar as they believe that Western experience is unique in bringing men into closer touch with essential and "natural" self than can happen in cities where "trivial" concerns dominate, they are forced to repudiate language. The effect of believing in the myth is silence. Yet that very belief exerts undue pressures on words, so that the real arguments are about style. Add to this the deep--and in some ways deserved--animus felt against the hacks who have turned these convictions into a series of cheap but profitable gestures, and the difficulties of imagining, and assessing, the fictional West are apparent.

Wright Morris, though rarely regarded as a Western writer, has made fictional subjects of the conundrums I have been discussing, and in The Territory Ahead[9] he discusses them directly. The American fondness for fact, he says, is reflected in our novelists' devotion to the "raw material myth":

A permissible illusion of rawness exists on each frontier. And in a nation of expanding frontiers, the illusion of rawness expands along with them. Technique [fictional technique], in this pioneer picture, is therefore little more than a clearing operation--the raw material is the thing, and the technique is the method of collecting it. There usually appears to be an inexhaustible supply of it. But if you happen to run out of it where you are, why then you move on to where it is waiting. It exists, that is. It is not something the artist conjures up (p. 4).

Fitzgerald's lament that his experience was limited compared to Hemingway's, Twain's proud claim that he was well-qualified to be a novelist since he knew nothing of books, Thoreau's sly insistence that he went to Walden to face the facts--these are instances for Morris of the peculiar conviction among American writers that the shaping imagination has a minor role in their accomplishments. As a result, the occasional stray masterpiece has "about it the air of an accident; not so much a crafty man-made thing, as a gift from above. The author usually took pains not to repeat it, or to learn from his experience" (p. 7). Yet it is as artists that Twain and the others live for us; their craft shaped "the transitory, elusive facts...into a fiction of permanence" (p. 5). Not the quality of raw experience, but the force of language fixes Huck's river, aching and lovely, in our minds, and it is finally Thoreau's care in chiselling sentences that floats Walden Lake as a "fact" in our minds, so that we view other bodies of water and even the dry reaches of the West through it. Fiction, thus, becomes the fact that matters:

Life, raw life, the kind we lead every day, whether it leads us into the past or the future, has the curious property of not seeming real enough. We have a need, however illusive, for a life that is more real than life. It lies in the imagination. Fiction would seem to be the way it is processed into reality. If this were not so we should have little excuse for art. Life, raw life, would be more satisfactory in itself. But it seems to be the nature of man to transform-- himself, if possible, and then the world around him--and the technique of this transformation is what we call art. When man fails to transform, he loses consciousness, he stops living (pp. 228-29).

Edson Lee would save the literary West by peeling back layers of artifice to recapture raw experience, thereby rendering fiction "truthful." But Morris shows that the choice is not between fact and fiction, but between kinds of fiction, some of which have become so furrowed into our consciousness that we regard them as truths. History has happened, and our only inexhaustible resource at the moment is cliche--that is, those successful fictions of the past. The problem, then, is not to peel back, but to transform; the writer has to repossess his inherited fictions for himself, and "repossession is reappraisal." In Quixote's wondrous transformation of the barber's basin--to use one of

Morris' favorite illustrations--we see the essential fictional act, yet it is the shaping act, not the "truth" of Mambrino's helmet, that can be our guide. To repossess for ourselves Mambrino's helmet, to make it more than an object in a literary museum, we have to escape the alluring amber of Quixote's transformation with our own repossession. Something of Morris' wonderfully rich approach to imagining the West can be glimpsed in a scene from his novel, Field of Vision. Here Mambrino's helmet is a Davy Crockett coonskin hat, worn by five-year-old Gordon McKee to a bullfight in Mexico City. The boy, one of a group of Nebraskans in Mexico, is being watched by Gordon Boyd who is reminded of his own youthful promise by the ritual heroism in the bull-ring, and the older man wonders what the boy is, how he has been affected:

> At the moment a miniature frontier hero, one of Disney's rubber-stamp midgets, chewing on the non-poisonous paint of the barrel of his gun. Any danger? No, the dangerous elements had been removed. From both the paint and the gun. . . . The way the coon had been removed from the coonskin hat, the way the Crockett had been removed from the frontier pants. . . . These things were safe now. . . . The strangest transformation of all, that is, had taken place . . . the objects did not enlarge the heart. They were there, but they were no longer possessed. What had happened? the neatest trick of the week. All that one had to do to tame the bull was remove the risks. Along with the means, that is, the meaning dropped away from it. Instead of bulls, prime rib on the hoof; instead of Crockett, nurseries full of records; instead of frontiers, a national shortage of coonskin hats. The transformation to end all transformations had taken place. One had the object. One wondered what the hell to do with it (p. 173).

If those artifacts of frontier bravery and independence are to be more than empty emblems, the heroic cliches have to be possessed as living, not dead, truths. So Boyd attempts to show the boy how to make his heroic past real for himself by plucking the hat off the boy's head and throwing it into the ring. The boy jumps the rail and reappears

> like a spring-wind toy in the costume of a frontier doll...and scooted like a BB across the ring. A troop of small fry, all of them authentic Indians, who had come in with the mules when the gates had opened, also headed for the coonskin, but Davy Crockett got there first. He had recovered his hat, but in the process lost his senses. He ran around wildly, pursued by Indians, wheeling to shoot one dead, scalp another, then ride off in all directions (p. 209).

The boy "recovered his hat" and has therefore experienced what is, for Morris, most valuable in the pioneering legacy--the absurd risks, the high wax-winged flights of audacious transformation, the suppleness of living beyond the fixed fictions.

Morris offers one lead out of the tense conundrums posed by custodial attitudes toward "art" and "reality" in the West. He has moved somewhere beyond those either-or possibilities for Western fiction announced by Jay Martin: "Romantically reconstructing myth or realistically destroying it--these are the two ways of regional literature."[10] This either-or attitude toward fictional possibilities is also discernible in Leslie Fiedler's The Return of the Vanishing American. Even though Fiedler is a critic who can always describe for his readers the fictional performance of a book, he falls into such statements as these: for everyone who tries to evoke the West "in fiction by reconstructing its past...two kinds of truth come immediately into conflict...: the truth of history, which is the truth of reason; and the truth of myth, which is the truth of madness." Or, in a somewhat different formulation: "But the real opposite of nostalgic is psychedelic, the reverse of remembering is hallucinating, which means that, insofar as the New Western is truly New, it, too, must be psychedelic."[11] In one sense, of course, both Fiedler and Martin have described accurately a quality of some Western novels. There are books which are deliberately anti-heroic, such as David Markson's The Ballad of Dingus Magee, in which "Yerkey's Hole" is a place named for a pioneering prostitute rather than for being a watering place. And in Mel Brooks' movie "Blazing Saddles" shuffling, taciturn cowboys fart noisily around a campfire. But his parodic stance, which poses seamy possibilities of Western history as the corrosive antidote to sentimentalities, seems finally as confining as the stance it attacks. The problem of fiction still remains. And it is precisely in imagining that the West can be imagined fictionally that Morris and a few other writers have distinguished themselves.

For fiction about the West can be "compelled and compelling about its own inventions," and "romantically reconstructing" or "realistically destroying" are not its only possibilities. There is also the "truth" of fictional performance, that element called to our attention by Robert Frost in an interview with Richard Poirier:

> So many talk, I wonder how falsely, about what it costs them, what agony it is to write. I've often been quoted 'No tears in the writer, no tears in the reader. No surprise for the writer, no surprise for the reader.' But another distinction I make is: however sad, no grievance, grief without grievance, how could I, how could anyone have a good time with what it cost me too much agony, how could they? What do I want to communicate but what a hell of a good time I had writing it? The whole thing is performance and prowess and feats of association. Why don't critics talk about those things--what a feat it was to turn that that way, and what a feat it was to remember that, to be reminded of that by this? Why don't they talk about that?[12]

Critics don't usually "talk about that" when the subject is Western fiction for some of the reasons I've been discussing. In general, "Western" receives such heavy stress that "fiction" is left to wander unmoored and unexamined. One knows, with some charity, how difficult it is to describe critically that element of fiction Frost points to, difficult because it is always harder to describe process than it is to describe results. To use Frost's metaphor in a perhaps extreme way, it is far easier to report box scores than it is to describe the astounding way that Elgin Baylor seemed to hang in the air at the top of his shot. Yet any fan knows that the quality of his experience, the very feel and flavor of it, comes from such moments or from a short flow of sequence. Just so, I think, with a reader's experience of the fictional West: the "subject" and the result of a novel is always of less interest, always less shaping, than are the turns of performance.

But to assert that authority in fiction resides in style--which means, finally, the manner in which words and tones jostle and build and modify each other--and not in theme or subject is to imply that I occupy a critical territory that I do not, in fact, wish to occupy. In objecting to the way in which Fisher and others have subscribed to the raw material myth I have not intended to say that fiction should be measured by complexity of structure, by sophisticated deployment of "point of view," or by other manipulations of the techniques available to fiction. Technique in fiction can't be an end in itself; to borrow a phrase from George Eliot, it is only "an admonition to the writer to be wise," not a measure of value. Novels written with great technical finesse can be boring, as many novels written during the 1950's testify, at least to me. We can insist upon style as the primary authentication of fiction without giving over helplessly to any manipulation which is adroit or knowing. It matters what the words say.

Since I have been arguing that Western fiction has not often been seen as fiction, it is appropriate to close with a notice of James K. Folsom's book, The American Western Novel, since some assumptions about value in fiction, and some others I would like to identify, operate in it. In one sense, Folsom's book is as "literary" as it could be: his central contention is that "the Western is usually a 'myth' or a 'fable,'" the nature of which has been misunderstood by critics who have confused the difference drawn by Hawthorne and Simms between "novel" and "romance." "The material of this fable is based...upon American history, but the purpose of the fable is not the realistic explication of a colorful chapter of the American past. It is rather a metaphorical parable of the inconsistencies and contradictions which inhere in the American's paradoxical views about himself, his country, and his destiny" (p. 29). In the main Folsom works toward a generic definition of the Western, stressing the unresolved paradoxes he has mentioned--"the world of the Western is commonly the world of self-contradictory ideas, all of which the American is tempted to affirm at once"--and drawing attention to the structural dimensions of the parable.

Folsom's book in general is careful not to claim too much for itself, and is useful for showing that the realism Mark Twain scored Cooper for ignoring is not, after all, the only benchmark of fiction. Yet Folsom's critical approach deadens the fiction he discusses. His generic approach demands that he treat

novels as tiles in a mosaic, judging them by what they add to the pattern which
is his primary subject. Given his concerns, Folsom cannot witness the novels
unfolding or describe the energies of the language; instead he sees the novels
as completed things, dead in themselves, extracting from them themes, ambi-
guities, structural parameters. His eye is trained for irony, but strangely,
not in order to record the discordances of genuine ambiguity, but to show a
final organic shape for the Western fable. He seems to assume that all parts
of a successful work will tuck themselves into a balanced organism, and the
effect of this assumption is to make it seem proper to regard a poem or novel
as a completed, finished artifact, rather than to see it as a process which creates itself, and us, anew as it proceeds. Because Folsom is interested in the
mosaic and not the parts, in the "Western story" rather than in a novel named
The Track of the Cat or The Virginian, he can say about Conrad Richter's Sea
of Grass that "the novel's success is partially due to Richter's stylistic competence; for in marked contrast to many westerns, this book is beautifully written" (p. 97). "Beautifully" written or not, novels are written, and to make one's
critical response subservient to the assumed demands of "unified sensibility"
rather than attempting to describe and locate what happens in and to the language and oneself as a reader is to forsake, to my mind, the essential joy and
meaning of fiction.

While I do not want to sound mean-spirited toward Folsom, I do want to
say that, for me, his discussion is a fairly typical example of ignoring what is
interesting in fiction in the name of criticizing it. Does one really experience
those structures that Folsom works so hard to identify? I do not. If I go back
to the novels he discusses, his critical road-map in hand and looking for what
he asks me to see, I wonder why I've gone back. The problem seems to be
that Folsom appropriates a body of Western novels and looks for organic relationships among them; but the whole enterprise curiously lacks conviction about
why one might want to read or write such a book, since the impression given is
that the nearest object of scrutiny has little inherent interest.

It is, then, in a loose and large literary sense that Folsom's attitude toward Western fiction is "custodial." It is a problem that he attempts to be
thorough and scholarly about. He attempts to dignify the fiction, lift it above
its poor-cousin state, by showing that it is "complex" as that word might be
used in a graduate seminar in literature. But there are other ways of seeing
values, and D. H. Lawrence can point us in one direction:

> Man struggles with unborn needs and fulfillment. New unfoldings
> struggle up in torment in him, as buds struggle forth from the
> midst of a plant. Any man of real individuality tries to know and
> to understand what is happening, even in himself, as he goes along.
> This struggle for verbal consciousness should not be left out in
> art. It is a very great part of life....It is the passionate struggle
> into conscious being.

That "struggle into conscious being" need not be taken, as it sometimes

45

has, for only another expression of romantic anguish. Lawrence, who wrote his own Western in St. Mawr, can open us to richnesses that taxonomic criticism is obliged to disregard in fiction. For serious Western fiction in particular struggles against itself: against the tyranny of fact in misunderstood "realism," against the banked dead weight of frozen legend, against the confining and conservative claims of nostalgia, against, even, its very medium--words. And all of these struggles are "a very great part" of the life we find in Western fiction and "should not be left out" of criticism. Yet Folsom cannot take account of them.

So what Lawrence and Morris and Frost tell us, in their various ways, is what we have always known in our best moments as readers: that we are being shaped by (and shaping ourselves), a "struggle toward consciousness," a transformation, a performance. Nabokov, an unlikely witness here, has called fiction the "good cheat," and one need not be wholly in the modern fictional camp occupied by Barth, Mailer, Barthelme, Pynchon and Nabokov himself to grant that all fiction is in some sense just that. However jarring to some Westerners, the most documentary realism, with authentic objects properly displayed, is a "good cheat." We have been talking prose all this time, and even though we have needed to set the argument in terms of "reality" and "artifice," what we have been talking about is prose: the ways in which style and gesture of language can uphold or authenticate or insult our fixed fictions.

University of Washington

NOTES

[1] "History, Myth, and the Western Writer," The American West, IV (May 1967), 61. The essay was later reprinted in The Sounds of Mountain Water (New York: 1969).

[2] Among them, Leslie Fiedler's The Return of the Vanishing American, John Cawelti's Six-Gun Mystique, Jay Gurian's Western American Writing: Tradition and Promise, Larry McMurtry's In A Narrow Grave: Essays on Texas, and The Popular Western, edited by Etulain and Marsden. This is by no means an exhaustive listing.

[3] The Performing Self (New York: 1971), p. 67.

[4] See, for example, Herbert J. Gans, Popular Culture and High Culture (New York: 1974).

[5] "The Western Writer and the Eastern Establishment," Western American Literature, I (Winter, 1967), p. 253.

[6] From West to East (Urbana, 1966).

[7] Quoted by W. H. Hutchinson in his introduction to Eugene Manlove Rhodes, Beyond the Desert (University of Nebraska: 1967), p. ix.

[8] Hondo (Gold Medal Books: 1953).

[9]The Territory Ahead: Critical Interpretations in American Literature (New York: 1963).

[10]Harvests of Change: American Literature 1865-1914 (New Jersey: 1967), p. 188.

[11]The Return of the Vanishing American (New York: 1968), pp. 164, 175.

[12]Quoted in The Performing Self, p. 90.

"ACROSS THE MEDICINE LINE: PROBLEMS IN COMPARING CANADIAN AND AMERICAN WESTERN FICTION "

by Dick Harrison

When I began to compare Canadian and American western fiction, I found there was a good deal of geography to get through before I could concentrate on the literature. As scholars of the American West freely admit, the area is so vast and so various that it mocks all efforts to generalize about it. Often the term "Wests" is more useful than "West." The Canadian West may be slightly less intractable, but with which of the American Wests does it share enough regional and literary similarities to sustain fruitful (or even sane) comparison?

Existing commentaries offer some help in limiting the field: Wallace Stegner, for example, says in The Sound of Mountain Water that California is not the West, [1] and Edward McCourt, in his The Canadian West in Fiction, also eliminates the West coast, contending that "Alberta is the far West; British Columbia the near East."[2] Even these convenient restrictions, which would obviously have to be disturbed in any exhaustive comparison, leave an awesome territory to cover. How do you get from Tombstone to Moosejaw, or more significantly, from Harvey Fergusson's The Conquest of Don Pedro to Robert Stead's Grain? Probably you don't, since Fergusson's Southwest has a history of settlement which sets it apart not only from the Canadian West but to a degree from the rest of the American West. Writers like Fergusson, Frank Waters, and William Eastlake reflect this regional difference in their preoccupation with the collision of cultures, with what T. M. Pierce describes as "The 'Other' Frontiers of the American West."[3] And if, as Raymond Gastil argues, the Pacific Northwest can claim to be a separate cultural region, then that area too might be left for separate comparison with British Columbia. [4]

For a number of reasons the Mid-west would seem the most likely area to compare with the Canadian prairie. Both are flat, agrarian, relatively peaceful and orderly, and have sustained their ties with the East, but anyone reading their literatures will be struck more by the differences than the similarities. In Canadian prairie fiction the land is a dominant presence and the other characters are constantly aware of its immensity, its power, and especially its menace. This is rarely so in the fiction of Willa Cather, Hamlin Garland, or Wright Morris, and to judge by what Ray B. Meyer says about the Mid-western farm novel, these writers can be taken as representative.[5] Mid-western fiction also lacks that pervasive sense of the individual isolated and exposed to the elements which characterizes the fiction of the prairie and of the Great West in America. There may be a simple enough explanation for these differences. The Mid-west was settled around the same time as Southwestern Ontario and has developed the same sense of long-sustained habitation.

The land is subdued; it is the human arrangements that need attention. In many ways Cather, Garland, and Morris have more in common with rural Ontario writers like Raymond Knister and Alice Munro than with westerners like Frederick Philip Grove, Sinclair Ross, and Rudy Wiebe.

There are exceptions, of course; Ross's As For Me and My House can fruitfully be compared with Mainstreet because Ross was evidently under the influence of Lewis' novel. Giants in the Earth makes a very useful comparison with some Canadian prairie novels, especially Grove's, but in Giants we are getting from the settled Mid-west out onto the arid plains, and besides, Rolvaag remains to my mind an eccentric to the general design of western American literature.

If we set aside, tentatively, the areas I have mentioned, the regions we are left with still make an incongruous pair geographically: on the Canadian side the prairies (usually taken to include parkland and foothills), on the American side the high plains, the mountains, and the vast intermountain regions. But there are reasons for beginning the comparison here. Both regions have accommodated the fur trade, the cattle industry, and grain-farming. They share most of the qualities Stegner isolates as the lowest common denominator of the West; they are late, large, new, and relatively arid.[6] The two are for great distances contiguous along an imaginary line, and both gave rise to the fiction which helped to form the classic meanings of the term West in the minds of the two nations. These regions are where the people worked out nationally distinctive ways of adapting, imaginatively as well as physically, to the immensity of the West.

Assuming, for the sake of argument, that we have found the two Wests to compare, we are still faced with another problem endemic to the study of western American literature: which type of fiction do we choose to compare? Since the "Medicine Line" historically expressed cultural as well as political differences, the popular fiction should be a convenient place to begin. As John Cawelti says, popular art has the function of "articulating and reaffirming the primary cultural values," and the early popular fiction does illustrate some of the root differences between the American frontier and the Canadian pioneer West.[7] The most succinct examples I can offer are a pair of barroom showdowns, the first from The Virginian, which is useful not only as a progenitor of the popular tradition but also as a novel in which Wister is quite explicit about his western actions being paradigms for the development of American character. The scene is at the meeting of the Virginian with his enemy Trampas. During a poker game Trampas calls him a "son-of-a_____," at which the other takes out his gun, and holding it unaimed on the table, says those memorable lines:

"When you call me that, smile." And he looked at Trampas across the table.
Yes, the voice was gentle. But in my ears it seemed as if somewhere the bell of death was ringing; and silence, like a stroke, fell on the large room.[8]

Confronted in this way, Trampas declines to "draw his steel," and so the Virginian has righted a wrong, and restored order to the card game. The second showdown is in Ralph Connor's <u>Corporal Cameron,</u> published around the same time as <u>The Virginian,</u> but set north of the border. Here Connor presents what may be the central archetype of the Mountie, a slim youngster in a scarlet tunic and pill-box cap, who walks into a gambling den where a desperado is flourishing his gun:

> "Put it down there, my man. Do you hear?" The voice was still
> smooth, but through the silky tones there ran a fibre of steel.
> Still the desperado stood gazing at him. "Quick, do you hear?"
> There was a sudden sharp ring of imperious, of overwhelming
> authority, and, to the amazement of the crowd of men who stood
> breathless and silent about, there followed one of those phenom-
> ena which experts in psychology delight to explain, but which no
> man can understand. Without a word the gambler slowly laid upon
> the table his gun, upon whose handle were many notches, the tally
> of human lives it had accounted for in the hands of this same des-
> perado.
> . . . .
> "Now, listen!" gravely continued the youngster. "I give
> you twenty-four hours to leave this post, and if after twenty-four
> hours you are found here it will be bad for you. Get out!"
> The man, still silent, slunk out of the room. Irresistible
> authority seemed to go with the word that sent him forth, and
> rightly so, for behind that word lay the full weight of Great Britain's
> mighty empire. [9]

Beneath their comic naivete, both scenes are simple, unambiguous op-positions of right and wrong, and in each case right is made to prevail not by violence but by the exertion of a somehow uncanny power. Here the differences begin. The Virginian draws the gun with which he will enforce the right, while in Connor's scene it is the man with the gun who backs down. The young Moun-tie represents the constituted law of the territory, while the Virginian's jus-tice is extra-legal. He speaks of living in a territory where "an honest man was all the law you could find in five hundred miles" (p. 372). And in this show-down, the power which overcomes Trampas and which electrifies the barroom is a force of personality emanating from within the Virginian himself. The young Mountie is quite pointedly not credited with any special capacities or any personal force beyond a character for being devoted to his duty.

Probably the most significant difference between these scenes is in the source of the justice which is asserted. In Wister's Wyoming, justice is roughly defined by codes of behaviour developed to suit the local conditions of life. As his wise old Judge says, "many an act that man does is right or wrong accord-ing to the time and place which form, so to speak, its context..." (p. 430). Justice is more particularly arbitrated on the moment, by men like the Virginian.

The law, as the Judge says in explaining a lynching, comes originally from the people; when they take it back into their own hands, it is not a defiance but an assertion of the law.

The young Mountie, on the other hand, is merely an instrument of a law which, like the whole system of order he maintains and the whole code of values by which he lives, is created elsewhere. His strength lies in his total acceptance of an authority emanating from a remote centre of Empire. One could say that the conception of order in Wister's West is inductive--order is generated from the immediate particulars of experience--while that of Connor's West is deductive--order descends logically from higher precepts to which the individual has no access.

Like Wister's Virginian, Connor's young Mountie is a figure designed to reaffirm the primary cultural values of his society. The Virginian's are recognizably those frontier values which continue to invest the popular Western and which have been so well articulated in American literary studies since the publication of Henry Nash Smith's Virgin Land. The young Mountie's values belong rather to an anti-revolutionary society. They fit in with a garden myth which was prominent in the work of Connor and such contemporaries as Nellie McClung, Arthur Stringer, and Robert Stead. Throughout this early fiction there is a hazy identification of the human order of Empire, the natural order, and the divine order. The Canadian West was not, of course, a frontier in the sense that the American West was, and this was not merely because order usually preceded settlement. It had as much to do with what the West represented to the country as a whole. The prairies were not thought of as the leading edge of a continuously expanding nation but as a colony developed separately which had to be tied in to confederation with a railroad and two armies. Canada itself was not an Atlantic seaboard nation seeking cultural independence from Europe but a landlocked nation struggling to maintain its British character. Canadians were not looking to an advancing frontier to provide their identity or mature their national character, and western writers could not think of themselves as at the centre of forces which were shaping their nation's ideals. The fact that the Canadian fictional prairie is not a frontier in the usual sense and does not yield to the application of Turner's thesis remains the most salient and the most consistent distinction between the literary fictions of the two Wests as it was between popular fictions.

A comparison of the popular fictions should yield many more worthwhile insights but it has some obvious and some unexpected limitations. The most obvious is that such studies tend to be rich in cultural implications but lean in literary interest. The most unexpected is that about fifty years ago the Canadian West ceased to have a popular fiction of its own.

In any case, it is finally not the most popular but the best fiction of the two Wests we want to compare. There are various ways of designating the more accomplished fiction. John R. Milton's term the "Western Novel" is probably the most effective for the American West, though in Canada the term "serious fiction," with its faint aroma of Matthew Arnold, seems to suit our Victorian origins. Literary study of the serious fiction in a sense includes the cultural questions already raised. While popular fiction may reaffirm the basic cultural values, the serious fiction which subjects those values to critical scrutiny also has the effect of defining and distinguishing them more precisely. The question of justice presented in gross terms in The Virginian, for example, is finely honed to its point of moral responsibility in The Oxbow Incident. Comparing the best fiction is necessarily more difficult, since original creations cannot be reduced to convenient formulae, and it may even be perilous to cite a novel as typical. In the present instance that difficulty is aggravated by the fact that the types of fiction to be compared are so disparate. How do you compare The Oxbow Incident with As For Me and My House, or Settlers of the Marsh with The Big Sky?

I am still a long way from a solution to this problem. Like Carlyle's Teufelsdrockh I can offer "nothing but innuendoes, figurative crotchets: a typical Shadow, fitfully wavering," but I hope these first impressions are suggestive enough to indicate that the work is worth doing. [10] There are some similarities with which to begin a comparison. In both bodies of fiction, for example, the implied criticism of basic values reveals characteristic human failures which seem to grow out of those values themselves. These failures are commonly signalled by the final isolation of the hero. Boone Caudill at the end of The Big Sky belongs in neither world; Hugh Glass in Lord Grizzly is left with only his mule and the wilds; Sam Minard in Mountain Man turns away from the wagon train to lay flowers on two lonely graves; Cain Hammett in Riders of Judgement dies fighting alone in his cabin; most of the characters in The Oxbow Incident withdraw from each other in shame. In western Canadian novels the heroes, if heroes they can be called, are similarly isolated. Abe Spalding in Fruits of the Earth is a lonely figure of authority; the Bentleys in As For Me and My House are isolated from the townspeople and from each other; Gander Stake in Grain goes alone to the city; Neil Fraser in Music at the Close dies in maudlin solitude on the battlefield; John Elliott in Our Daily Bread dies beyond all help in his decaying cabin.

The isolation, the exclusion of these figures from their desired community with man or nature, is a traditional tragic pattern, but the failures which produce the isolation are distinctive. Cawelti says that the hero of the formula Western is often excluded from civilized community by the exercise of those very skills of violence with which he has protected the civilized order from savagery, as well as by his stock in the savage way of life and his ambivalence toward the pioneer values of progress. [11] Delbert Wylder, writing of serious western fiction, extends the argument, saying that the western hero is "a man who, through love of freedom, has sacrificed his connection to the rest of humanity and has become impotent in the process." [12] The failure seems to lie consistently in an excess of frontier virtues, especially in a fascination with individualism which makes the hero unable to submit to the social contract even when he has helped to draft it.

By contrast, the isolation of characters like the Bentleys results from a life of self-abnegation. They have submitted themselves too long to what is for them a sterile social order; they have come to depend upon the huddled pettiness of the small town for their self-justification and upon a view of nature as actively hostile. As Mrs. Bentley says:

> We shrink from our insignificance. The stillness and solitude--
> we think a force or presence into it--even a hostile presence,
> deliberate, aligned against us--for we dare not admit an indif-
> ferent wilderness, where we may have no meaning at all. [13]

Mrs. Bentley's experience of feeling isolated from nature is a consistent effect of the submission to social order which characterizes Canadian western fiction. Perhaps the best example is in Grove's _Fruits of the Earth_. Abe Spalding has asserted his will upon the landscape without becoming vitally aware of it.

> He had looked down at his feet; had seen nothing but the furrow;
> had considered the prairie only as a page to write the story of his
> life upon. His vision had been bounded by the lines of his farm;
> his farm had been floated on that prairie as the shipwright floats
> a vessel on the sea, looking not so much at the waves which are to
> batter it as at the fittings which secure the comfort of those within.
> But such a vessel may be engulfed by such a sea. [14]

Spalding has succeeded through his single-minded devotion to the pioneer ideals of order and progress, but eventually finds that he has isolated himself from nature, from his own inner nature, and from those he loves. Again the failure appears to stem from an excess of the prevailing virtues of Abe's West.

These contrasting ways of failing suggest a basic difference between the fictions of the two Wests which seems to lie in that central relationship in which the individual stands between the community and nature. In the American western novel the relationship between the individual and nature is relatively stable. If, as James Folsom says, the central question in this fiction is whether man is more blessed in a state of nature or in a state of civilization, it is at least assumed that an individual's freedom and harmony with wild nature are possible. [15] It is on the other side of that relationship, in the gap between the individual and his community, that the crucial tensions develop to generate the vital action which shapes the fiction. Spring still comes to the young cowhands who leave Oxbow, old Hugh Glass can still get on his mule and go out to "make meat"--it's "them haunt sons" that trouble him.

In prairie fiction, possibly because of the values which have dominated the development of the Canadian West, the stable side of the three-way relationship tends to be between the individual and his society. The critical action is likely to be in the gap between the individual and nature. For pioneers identified with civilized values of order and progress, nature is not necessarily beneficent, and wild freedom is simply an illusion. We should not be misled by the popularity of the garden motif in the early fiction. Most of the serious fiction has been a reaction against that idea, and besides, as anyone knows who has gone through the suburban outdoor routine of uprooting, poisoning, and mutilating living things, a gardener is not a lover of nature but a lover of order. The garden myth, in fact, tended to obscure the uneasy truce between nature and civilization on the northern plains. As the man-nature theme develops in the serious fiction it becomes increasingly apparent that in losing touch with external nature the characters have, like Abe Spalding, lost touch with their own natures. The Bentleys' repression of their unconscious natures, for example, is imaged in the stifling of their creative imaginations. The Waste Land image of the natural environment becomes a reflection of their own sterility. What D. G. Jones says of Canadian culture as a whole is especially pertinent to western fiction:

> The land is both condition and reflection, both mirror and fact.
> Particularly in literature it comes to symbolize elements of our
> inner life. As these elements are ignored or suppressed, the
> land becomes a symbol of the unconscious, the irrational in the
> lives of the characters. And the more powerful those elements
> are, the more disturbing and demonic the land and the figures
> associated with it may become. [16]

In prairie fiction the opposition between man and nature becomes an opposition between man's will and his own nature, between conscious and unconscious.

These differences in the central concerns of the serious fiction on either side of the border bring to mind some possibly related differences in form and technique. If, as John Milton says, "the Western novel is extensive, constantly engaged in an opening-out, from character to action to landscape to a concern with racial consciousness," the prairie novel is inclined to move downward and in, toward an individual consciousness of man's relation to the universe. [17] While the Western novel tends to be more public, more given to action, the prairie novel tends to become private, domestic, personal, confessional. While the form of the Western novel is often romantic, tending toward myth or fable, the form of the best prairie fiction is more novelistic, tending toward documentary or argument. The contrasts could be extended, but these few are probably sufficient to suggest the difficulty of setting up close comparisons between novels.

Immediately contemporary novels seem to offer more accessible ground for comparisons across the 49th parallel. Read Thomas Berger's Little Big Man, Robert Kroetsch's Studhorse Man, Rudy Wiebe's Temptations of Big Bear, Wallace Stegner's Angle of Repose, Margaret Laurence's The Diviners, and you will probably get the impression that the two literatures are converging. One of the most striking similarities is that writers on both sides of the border feel themselves cut off from a living past, but here again their reasons for feeling cut off seem to differ. Wallace Stegner says "westerners...have no sense of a personal and possessed past, no sense of any continuity between the real western past which has been mythicized almost out of recognizability and a real western present that seems as cut-off and pointless as a ride on a merry-go-round that can't be stopped." [18] The intense concentration upon historical authenticity in western studies may spring from a desire for this lost continuity. Western Canadian writers speak less of a discontinuity than a lack of roots. Images from two recent novels may help to characterize the difference. Stegner's Lyman Ward says, "As a modern man and a one-legged man, I can tell you that the conditions are similar. We have been cut off, the past has been ended and the family has broken up and the present is adrift in a wheelchair."[19] Severance from the past has been traumatic, an accident brought on by modern life, technology, urbanization, whatever. In The Diviners Laurence's novelist-narrator, Morag, is represented not as crippled but as orphaned; looking through some photographs of her Manitoba childhood, building pleasing recollections around them, she suddenly says "that is the end of the totally invented memories."[20] Her parents have died without leaving her any coherent memories of themselves, but she is more completely without a "possessed past" because her regional as well as her personal past is made up of conflicting "invented memories": the legends of Piper Gunn told by her Scots foster-father, the songs of "Rider Tonnere" sung by her Metis friend, the Ontario school histories she has been forced to learn. In effect, she is cut off from a living past not because anything traumatic has intervened but because the local past has never been given a living form. If she is to regain it, to find her roots, she must recapture not the authentic detail of her past but its form and significance. A similar impulse can be seen in the myth-making of Robert Kroetsch and the historical fictions of Rudy Wiebe.

It may be that American writers, faced with an over-mythicized West, go back to find the facts, something solid, verifiable, and prosaic enough to draw that past into their known world. The Canadian writer, faced with an under-mythicized West, goes back to find the spirit, the human significance which he knows intuitively must have inhabited the bones of history he has inherited. The past is, for him, a way to the present, a way of knowing at last who and where he is.

University of Alberta

NOTES

[1] The Sound of Mountain Water (New York: Doubleday, 1969), p. 177.

[2] The Canadian West in Fiction, Revised (Toronto: Ryerson, 1970), p. 6.

[3] "The 'Other' Frontiers of the American West," Arizona and the West, IV (Summer 1962), 105-112.

[4] "The Pacific Northwest as a Cultural Region," Pacific Northwest Quarterly, LXIV, No. 4 (October 1973), 137-184.

[5] The Middlewestern Farm Novel in the Twentieth Century (Lincoln: University of Nebraska Press, 1965).

[6] The Sound of Mountain Water, p. 196.

[7] *The Six-Gun Mystique* (Bowling Green: University Popular Press, 1975), p. 31.

[8] *The Virginian* (London: Macmillan, 1902), p. 29.

[9] *Corporal Cameron* (Toronto: Westminster, 1912), pp. 307-308.

[10] *Sartor Resartus* in *Prose of the Victorian Period* (Boston: Houghton Mifflin, 1958), p. 99.

[11] *The Six-Gun Mystique*, p. 73

[12] "The Western Hero From a Strange Perspective," in Richard Etulain et al, ed. *Interpretive Approaches to Western American Literature* (Pocatello: Idaho State University Press, 1972), p. 23.

[13] *As For Me and My House* (1941; rpt, Toronto: McClelland and Stewart, 1957), p. 100.

[14] *Fruits of the Earth* (1933; rpt. Toronto: McClelland and Stewart, 1965). p. 138.

[15] *The American Western Novel* (New Haven: College and University Press, 1966), p. 53.

[16] *Butterfly on Rock* (Toronto: University of Toronto Press, 1970), p. 34.

[17] "The Western Novel: Whence and What," in *Interpretive Approaches to Western American Literature*, p. 19.

[18] *The Sound of Mountain Water*, p. 225.

[19] *Angle of Repose* (Greenwich, Conn.: Fawcett, 1972), p. 13.

[20] *The Diviners* (Toronto: McClelland and Stewart, 1974), p. 9.

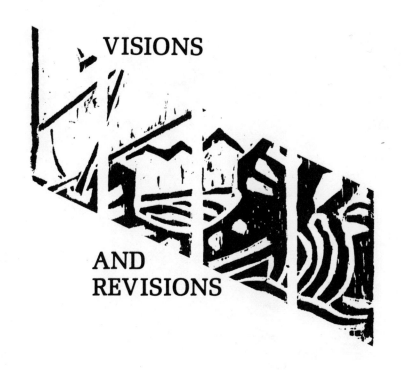

VISIONS

AND
REVISIONS

"AS FAR AS THE SOUTH SEAS": THE DIVIDING LINE AND THE WEST IN WILLIAM BYRD'S HISTORIES

by Kenneth A. Requa

Between the two accounts William Byrd developed out of his journal record taken during his participation in the commission appointed in 1728 to map out the North Carolina-Virginia border line, the difference of purpose is obvious enough: he made the first version, the Secret History of the Dividing Line, an entertainment, a personal history that highlights, often comically, the conflicts among the commissioners themselves, and he larded the second version with enough data on flora, fauna, native Americans, and immigrant settlers to make it serve as a natural history of the area.[1] Less apparent than these conscious and evident designs (and virtually ignored by commentators on Byrd) is another deeply significant matter in these histories: the revelation of Byrd's attitude toward the West, which to him was the Piedmonts, the region he had seen for himself up to 241 miles from the Atlantic coast, and then the mountains and the strange territory beyond that stretched, as the North Carolina charter declared, "as far as the South seas."[2] Fundamental in both accounts is his conviction that the West was a disordered wilderness, an uncultivated land that challenged the cultured Virginian to maintain at least his own order and perhaps like God himself to create order in so chaotic a landscape.

To understand his predetermined perception of the West, it is important to see that there was nothing Byrd, a "citizen of the Enlightenment," as Louis B. Wright has called him, craved so strongly as order, an ideal as old as Aristotle and, to Byrd, as new as Newton.[3] At the time of his appointment to the dividing line commission, he had spent more than half of his life in England. Like other children of wealthy Virginians in the late seventeenth century, he had been sent off to school in England and had stayed on even after he had completed legal studies at the Middle Temple and been called to the bar.[4] Both his experience in England and his reading reinforced his sense that he was now in a raw new world. Like other Virginian aristocrats who, as Byrd's contemporary Hugh Jones pointed out, considered themselves citizens of London as well as of the colony, Byrd tried to make his plantation an outpost of order.[5] The Secret Diaries he kept while in Virginia certainly reveal a man whose sense of order extends all the way from the daily operation of the plantation into his private life, presented in his Diaries, as a measured dance whose steps--sleep, meals, readings, and prayers--rhythmically recur. But the most concise glimpse of this preoccupation is in a letter Byrd wrote to the Earl of Orrery not long after his final return to Virginia in 1726. Although he misses the amusements of London, he says he enjoys the sunny, clear air of Virginia. He finds life on the plantation generally acceptable, but he notes one source of trouble, disorder: "I must take care to keep all my People to their duty, to set all the springs in motion and to make every one draw his equal share to carry the machine forward."[6] The metaphor is the key: it stresses an order as regular as machine-work and the need for an operator to maintain it. Byrd, who believed that as a gentleman he should be moderate in his personal life, believed as well that he should extend this principle of good order into the new world around him.

From the tidewater region, the Virginia gentleman could look past the edges of his world into the region where he most certainly could extend his civilization, the West. Byrd who perfected the plantation founded by his father, a planter and trader well informed about the western wilderness, knew the promise the new lands held. Nine years before his journey along the line, he wrote to the Earl of Orrery: "We have some Men here who have been on some of the Branches of [the] Massasipi River. The nearest to us are 500 miles from this Country; lying about the Latitude of 30, and these Travellers say they never saw either a finer Soil or a finer Clymate."[7] Byrd's emphasis on the qualities of soil and climate reveal his interest in new lands suitable for the westerly extension of his plantation world. When the appointment to the commission came, Byrd did not hesitate, for it not only appeased his hunger for political preferments and his thirst for new acres but also it offered him the opportunity to demonstrate the victory of the Virginia gentleman over all obstacles. As the leader who would steer the men to their goal, he knew they would have little immediate impact on the vast wilds ahead, but in his accounts of the journey he would show the West could not conquer him. Rather than presenting a series of notes on travels, like John Fontaine's account of the Spotswood expedition in 1716 or an account of the terrors of exploration, like John Lederer's narrative of his journeys in 1669 and 1670, Byrd's Histories emphasize the conflict between the uncultivated land and the cultured gentleman.[8]

Some critics have commented that Byrd's Secret History resembles English satirical verse and Restoration comedy. But though strains of these genres are apparent and though Byrd emphasizes the peculiar traits of his characters to such an extent that he came close to writing a comic novel, rather than a history, the deepest unity of the work is not the satiric portraiture itself but the common purpose these portraits reveal: the demonstration of order and disorder in the wilderness.[9] Just as surely as the diet becomes more wild as the party travels west, changing from pork to mixtures of the beef they carry and the game they shoot--deer, wild turkey, buffalo, and bear--so too the men become progressively unruly and even mutinous. Even early in the journey, cowardice interferes with the smooth proceeding of the party. Capricorn makes excuses to avoid the journey (48-49), and men along the way fear joining them: "We endeavored to hire two or three men here to go along with us," Byrd says, "but might for the same price have hired them to make a trip to the other world. They looked upon us as men devoted, like Codrus and the two Decii, to certain destruction for the service of our country" (52).[10] One man volunteers but overnight, reports Byrd, so disturbs himself with dreams of the dangers ahead that he "declared off in the morning" (50).

Once the cavalcade is under way, Byrd focuses his satiric thrusts at disorder within the group itself. The commissioners from North Carolina, in Byrd's account, disrupt the mission. They arrive ill-prepared to travel, "better provided for the belly than the business" (55); they bring more supplies than their horses can carry (95, 99-100). Their contribution to the running of the line is small, but their contribution to disorder--quibbling, drinking, eating--so large that Byrd considers himself well rid of them when, some forty miles before the Virginia party finishes, they decide to abandon the mission. Byrd's final comment on them is in the form of a matrimonial joke, one of his favorite kinds of wit: after all their disagreements, the commissioners from the two colonies part in peace, "just like some men and their wives who, after living together all their time in perpetual discord and uneasiness, will yet be very good friends at the point of death when they are sure they shall part forever" (112). More than simply a random witty aside here, the humorous remark aptly highlights the common strain of disorder in matrimonial combat and the behavior of the commissioners from North Carolina.

The comments Byrd makes on two members of the Virginia party, the Reverend Humdrum and Astrolabe, produce consistent portraits of minor disorders. Chaplain Humdrum is immoderately fond of bear-meat. As they travel west into the mountains, and the country of the bear, the hunger devours the virtuous restraint Byrd implies one should expect of this man of God. Beneath the obviously humorous contrast of a man dedicated to things of the spirit falling into something as unlikely as a craving for bear, the implication is clear as in Byrd's treatment of the other men: Humdrum is overwhelmed by the wild. Metaphors of intemperate love underscore this vicious attachment: "Our chaplain loved it so passionately that he would growl like a wildcat over a squirrel" (118); [Humdrum] "discovered his passion for the delicious flesh of bear" (122). Byrd dubs him the "Bishop of Beardom" and wishes "other bishops loved their flock as entirely as our Doctor loves his" (133). When they leave the western region of the bears, Byrd finds Humdrum is "quite peevish," as if separated from his lover (138).[11] Orion, on the other hand, demonstrates another problem--the failure of the incompetent fop in the hard test of western travel. One of the principal surveyors for Virginia, he performs so badly that Astrolabe, the other surveyor, must cover for him (see, for example, 84-85). He is so impractical a man that going into the most impassible region of the journey, the Dismal Swamp, he takes his Sunday-suit (62). Growing more insecure as the party travels west, he makes himself the disciple of the troublesome Virginia commissioner Firebrand. Byrd, the eminently self-sufficient man of the journey, scorns this cowardly attachment: Orion, he notes, "stuck as close to his patron Firebrand as the itch does to the fingers of many of his country folks" (73). Orion is the "shadow" and "echo" of Firebrand, a "burr" stuck to him. In the Dismal Swamp, apart from his champion, he alone of all the men complains. In all cases, Byrd presents him as a faulty part of the machinery, a man who cannot stand up to the demands of the trip and who, to function at least adequately, must return to the less tasking civilization of tidewater Virginia.

More particularly than these men, Byrd, by his emphasis and selection of detail, placed two of the commissioners at the center of the conflict between order and disorder. The prince of disorder in the Secret History is the man whom he aptly names Firebrand and who from the very first disrupts the progress. [12] Remarking on Firebrand turning up late for their departure, Byrd says: "This disorder at first setting out gave us but an indifferent opinion of Firebrand's management" (50). This ominous beginning is only too well fulfilled, for Firebrand will side with the North Carolina commissioners in all disputes and thus be both disloyal and as low as those commissioners in Byrd's eyes. He will be rowdy, drunk, petty and vain. Throughout, disorderly Firebrand is virtually the counterpart of the disorderly wilderness; in the west, his thin veneer of culture quickly peels away. The man who opposes and ultimately triumphs over Firebrand is Byrd himself, aptly named Steddy; it is the only name Byrd keeps free from ironic connotations. If Firebrand comes close to Byrd's allegorical embodiment of the wild, Steddy is carefully identified with the cultivated landscape of the mother-country. At the very beginning of the journey, Steddy, who has arrived on time, looks from the American coast across the sea toward the old world: "I often cast a longing eye toward England and sighed" (55). The remark might pass for no more than amusing nostalgia, if it did not fit so well the pattern Byrd maintains for Steddy, the true center of whose conscious world is England, the opposite of the pathless western woods he must face. He will show how one man at least maintains order in the wilderness. In his first speech to the men, attempting to set forth for them his own modus operandi, Steddy instructs them "to set...a constant pattern of order, industry, and obedience" (48). In Byrd's account, Steddy is vindicated, for his orderly procedure wins out over all the others, especially the mutinous Firebrand, and he runs the line steadily west. Steadfast through all disorders, natural and human, Steddy so controls the men that the mission is completed. The prince of disorder fails to subvert the commission and leaves before the line is run to its ultimate point; Steddy not only sees it through but more than all the others assumes the credit for the accomplishment.

Byrd makes the conflict between the two men apparent in virtually everything they do. Firebrand refuses an invitation to dinner from one of their hosts along the way because the host failed to send it in the proper form, but Steddy ignores this and accepts the hospitable offer (52). Firebrand will not see the men off on their dangerous mission into the Dismal Swamp, but Steddy accompanies them to the very brink and sends them off with one of his inspiring harangues (62). Firebrand joins with the North Carolina commissioners in their low jokes on the chaplain; Steddy, however, above such pranks, comments: "I was grave and speechless the whole evening and retired early; by all which I gave them to understand I was not fond of the conversation of those whose wit, like the commons at the university and Inns of Court, is eternally the same" (96). Firebrand is proud and vain, a man who insists the common men call him "master" and who claims as his own a boar dead before he shot (98, 102). Steddy is modest and acts honorably, rather than seeking honors. Perhaps the best example of their differences in behavior, however, is the contrast implied in Steddy's reaction to slipping from his horse into a creek (Firebrand, of course, would have sworn, his reaction to even lesser discomforts, but not Steddy): "I wet myself all over and bruised the back part of my head, yet made no complaint but was the merriest of the company at my own disaster" (133) . The juxtaposition of merriest and disaster is the key: the "well-bred gentleman and polite companion" maintains his poise, even in pain.[13] But Byrd stresses even more strongly than these conflicts of manners the sexual conduct of the two men. Steddy is virtuous throughout the journey, Firebrand rapacious. Before the cavalcade leaves the settlements behind, Firebrand assaults two of their hostesses. Once, he nearly rapes the woman (Byrd stops short of that charge), as does his servant, over whom, Byrd suggests, Firebrand should have some control; and the other time, Firebrand contents himself with tormenting the woman by picking her scabs (73, 61). Steddy, who characteristically sleeps away from the houses, scorns such conduct. As his account would have it, Steddy plays the gentleman at all times. Others may go too far, but Steddy contents himself with a few saucy remarks and chaste kisses. Byrd's Diary, of course, reveals that at least during his time in London he tended to slip down to the suburbs of moderation, but he presents Steddy on this journey, aware of his position, as always remaining discreet. In the Indian camp, Nottaway Town, he is not one of those men who soil their linen seeking favors from the women (82), and on occasion, he even plays the chaperon to save women from his lusty companions (60, 64). In fact, the only personal indiscretion Byrd records is confined to Steddy's dream of the three graces, with one of whom he has an "intrigue" (120). The major confrontation of the two men, however, comes on the last night of their time together. Firebrand, arguing with Meanwell, the third Virginian on the commission, loses all control and flourishes a table-leg; Steddy calls on his authority as chief commissioner to restore order. Completely out of control, Firebrand defies him until Steddy falls back on the most prudent way to calm the storm--summoning his men and threatening Firebrand with arrest. The language of this climactic scene distinguishes the orderly gentleman from the troublemaker: Firebrand angers and takes "fire," he speaks in a great fury, but Byrd has Steddy sound unruffled: "I desired him to forebear or I should be obliged to take him in arrest" (107). The result of the conflict is the inevitable final victory of Steddy over Firebrand, of the well-maintained man over the wild one.

Even apart from these conflicts with the other members of the party, Byrd presents Steddy as serene throughout the journey. Although occasionally he is "almost dazzled" by the "wild prospect" of the western landscape, he does not essentially alter his way of perceiving the wilds. Part of his serenity is maintained by what he avoids, as is the case with the Dismal Swamp and the bear. Not perceiving the grim possibilities Melville suggests (that the Dismal Swamp might stand as an image of the dark disorders of the world), Steddy treats it only as difficult terrain that will inconvenience his men. The animal most associated with the West in the Secret History, the bear, does not loom in Steddy's imagination as a grand symbol of the wilderness itself, as it did for Faulkner's Ike McCaslin; rather, Steddy sees in it a providential supply of meat, provided to help the mission succeed (137). His equilibrium is supported at least in part by his ability to reduce the strange to the familiar. The witty names he gives mountains, such as "Pimple," "Wart," and "Maiden's Breast" (122, 123, 132) could suggest the whistling-in-the-dark of a man surrounded by the unknown, but the tone controls the report, so that Steddy betrays no fear or even hesitation. The naming of Matrimony Creek is typical: "Something more than four miles from our camp we crossed Matrimony Creek, which received its name from being very noisy, the water murmuring everlastingly amongst the rocks" (123). Nothing is betrayed here in this straightforward account. Placing the familiar name on the strange creek, recalling homey wit, rather than attempting to capture the distinct natural phenomenon is simply a gentleman's pastime in the wilderness. Steddy, the Secret History shows throughout, does not succumb to the wilds. With such a man at the center of the account, from his first call to the men to remain orderly to his happy return home where he finds all in good order, nothing is so overwhelming as Byrd's urge to make this entertaining account reveal the triumph of a civilized gentleman who travelled through the wild untouched as if his own orderly self had created for him a magic circle.

Byrd was not finished with his materials yet. Since the chief audience for the Secret History would have been his plantation neighbors who knew the actual men behind the pseudonymous caricatures Byrd had created, he apparently returned once more to his materials with a larger audience in mind. Once again, he imposed his literary imagination on the factual material to make it take another shape. That he worked to make his new account reflect the order he believed in so strongly is evident in the letter he wrote to Peter Collinson in July, 1736. Byrd claims he would not let his manuscript out to a general audience until it met his own exacting standards: "I have an infirmity, never to venture anything unfinisht out of my hands. The Bashfull Bears hide their Cubbs, 'til they have lickt them into shape, nor am I too proud to follow the example of those modest animals. If Solomon sends lazy people to the Ants, to learn industry, all authors, should not be ashamed to go to the Bears, to be instructed, never to produce any offspring of theirs, 'til they have brought it into Shape fit to be seen."[14] Although Byrd never licked the History into the shape he wanted, and so kept it back from publication, he did produce a significantly new work from the same basic material as the Secret History. He took this new account far in the direction of a natural history, adding a prefatory history of the founding of the colonies, detailed observations on animals seen along the way (opossums, beavers, and bears) and some not seen (alligators and whales), as well as descriptions of frontier conditions, but he still maintained the same basic pose as the gentleman in control. His method is different from before, for the men in the dividing-line party receive much less attention. He makes brief mention of the North Carolina commissioners (they come supplied in September, Byrd cannot help mentioning, with so much food, "we were afraid they intended to carry the line to the South Sea" [223]), and of Firebrand and Orion, here under their own names, but the conflicts they engendered and the gallant efforts Steddy made to hold the crew together are either deleted or so deemphasized that they have little importance in the new account. One example

of the kind of changes Byrd made is his two accounts of October 15. In the
Secret History, he provides the basic detail of distance advanced, but he
emphasizes especially two episodes of disorderly conduct. In the first case,
Steddy maintains order: "I interposed very seasonably to decide a wager betwixt two of the warmest of our men, which might otherwise have inflamed them
into a quarrel" (120). The second is a case of theft: "This night Astrolabe's
servant had his purse cut off, in which he lost his own money and some that my
man had put into his keeping. We could suggest nobody but Holmes of the kingdom of Ireland, who had watched, it seems, that night for several of the men,
without which he could not have had an opportunity" (121). The History provides
the same geographic details, but Byrd omits the disputes and introduces material on wild geese and bears. He begins with personal observation and fills
out the accounts with details learned from other sources. From the Indians he
learns their name for geese and comments on the quality of the down and meat.
He begins his comments on bears with the observation of a bear sitting on gravel in the middle of a stream and goes on to explain how the gravel gets piled:
"[I] wondered very much at first how so many heaps of small stones came to be
piled up in the water, till at last we spied a bear sitting upon one of them, looking with great attention on the stream and raking up something with his paw,
which I take to be the shellfish above-mentioned" (251). The shifts Byrd made
from personal matters to observations of nature change his picture of the men
so much that a statement he makes about the group early in the History (February 28) could stand as well for the entire journey: "They proceeded in good order" (172).

Although Byrd comes across most strongly in the History as the natural
scientist serenely recording the wonders of the west, his sense of order creeps
into the work in another way. The deemphasis of conflicts among the commissioners allows him to let them be his standard for measuring the people they
pass along the way. The few industrious and frugal people they pass receive
due praise. Of Norfolk, Virginia, he says: "The two cardinal virtues that make
a place thrive, industry and frugality, are seen here in perfection; and so long
as they can banish luxury and idleness the town will remain in a happy and
flourishing condition" (173; see too 192). But as they travel west, Byrd finds
more often lazy and idle settlers he must chastize. The famous passage on
Lubberland is the most explicit example of Byrd's abhorrence of disorderly
people, for here is a place that attracts the indolent and stands as a contrast
to Byrd's ideally run plantation: "To speak the truth, 'tis a thorough aversion
to labor that makes people file off to North Carolina, where plenty and a warm
sun confirm them in their disposition to laziness for their whole lives" (205).
The slothful inactivity of such people implicitly contrasts to the energetic progress of the dividing line party. In the History, it thus becomes clear, Byrd's
strategy has changed but not his stance. Like the Secret History, this account
celebrates orderly procedure under disorderly circumstances. As a natural
history, it celebrates the control the Enlightened mind maintained over the raw
materials of the new land.

More land-owner and planter than writer, Byrd was not content to merely let his mind play with literary versions of his western journey along the line. He tried two schemes to act upon the implication in both Histories that the cultured gentleman could control the uncultivated lands. His first proposal, made a year after his return from the journey, was that the English Commission for Trade and Plantations oversee construction of a canal between rivers in North Carolina and Virginia. Byrd told the commissioner, Colonel Martin Bladen, that he was convinced such a canal would benefit the public in general but especially the land owners along the line, of whom Byrd hoped to be one, whose property, he estimated, would increase ten-fold in value.[15] Perhaps because this proposal did not work out, Byrd tried his second plan to civilize the western lands. By a large purchase from the North Carolina commissioners, who had received acreage for their services on the dividing-line survey, Byrd brought some 20,000 acres under his personal control and planned to bring immigrants to cultivate this new land along the dividing line. He told Governor Johnston of North Carolina that the colony he envisioned "would not only be a Guard to the Frontiers, but would encourage the taking up of Lands, in those parts."[16] To help begin this westward movement, Byrd made another trip west in 1733 to see his new purchase. This "Land of Eden"as he called it, after the former governor of North Carolina, Charles Eden, and the paradise he thought it resembled, Byrd hoped would take on the civilized ways of the world he knew. In a passage that recalls Steddy sighing as he glances back toward England, Byrd in his account of the "Journey to the Land of Eden" looks back at his new western land as he and his friends depart for home: "I could not quit this pleasant situation without regret but often faced about to take a parting look at it as far as I could see."[17] What Byrd perhaps saw in his imagination is what many other American exploiters-to-come would also see: the untouched land not as something worthy of awe and perhaps preservation but rather as the raw material upon which the commercial mind could impose its shapes.

University of Washington

NOTES

[1]The exact dates of composition remain unknown, but William K. Boyd and Richard B. Davis argue for the following order: The Secret History, sometime between Byrd's return in 1728 and 1732; the History, between 1732 and 1738. Davis, "William Byrd: Taste and Tolerance," in Major Writers of Early American Literature, ed. Everett Emerson (Madison: Univ. of Wisconsin Press, 1972), pp. 168-69; Boyd, "Introduction," William Byrd's Histories of the Dividing Line Betwix Virginia and North Carolina (1929; New York: Dover 1967), pp. xxvii-xxviii.

[2]"The Second Charter granted by King Charles II to the Proprietors of Carolina," in The Prose Works of William Byrd of Westover: Narratives of a Colonial Virginian, ed. Louis B. Wright (Cambridge: Harvard Univ. Press, 1966), p. 323. Two exceptions to the commentators alluded to are Carl Dolmetsch who would claim the History for "the very 'American' literature of

westering" and Robert D. Arner who sees the dividing line itself as Byrd's "frontier...as Europeans understood [the term], to denote a firmly fixed border between two hostile states, the comforting known and the disquieting unknown." Dolmetsch, "William Byrd II: the Augustan Writer as 'Exile' in His Own Country," Virginia Quarterly Review, 48 (Winter, 1972), 149; Arner, "Westover and the Wilderness: William Byrd's Images of Virginia," Southern Literary Journal, 7 (Spring, 1975), 119.

[3]Wright, "William Byrd: Citizen of the Enlightenment," in Anglo-American Cultural Relationships in the Seventeenth and Eighteenth Centuries (Los Angeles: William Andrews Clark Library [1958]), pp. 26-40. Using the distinctions of Henry F. May, I would qualify the title to Citizen of the Moderate Enlightenment, that is, the first phase of the British-nurtured, American phase of the movement, which maintained as one of its highest ideals order. May, The Enlightenment in America (New York: Oxford Univ. Press, 1976), pp. 3-41.

[4]The best biography is in Pierre Marambaud's William Byrd of Westover, 1674-1744 (Charlottesville: Univ. Press of Virginia, 1971), pp. 15-57.

[5]Jones, The Present State of Virginia from Whence Is Inferred a Short View of Maryland and North Carolina, ed. Richard L. Morton (Chapel Hill: Univ. of North Carolina Press for the Virginia Historical Society, 1956), pp. 74, 80. See too Louis B. Wright, The First Gentlemen of Virginia: Intellectual Qualities of the Early Colonial Ruling Class (San Marino: Huntington Library, 1940).

[6]The Orrery Papers, ed. Countess of Cork and Orrery (London: Duckworth & Co., 1903), I, 60-61.

[7]Orrery Papers, I, 32.

[8]The Journal of John Fontaine: An Irish Huguenot Son in Spain and Virginia, 1710-1719, ed. Edward Porter Alexander (Williamsburg: Colonial Williamsburg Foundation, 1972), pp. 101-109; The Discoveries of John Lederer..., trans. Sir William Talbot (1672; facs. rpt. Ann Arbor: University Microfilms, 1966).

[9]See Maude H. Woodfin, "Introduction,"Another Secret Diary of William Byrd of Westover, 1739-1741 (Richmond: Dietz Press, 1942), p. xxxix; Willie T. Weathers, "William Byrd: Satirist,"William and Mary Quarterly, 3rd ser., 4 (January, 1947), 33; Dolmetsch, "William Byrd: Comic Dramatist?" Early American Literature, 6 (Spring, 1971), 28; Dolmetsch, VQR, 149.

[10]All quotations from the Histories follow Wright, ed., Prose Works and are cited in the essay by page numbers only.

[11]In these passages, Byrd could well have a submerged sexual joke about the prissy parson's carnal appetite, for Byrd elsewhere reports that Indians consider bear-meat an aphrodisiac, and, in the History, he notes the Indian women some of the men find so irresistible are coated with bear oil (141, 218).

67

[12] Robert D. Arner has called attention to the metaphorical language through which Byrd casts Firebrand as a devil. Byrd is even more specific than Arner suggests, however, for the major moral threat throughout from Firebrand is disorder. Arner, 114.

[13] The phrase quoted is part of the epitaph on Byrd's monument. See Marambaud, p. 57.

[14] "Letters of the Byrd Family," Virginia Magazine of History and Biography, 36 (October, 1928), 355.

[15] "Letters," VMHB, 36 (April, 1928), 115-16.

[16] "Letters," VMHB, 36 (July, 1928), 210.

[17] Prose Works, p. 398.

WONDERS OF THE VISIBLE WORLD: CHANGING IMAGES OF THE WILDERNESS IN CAPTIVITY NARRATIVES

by Andrew Wiget

The task of westering not only taxed the settlers' economic and physical resources to the limit, forcing innovations in finance, technology, and social systems; it also forced changes in their imaginative perception of the wilderness, a continual revaluation of the meaning of the unknown land beyond the margins of civilization. The captivity narrative enduring as a genre throughout the frontier experience, reflects at various moments in its development those critical turning points at which the social and imaginative forces which stirred in the contemporary mind changed the image of the wilderness from Desert to Garden.[1] As the Puritan providential view of history disintegrated in the last decades of the eighteenth century under the impact of new ideas, especially sentimentalism and a growing interest in various aspects of the Romantic vision, narrators of the Indian captivities began to separate the Indian from his forest or plains background. The providential perspective which had served for over a hundred years as a frame to hold the foreground and the background of the desert portrait of the hostile and alien wilderness together and in focus was broken. This effective dissolution of the ties between native and nature permitted narrators to continue to malign the Indian while marvelling at the wonders of the visible world. Americans began to represent the wilderness landscape as the source of wonder, the ground of possibilities, even a potential Garden.

Though the Puritans came to America to escape religious persecution, they mortgaged their way on the promised benefits of the fur trade. Abuses in the New England trade, its ultimate failure, and the tension produced by steady encroachment on Indian lands, precipitated the early forest wars of the sixteenth century, a conflict aggravated by the involvement of colonies in the European wars that carried France and England into the eighteenth century. But the Puritans were possessed of a peculiar ideology whose imaginative energy colored not only their interpretation of these events, but their vision of the Indian and the wilderness landscape through which he roamed. In the words of William Hubbard, chief chronicler of King Philip's War, the New World wilderness was a "howling desart." He described the Plimoth forces, who abandoned chasing the Indians into the infamous Poccasset swamps, as unwilling

> to run into the mire and dirt after them in a dark swamp
> being taught by late experience how dangerous it is to fight
> in such dismal woods, when their eyes were muffled with
> the leaves, and their arms piniored with the thick boughs
> of trees, as their feet were continually shackled with the
> roots spreading every way in those boggy woods.[2]

Nathaniel Saltonstall, another war reporter, also featured the wilderness landscape as one vast tract of forest and swamp. In 1682 when her classic captivity narrative was published, Mary Rowlandson, too, described the wilderness as "vast and howling," filled with snow, cold, wild rivers, vast swamps, dense forest, and inhabited by "wild beasts."[3] By 1699, when Cotton Mather published his history of the wars, Decennium Luctuosum, the descriptive language was already stereotyped. Recounting the captivity of Sarah Gerish, Mather describes her

> terrible march through the Thick Woods, and a thousand
> other Miseries, till they came to the Norway-Plains.
> From thence they made her go to the end of Winno-pisseag
> Swamps, where sometimes they must Scramble over huge
> Trees fallen by Storm or Age for a vast way together, and
> sometimes they must Climb up long, steep, tiresome, and
> almost Inaccessible Mountains. . . .
>   A Long and sad Journey she had of it, thro' the midst
> of an hideous Desart, in the midst of a dreadful Winter.[4]

Mather continues, urging the reader to imagine the captive's fear when the Indians had abandoned her: "What Agonies you may imagine she was in, to find herself left a prey for Bear and Wolves, and without any sustenance, in a howling Wilderness many Scores of Leagues from any Plantation?"

The emotional energy necessary to sustain the violence of this wilderness imagery was rooted in the Puritans' inability to separate the landscape from its Indian inhabitants with whom they were forever involved in a real and bloody war. In this howling desert, the Indian was naturally a wild beast, the most ferocious animal, literally a man-eater; the imagery of the landscape was inextricably bound to this image of the Indian. Of the Poccassett swamp, Hubbard remarks, "it is ill fighting with a wild beast in his own den."[5] And Saltonstall notes the Indian's uncanny, almost supernatural mastery of that swamp:

> This Pocassit Swamp, is judged about seven or eight Miles
> long, and so full of Bushes and Trees, that a Parcel of
> Indians may be within the Length of a Pike of a Man, and
> He cannot discover them; and besides, this as well as all
> other Swamps, is so soft Ground, that an Englishman can
> neither go nor stand thereon, and yet these bloody savages
> will run along over it, holding their Guns cross their Arms
> (and if Occassion be) discharge them in that Posture.[6]

Mather emphasizes the Indian's peculiar, yet natural, relationship to the wilderness by using animal images. The forests were "The Dark places of New-England, where Indians had their Unapproachable Kennels, were Habitations of Cruelty"; and the Indian was variously portrayed in his den or lair as a dragon, tiger, werewolf, bear, adder, wolf, and finally, as the Devil.[7]

The Puritans, of course, considered themselves God's chosen people. In the battle to carve a New Israel out of the heathen Canaan to which He had led them, they were His army and the Indians were the heathen oppressors of Israel and allies of the devil. The land could be made clean only through blood; it had to be wrested in mortal and immortal combat from the hands of the implacable savage demons that possessed it. As long as this providential perspective persisted, the colonial mind could never see the wilderness as a land of promise, a native Eden.   The wilderness continued to be imaged as hell in the minds of some individuals until the end of the nineteenth century. However, this hellish wilderness of the Puritans and of the Rowlandson-Mather narratives, though it persisted in the popular imagination and was reflected in captivity narratives through the period following the French and Indian war, began very early to be undermined by the seeds of sentimentalism.

The seeds had been planted in the captivity narrative genre from the first; the Puritan narratives consistently displayed a white heroine, often with babe in arms.[8] Rowlandson, for instance, finds herself alone in the wilderness with only her "poor wounded babe, and it seemed a present worse than death that it was in such pitiful condition, bespeaking compassion."[9] Elizabeth Hanson in her 1724 narrative complains of "being tender and weakly," since it had been "but fourteen days since my lying in."[10] By the end of the eighteenth century the Madonna of the Wilderness had become a captivity narrative motif. When the Indians attack the house of Mrs. Frances Scott, the editor of her 1786 narrative describes the parent-child relationship in clearly sentimental terms:

> the eldest, a beautiful girl of eight years old, awoke and
> escaped out of the Bed, and ran to the Parent, and, with
> the most Plaintive Accents, cried, 'O Mamma! Mamma!
> Save Me! The Mother, in the deepest anguish of spirit
> and with a Flood of Tears, entreated the Savages to spare
> her child; but with brutal Fierceness they tomahawked
> and stabbed her in the Mother's Arms.[11]

Melodrama, of course, was inherent in such situations. In her narrative of 1792, Jemima Howe, describing her winter captivity, notes that "The lips of my own child were sometimes so benumbed that when I put it to my breast, it could not, till it grew warm, embibe the nourishment requisite for its support."[12] The fictional captivity narrative exploited these incidents more frequently; in the narrative of Maria Kittle, written by Ann Eliza Bleecker in 1797, Maria's daughter, the "smiling Anna," wins the affection of everyone; including the Indians who bring her, "the earliest strawberries, the scarlet plumb and other delicate wild fruits in painted baskets."[13] Under such circumstances the audience appeal of the narrative drifted away from religious concerns with Providence towards an emotional involvement with the Heroine.

This change in attitude is made clear by a subtle and distinctive shift in the stock opening of captivity narratives.   The standard motivation of Puritan narratives was the sin of pride; a proud person was made subject to the test of

71

God's wrath, his "refining fire." Rowlandson explains the Indian attack by remarking, "The Lord hereby would make us the more to acknowledge his hand, and see that our help is always in him."[14] John Gyles strikes a similar note in the opening of his narrative, published in 1736, as does Peter Williamson in his narrative of 1757. But by the last third of the century, under the impact of sentimentalism, the situation which precipitated the attack in both fictional and non-fictional narratives was not the would-be captive's pride but his idyllic pastoral and nuptial happiness. The fictional narratives written by Miss Bleecker (1797) and by the pseudonymous Abraham Panther (1787) begin similarly. Panther's captive tells of spending with her husband "many happy evenings vowing mutual love and fondly anticipating future happiness."[15] Bleecker's Mrs. Kittle and her husband, visited and loved by everyone, occupied a "small, neat" farm; and Mr. Kittle, out hunting with his brother, exults in the outdoors, his wife and his children, exclaiming "I anticipate my heaven."[16] Sentimentalized bliss rather than pride went before the fall in non-fictional captivities as well; Mary Kinnan, in her 1795 narrative described her pre-captivity state thus: "Happiness smiled on our cottage; -- content spread her influence around; --the voice of grief was not heard."[17] Even John Filson, in his 1784 narrative of the captivity of Daniel Boone, describes the tranquil, Edenic qualities of the Kentucky wilderness just before the Indians attack.

The sentimental appeal of the fictional narrative was often made openly. Panther's captive, awakening from a swoon, begins with the ingenuous disclaimer that it "cannot be very interesting or entertaining -- yet it may possibly excite your pity, while it gratifies your curiosity."[19] Maria Kittle's "smiling Anna" asks her father, when he leaves the day before their captivity, "who will tend me when my papa, my mama's papa is gone?"[20] This overt sentimental appeal in sentimental language colored nonfictional narratives as well. The impassioned Mary Kinnan began her 1795 narrative in this manner:

> Whilst the tear of sensibility so often flows at the unreal
> tale of woe, which glows under the pen of the poet and the
> novelist, shall our hearts refuse to be melted with sorrow at
> the unaffected and unvarnished tale of a female, who has
> surmounted difficulties and dangers which on a review ap-
> pear romantic, even to herself.[21]

Susannah Johnson (1807), while remarking that "The air of novelty will not be attempted in the following pages; simple facts, unadorned, is what the reader must expect," added that "pity for my sufferings and admiration for my safe return is all that my history can excite."[22] And when Mrs. Johnson is "Taken with the pangs of childbirth," she urges "The compassionate reader to drop a fresh tear, for my inexpressible distress."[23]

Perhaps the most dramatic element in this deterioration of the Puritan perspective was the secularization of the wilderness experience. This is most marked by the decline in the use of Biblical quotation. The numerous quotations, complete with textual references, served to create for the Puritan a wilderness experience that was a nearly-allegorical "type" of the Babylonian captivity, investing the narrative with the religious themes of the test of faith, the chosen people in the land of the heathen, and the intervention of Providence. Almost all the references in Rowlandson, for instance, come from the Psalms and prophetic books written during or about the Babylonian captivity. The Puritan captivity narrative was perhaps the highest New World embodiment of a grace rather than works theology of salvation. [24] Extensive and exact quotation from the Bible seems to have been a function of the closely circumscribed Puritan religious community; as the frontier moved westward out of New England into the Appalachians and the eighteenth century, such exact quotations diminish considerably. Bartlett (1807) uses them extensively in his anti-Catholic captivity narrative of the French and Indian War, as does Zadock Steele (1818); notably, both are New Englanders. [25] Paraphrasings appear in the place of exact quotations in Eastburn (1758) and Marrant (1785), the last making open reference to Whitfield's preaching; hymns of Watts and Wesley are often quoted in place of Biblical quotations. [26] More common are general references to Providence, beginning with Hanson (1724) and persisting, though becoming fewer and fewer, into the nineteenth century. [27] By the end of the century, many narratives had dispensed with religious allusions almost entirely, supplanting them with literary allusions to Shakespeare and later Romantic poets. [28]

Even the "remarkable Providences" which so characterize the Puritan perspective were considerably secularized. In 1783, John Slover, about to be burned at the stake, found himself the gracious recipient of a sudden cloudburst out of a clear sky which drenched the fire and saved him: Slover does not emphasize his particular salvation, but seems more taken, as the reader is, by the wonder of it. [29] Mrs. Frances Scott, lost in the wilderness, is also the recipient of a miracle, but in her case no mention is made of Providence:

> Our Wanderer now left the River, and after proceeding a good distance, she came to where the valley parted in two, each leading a different Course. Here a painful Suspense again took place: A forlorn Creature almost exhausted, and certain, if she was far led out of the Way, she should never see a human Creature. During this Soliloquy, a beautiful Bird passed close by her, fluttering along the Ground, and went out of sight up one of the Vallies. This drew her Attention, and whilst considering what it might mean, another Bird of the same Appearance, fluttered past her, and took the same Valley the other had done. This determined her choice of the Way. [30]

Two days later, having chosen the right path, Mrs. Scott left the wilderness behind. Lacking divine reference, Providence has been reduced to chance. This is emphasized in Mary Kinnan's 1795 narrative. Planning to rendezvous in the woods with her brother who has come to rescue her, she misses him, each "having gone to different trees." The following night they are reunited, presumably under the right tree, though no reference to the tree or Providence is made in the text. [31]

Perhaps nothing illustrates more clearly the change in attitude that led to the destruction of the Providential perspective than a small passage in John Slover's narrative. Slover experiences a change of heart "sudden and perceivable as lightning, an assurance of my peace made with God," while he is at the stake awaiting the fire. But he prefaces the revelation of that experience with a statement that, "I knew myself to have been a regular member of the church and to have sought repentance for my sins."[32] It is clear that his "confidence in mind" about his salvation does not depend wholly upon that sudden grace from God, but also upon some sense of his own worth. The focus of the writer's as well as the reader's attentions here moves away from the arbitrary intervention of transcendent Deity to the interior life of the man.

This emphasis on sentimentalism and the personal ego perspective of the narrator also affected the treatment of the landscape. While Puritan narratives had used very emotional language to describe the wilderness, the source of that language was ultimately the peculiar communal, religious perspective furnished by their ideology. The appearance in the last third of the eighteenth century of a new Romantic aesthetic served to focus attention on the human source of wilderness imagery.

Beginning with the resurrection of Longinus' treatise, On the Sublime, at the beginning of the eighteenth century, English essayists began to pay attention to the capacity of the wilderness landscape to stir our emotions. In an important series of essays in the Spectator, Joseph Addison addressed himself to "The Pleasures of the Imagination," asserting that they arose primarily from "the Sight of what is Great, Uncommon, or Beautiful."[33] The scenes of storms, whitewater, and mountains which he used to exemplify his thesis were quickly appropriated by many who saw in the grandeur of nature the highest kind of beauty. MacPherson's Ossian, so often quoted in the eighteenth century as the highest expression of the sublime, is filled with such rugged, misty landscapes. In America, Jefferson, it appears, knew both the Spectator essays and Ossian and accepted that vision of the landscape.[34] His description of the magnificence of the Natural Bridge or of the grandeur of the Blue Ridge reveal his interest in the wilderness landscape; even Filson's Boone cannot describe the region with such open pleasure and excitement.[35]

But if landscape influenced emotions, elevating the soul in "a proud flight," it was also true that one's emotional state could affect the vision of the landscape. Hugh Blair, perhaps Ossian's greatest apologist in the eighteenth century, pointed this out, revealing the sentimentalism inherent in such a perspective; Ossian's poetry, Blair wrote, "deserves to be styled, The poetry of the heart. It is. . . a heart that is full, and pours itself forth."[36] Implicit in this aesthetic, in Ossian's poetry, and even in Jefferson's agrarianism, is an incipient primitivism which postulates a correspondence between the landscape and the soul. This primitivism is founded on the ambiguity of the relationship between the viewer and the landscape, an ambiguity Longinus perceived when he wrote that the soul "is filled with joy and vaunting, as if it had itself produced what it has heard."[37]

This ambiguity had a lasting effect on the captivity narrative: man could be depressed and see the wilderness as hostile and oppressive, while in fact the wilderness may be exceedingly beautiful. Bleecker makes this clear in her fictitious narrative of Maria Kittle:

> When our souls are gloomy, they seem to cast a shade
> over the objects that surround us, and make nature
> correspondent with our feelings. So Mr. Kittle thought
> the night fell with a deeper gloom than usual.[38]

And elsewhere she describes Maria waking:

> As the sun began to exhale the crystal glories of morning,
> . . . half rising, and reclining on her elbow, [Maria]
> surveyed the lonely landscape with a deep sigh; they were
> on an eminence that commanded an unlimited prospect of
> the country every way. The birds were cheerful; the deer
> bounded fearless over the hills; the meadows blushed with
> the enamel of Flora; but grief had saddened every object in
> her sight; the whole creation seemed a dark blank to the
> fair mourner.[39]

The ambiguity between objective and subjective landscape was not restricted to fictional narratives, though it was certainly more prominent there. Mary Kinnan, in her narrative of 1795, implies that there are two landscapes when she says: "Nature too <u>seemed</u> to conspire against me."[40] (My emphasis) And in 1872, Fanny Kelly wrote of the Plains, "with a mind free from fear and anxiety, the whole picture would have been a dream of delight."[41] Her mood, however, precluded any enjoyment.

The belief that there were two landscapes, one in the imagination and one in reality, wrought havoc with the Puritan landscape. Rachel Plummer could write in 1839, "Notwithstanding my sufferings, I could not but admire the country,"[42] but for Mather, Hubbard, and Rowlandson such a distinction was impossible. The Puritan wilderness landscape of the mind was the real landscape, the only landscape, and it was hell. However, the doctrine of correspondence between soul and nature with its two landscapes opened the door to new treatments of the wilderness. The landscape could be both hell, reflecting the tortured state of the narrator's mind and emotions, and an Eden in and of itself.

In terms of the landscape as hell, a persistent motif in the captivity narrative from Rowlandson (1682) to Kelly (1872) is the belief that man can only be dehumanized in the wilderness. This is most clearly indicated by his being forced to eat "uncivilized" food and, out of sheer hunger, actually to like it; such food might be horsemeat, roots, grubs, the entrails of animals, even human flesh.[43] Tortures and treachery persist; new levels of savage Indian inventiveness seem to be uncovered in each succeeding narrative. In Peter Williamson's narrative (1757) a captive is buried with only his head exposed and a fire built around him just enough distance away that his brains slowly boil and eyes gush out. [44] The heightened emotional state of the narrator is often mentioned, even in the most objective treatments; Charles Johnston (1827) felt horror "thrill through his frame."[45] Such heightened states often induced forebodings, visions, and other psychological phenomena. Jemima Howe (1793) imagined she saw the tortured "Carcasses" of her children hanging in a tree; John Tanner (1830) had a vision of where he would kill a bear come true; Rachel Plummer (1839) saw a ministering angel who visited her in a cave; Mary Jemison (1842) saw a white sheet loom before her menacingly, seeming to obliterate her vision, and imagined very graphically possible tortures she might suffer; and Fanny Kelly (1872) was convinced she heard the voices of her husband and child crying out to her in the darkness. [46]

This Gothic strand of tortures, animalism, forebodings, and visions was linked closely with sentimentalism and the emotional state of the narrator. These events served as a kind of "objective correlative" by which the depths of the narrator's emotional suffering could be meaningfully communicated to the reader. It is clear, however, that the terror resides in the imagination of the narrator and is not an inherent quality of the wilderness environment. For it is in some of these same narratives which exacerbate earlier Gothic tendencies that the seeds of the wilderness Garden first bloom. Picturesque imagery of violent, but thrilling storms abound; the landscape is often treated in picturesque, even sublime images; curiosity about great natural wonders increases; fertility rather than sterility is a common theme; and an Eden of beauty, enchantment, even of plenty, is pictured for the reader.

Those thrilling but threatening storms that Romantic landscape artists in paint and prose found so attractive and which seem to represent so ideally the ambivalence of the landscape, its sublime but fearful aspect, abound. Jemima Howe (1793) describes a violent lightning storm and an earthquake; Mary Kinnan (1795) found, "the rain descended in torrents, the lightnings flashed dreadfully, and almost without intermission; whilst the thunder rolled awfully on high."[47] The fullest elaboration of these terrible but sublime storms in a captivity narrative appears in one of the first Beadle dime novels, the fictional Seth Jones: or, The Captives of the Frontier (1861) by Edward S. Ellis:

> The heavy clouds, growing darker and more awful, poured
> forward until they seemed to concentrate in the western sky,
> where they towered aloft like some old embattled castle.
> The thunder grew heavier, until it sounded like the rolling
> of chariot wheels over the courts of heaven, and the red
> streams of liquid fire streamed down the dark walls of
> Storm Castle. [48]

A similarly awesome thunderstorm was described less poetically by Fanny Kelly in her 1872 narrative. [49]

Though in their sublimity both were attractive to man, the grandeur of the frontier storms was more than matched by the grandeur of the frontier landscape itself. The "landscaping" tradition took two courses: on the one hand, the frontier was almost idyllically imagined, pastoral images abound and lead inevitably to the ultimate description of the wilderness as Garden; on the other hand, the picturesque tradition is less concerned with pastoral aspects of the wilderness than it is with descriptions of the natural wonders.

Picturesque scenery prevailed in captivity narratives by the end of the eighteenth century. Mrs. Frances Scott wanders through a pass in the Great Laurel Mountains amidst huge upheavals of rock, "numerous high craggy clifts along the Water-Edge."[50] Brown describes a similar picture of the Wilderness in Edgar Huntly:

> The hollows are single, and walled round by cliffs, ever varying in shape and height. . . The streams that burst forth from every crevice are thrown, by the irregularities of the surface, into numberless cascades, often disappearing in mists or in chasms, and emerge from subterranean channels and, finally, either subside into lakes, or quietly meander through lower and more level grounds.
>
> Wherever nature left a flat it is made rugged and scarcely passable by enormous and fallen trunks, accumulated by the storms of ages. . .[51]

The grandiose scenery and picturesque sights that fill the pages of the narratives of Rachel Plummer (1839) and Fanny Kelly (1872) take on the character of natural wonders. Knowing quite clearly that the water she is seeing was a mirage--she indicates this in a footnote to her readers--Plummer's description emphasizes wonderment, and she remarks, "Is there anything like magic in this." This wonderment continues as she discovers sea shells on the plains and concludes the land must have been covered by a great sea; when she finds "thousands of bushels of salt--yea, millions--resembling ice"; and when she describes the burning springs, yellow earth and thorny trees of the desert.[52] Some of her accounts border on the fabulous. She describes a "man-tiger" which inhabits the Rockies, is eight or nine feet tall, has the features of a man and claws instead of fingers; as well, she asserts, "a species of human beings live in caves" in the mountains; in both cases she is reflecting the mythology of her Comanche captors, the first in reference to the grizzly bear, the second, to a race of dwarfs that occur frequently in myth.[53] Her most elaborate and extensive description she reserves for the Rocky Mountains: "so incredibly high, and perpendicular are they in many places, that is impossible to ascend them."[54] In some places, Fanny Kelly's narrative (1872) approaches the same sense of the sublime and picturesque. She describes in extensive detail and in vivid language a prairie fire and a redrock canyon, imagining the latter as huge "carved columns supporting a mighty ruin."[55]

But by far the most noticeable change in wilderness imagery is the development of Edenic motifs in late eighteenth century captivity narratives. The rescuers of "The beautiful lady" in Abraham Panther's tale (1787) are amazed

77

at the scene that they view after two weeks march in the wilderness:

> The land we found exceedingly rich and fertile, everywhere
> well watered, and the variety of berries, nuts, ground-nuts,
> &c, afforded a very comfortable living.
> On the fourteenth day of our travels, while we were ob-
> serving a high hill, at the foot of which, ran a beautiful
> stream, which passing through a small plain, after a few
> windings, lost itself in a thicket--and observing the agree-
> able picturesque prospect, which presented itself on all
> sides, we were surprised at the sound of a voice, which
> seemed at no great distance. [56]

And Maria Kittle describes a landscape where "birds were cheerful; the deer
bounded fearless over the hills; the meadows blushed with the enamel of Flora;
. . . . and spotted trout, and other fish, dart sportively across the water."[57]
Both Maria Kittle and the "beautiful lady" also describe contrastive, menacing
scenery, but it is clear that the wilderness also includes Garden imagery.

Writers of "factural" captivity narratives also developed this Garden image, though tentatively at first. As early as 1785, Frances Scott began developing the image of the wilderness as a land of plenty by providing the first cata-
loging of flora and fauna found beyond the frontier.[58] Mary Kinnan (1795) was
taken by the Indians "into a fine country, [Ohio] where we had venison, and other
game."[59] Kinnan's observation was supported by Mary Jemison (1842), who
described Indian life in the Ohio region:

> The town where they lived was pleasantly situated on
> the Ohio, at the mouth of the Shenanjee; the land pro-
> duced good corn; the woods furnished plenty of game,
> and the waters abounded in fish. [60]

And Charles Johnston (1827) wrote of the same region, "During the whole march,
we subsisted on bear's meat, venison, turkeys, and racoons, with which we
were abundantly supplied, as the ground over which we passed afforded every
species of game."[61] Filson's narrative of Boone's captivity (1784) and Morrow's
narrative of the daughters' (1833) draw a similar Edenic picture of Kentucky. [62]

As the frontier moved westward across the Mississippi towards the Rockies, there were those who automatically saw this new wilderness as Garden and
so recorded their images for others back East to read. Rachel Plummer (1839)
for instance, seeing natural wonders, a profusion of timber and game, openly
admired the landscape. She described the vast slope of the southern Rockies as
"being prairie and timber, and very rich with many fine springs . . . . a very
diversified country; abounding with small prairies, skirted with timber of various kinds--oak, of every description, ash, elm, hickory, walnut, and mulberry
. . . . [and] the purest atmosphere I ever breathed."[63] She then proceeded to
catalogue all the game animals of the region. Forty years later, Fanny Kelly
did a similar service for the High Plains, describing a flower-covered landscape

crossed with streams.[64] Her description of the Powder River Valley is an open challenge to Eastern farmers:

> Between these ranges [Bighorn and Cloud Peak], that cul-
> minate in the queenly, shining crowned height that takes its
> name from the clouds it seems to pierce, are fertile valleys,
> in which game abounds, and delicious wild fruits in great
> variety, some of which cannot be surpassed by cultivated
> orchard products in the richness and flavor they possess. . . .
> Between these ranges [Bighorn and Wind River], and
> varying in breadth from twelve to twenty-five miles, are
> fine hunting grounds, abounding in noble orchards of wild
> fruit of various kinds, and grapes, as well as game of the
> choicest kind for the huntsman.[65]

Because writing is an art and a material form of communication, it is one thing to describe and explain the change in wilderness imagery from desert to Garden on an ideological level and another thing to illustrate how it may have come about in practice. Three factors materially contributed to altering the image of the wilderness in captivity narratives.

First, the lag between the time of the captivity and the publication of the narrative seems to have increased. Originally timely pieces reflecting current positions toward the Indian, British, or French, the narratives were usually published within one year after the experience. This changed, however. Though Frances Scott's 1784 captivity was published in 1785, Jemima Howe's 1755 experience was not printed until 1792; Susannah Johnson (1744) published her narrative in 1807, and Zadock Steele (1780) published his in 1818. The span of time between Joseph Bartlett's 1708 captivity and its 1807 publication was nearly a century. Therefore, as the time lag between experience and publication became common, the record of the experience was subject to a greater variety of social and ideological influence.

Also, by the end of the eighteenth century, writers of some note began concerning themselves with the captivity experience. The narrative written by the pseudonymous Abraham Panther may hardly merit anthologizing, but nevertheless it was reprinted twenty-five times and became something of an early American bestseller. On the other hand, Ann Eliza Bleecker, whose fictional Maria Kittle is the subject of a novel length captivity narrative, moved in a circle of New York literati that included her husband, Anthony, William Dunlap, and Charles Brockden Brown. The latter's fictional Edgar Huntly draws heavily on captivity narrative materials. In the nineteenth century, James Fenimore Cooper's The Prairie and The Last of the Mohicans feature Indian captivities prominently. In the last half of the nineteenth century, minor writers like Edward Ellis and Joseph Badger consciously exploited the captivity experience in dime novels.

The impact of conscious literary effort and elevated style must have been felt most heavily by the editors of later captivity narratives. Editors are creatures of their time, often homogenizing unique experiences told in an original manner by imposing a language and tone foreign to the captive himself on the material. The editors of Frances Scott's 1786 narrative felt compelled to add a preface to her narrative which included several handfuls of Biblical quotations. She had included very few in her narrative, perhaps because it was 1786; but, because the book was published in Boston, the quotation-riddled preface was mandatory. The publishers of Mary Jemison's classic narrative reacted strongly against the Gothic elements that had filled narratives at the turn of the century; they assured their readers that "no extraneous or equivocal matter has been introduced, for the purpose of exciting the wonder of a visionary imagination, or of ministering to the cravings of a morbid appetite." The author of the biography added that, "No circumstance has been intentionally exaggerated by the paintings of fancy, nor the fine flashes of rhetoric."[66] Disclaimers aside, Jemison's narrative has its share of rhetorical flash and fancy, though it is supposedly a verbatim record of what was told to the author by Jemison who was nearing one hundred years of age and had lived with the Shawnee, out of regular contact with English-speaking Americans, for seventy-eight years. The weight of probability suggests that it was the editor, closer to the literary and intellectual currents of his age than the settler and his wife, who introduced sentimental language into the narrative, exaggerated incidents of terror and pathos, shaped the theme and moral sentiment of the tale, and eventually contributed most to the changing image of the wilderness.

Clearly the Garden image of the wilderness, like the Desert image, developed in response to emotional, imaginative, and material needs. The "desert" had assisted in the development of closely-defined, stable communities; it prevented a too quick dissipation of spiritual and material resources. But the burgeoning population of a new nation needed, at the end of the eighteenth century, to get to the other side of the mountains, and half a century later to the other side of a great river. The Garden image developed to resolve the conflict between a wilderness foreign to man and man's need for water, timber, rich soil and open range. That it developed in the captivity narrative, the most unlikely of genres, is a reflection of the flexibility of the human imagination. Under the impact of social and intellectual forces focussed on the genre by its editors, the captivity narrative created an ambiguous wilderness, one both fruitful and attractive yet peopled with savages. Then only the extermination of the Indians stood between the farmer and the peaceful cultivation of his soil.

But the Indians did not die alone, and the wilderness Garden was not created without an additional price. The vitality of the captivity narrative, with its ability to stir our imaginations in great moments of real drama through coherent and powerful drawing of wilderness life, also dies. When sentimentalism undermined the savage wilderness, it also undermined the dramatic situation of the heroine. No longer fighting for her life in an alien and hostile land, she was reduced to an interested observer at best, to a whining female at worst, and her sufferings seemed the stuff of melodrama, arbitrary and meaningless. Two hundred years of a vital genre disappeared in tears and exclamation points, but not without radically changing our image of the wilderness.

University of Utah

N.B. Generally the dates within parentheses in the body of the paper refer to the dates of publication. Occasionally, however, they refer to the date of the experience. The proper reference should be made clear by the context.

[1] For evolutionary, environmental, and mythic interpretations of the impact of the Frontier on American life, see Frederick Jackson Turner, "The Significance of the Frontier in American History," Early Writings (1938), Walter Prescott Webb, The Great Plains (1931), and Henry Nash Smith, Virgin Land (1950), respectively. A challenging but debatable mythic interpretation of the Frontier is Richard Slotkin's Regeneration through Violence (1973).

The captivity narrative is treated extensively in Slotkin, but the standard remains Roy Harvey Pearce's The Savages of America (1953). See also Pearce's article, "The Significances of the Captivity Narrative," (AL, XIX, 1–20, 1947) as well as Richard VanDerBeets' "A Surfeit of Style: The Indian Captivity Narrative as Penny Dreadful," (Research Studies, XXXIX, 297–306, 1971) and "The Indian Captivity Narrative as Ritual," (AL, XLIII, 548–62, 1972); also, David Minter's "By Dens of Lions," (AL, XLV, 335–47, 1973).

[2] William Hubbard, The Present State of New England (1677, rpt. Bainbridge, New York: York Mail-Print, Inc., 1972) p. 27.

[3] Mary Rowlandson, Narrative of the Captivity of Mrs. Mary Rowlandson (1682) in Charles H. Lincoln, Narratives of the Indian Wars, 1675–1699, Original Narratives of Early American History (New York: Scribner's, 1913) pp. 129, 132.

[4] Cotton Mather, Decennium Luctuosum, in Lincoln, p. 200.

[5] Hubbard, p. 27.

[6] Saltonstall, The Present State of New-England with Respect to the Indian War, in Lincoln, p. 31.

[7] Mather, in Lincoln, pp. 192, 200, 201, 208, 212, 214, 267.

[8] A strong tradition of active feminine heroines like Hannah Dustan coexists with the tradition of the passive sentimental heroine of the Rowlandson type. Both persisted into the nineteenth century.

[9] Rowlandson, in Lincoln, p. 122.

[10] (Samuel Bownas) An Account of the Captivity of Elizabeth Hanson, Now or Late of Kchecky, in New England. . . Taken in Substance from her own mouth, by Samuel Bownas (1724), in Richard VanDerBeets, Held Captive by Indians: Selected Narratives, 1642–1836 (Knoxville: University of Tennessee Press, 1973) p. 134.

[11] A True and Wonderful Narrative of the Surprising Captivity and Remarkable Deliverance of Mrs. Frances Scott, An Inhabitant of Washington County, in the State of Virginia (Boston: 1786), p. 9.

[12](Bunker Gray) A Genuine and Correct Account of the Captivity, Sufferings & Deliverance of Mrs. Jemima Howe, of Hinsdale in New-Hampshire (Boston: 1792), p. 8.

[13] Ann Eliza Bleecker, The History of Maria Kittle (Hartford: Elisha Babcock, 1797) p. 6.

[14]Rowlandson, in Lincoln, p. 119; see also, Memoirs of Odd Adventures, Strange Deliverances, etc., in the Captivity of John Gyles, Esq., (1689) p. 93-94, and Adventures and Sufferings of Peter Williamson (1757), pp. 217-18, both in VanDerBeets.

[15]Abraham Panther (pseud.), A Very Surprising Narrative of a Young Woman discovered in a Rocky Cave after having been taken by the Savage Indians of the Wilderness, in the year 1777. (Brookfield, Mass.: 1800) p. 5.

[16]Bleecker, pp. 5, 11.

[17](Shepard Kollock), A True Narrative of the Sufferings of Mary Kinnan, who was Taken Prisoner by the Shawnee Nation of Indians. . . (Elizabethtown, N. J.: Shepard Kollock, 1795) in VanDerBeets, p. 321.

[18]John Filson, The Adventures of Col. Daniel Boon; containing a Narrative of the Wars of Kentucke (Wilmington, Kentucky: 1784) in Roy Harvey Pearce, ed., Colonial American Writing (New York: Rinehart, 1950) pp. 563-64.

[19]Panther, p. 4.

[20]Bleecker, p. 16.

[21]Kinnan, in VanDerBeets, p. 320.

[22]A Narrative of the Captivity of Mrs. [Susannah] Johnson (Windsor, Vt.: Alden Spooner, 1807, second ed.) p. 25.

[23]Johnson, p. 38.

[24]Even in the religious mind, however, new tests of salvation were developing. Most significantly, Jonathan Edwards assured believers that they could have a "sensible awareness" of the presence of God (Treatise on Religious Affections, 1746). The Great Awakening, together with the Wesleyan movement of the 1770's, insured American exposure to and acceptance of an emotional rather than a "dry" faith experience.

[25]Narrative of the Captivity of Joseph Bartlett (n. p.: 1807); and The Indian Captive; or a Narrative of the Captivity and Sufferings of Zadock Steele (n. p.: 1818), rpt. in John Prost, Indian Battles, Captivities, and Adventures (New York: Derby and Jackson, 1859), pp. 209-76.

[26]A Faithful Narrative, of the Many Dangers and Sufferings, as well as Wonderful and Surprizing Deliverances of Robert Eastburn, During His Late Captivity Among the Indians; and A Narrative of the Lord's Wonderful Dealings with John Marrant, A Black, Taken down from his Own Relation, both in VanDerBeets.

[27]Besides Hanson, see also Eastburn and Marrant.

[28]Besides Scott (1785), Howe (1792), and Kinnan (1795), all previously cited, see A Narrative of the Incidents Attending the Capture, Detention, and Ransom of Charles Johnston (1790) in VanDerBeets, and James W. Morrow, "The Captives [Boone's daughters]", The Western Monthly Magazine, Sept. 1833, pp. 285-91.

[29]In Samuel L. Metcalf, A Collection of Some of the Most Interesting Narratives of Indian Warfare in the West, 1821, p. 57.

[30]Scott, pp. 16-17.

[31]Kinnan, in VanDerBeets, 330.

[32]Slover, in Metcalf, p. 56.

[33]The series of essays was published in nos. 409, 411-21 of the Spectator. The quotation, from an essay in no. 412, appears in Walter Jackson Bate, Criticism: The Major Texts (New York: Harcourt, 1952), p. 184.

[34]See Jefferson's letters to Thomas Law, Esq., of June 13, 1814, and to Charles McPherson, February 25, 1773, in vol. XIV, p. 140 and vol. IV, pp. 21-22, The Writings of Thomas Jefferson (Washington, D. C.: The Thomas Jefferson Memorial Association, 1903).

[35]Filson, in Pearce, pp. 563, 565; Jefferson, Notes on Virginia, Query IV, vol. II, Writings, pp. 24-25.

[36]Hugh Blair, Critical Dissertation on the Poems of Ossian (1763), quoted by M. H. Abrams, The Mirror and the Lamp (New York: Norton, 1958) p. 83.

[37]Longinus, On the Sublime, in Bate, p. 65.

[38]Bleecker, p. 13.

[39]Bleecker, p. 32.

[40]Kinnan, p. 323.

[41]Fanny Kelly, My Captivity Among the Sioux Indians (1872, rpt. New York: Corinth, 1962) p. 52.

[42]Rachel Plummer, Narrative of the Capture and Subsequent Sufferings of Mrs. Rachel Plummer (1839), in VanDerBeets, pp. 338-39.

[43]Almost all of the narratives cited feature this motif. To them can be added the suggestion of cannibalism in A Brief Narration of the Captivity of Isaac Hollister, who was Taken by the Indians, Anno Domini, 1763 (Suffield, Mass.: Edward Gray, 1803), and Charles Brockden Brown's Edgar Huntly (1791, rpt. New York: Macmillan, 1928).

[44]Williamson, in VanDerBeets, p. 223.

[45]Johnston, in VanDerBeets, p. 255.

[46]Howe, p. 11; Plummer, in VanDerBeets, pp. 350-51; Kelly, pp. 54-55; and James E. Seaver, Deh-he-wa-mis: or a Narrative of the Life of Mary Jemison: otherwise called the White Woman, who was taken Captive by the Indians in MDCCLV, and who continued with them seventy-eight years (Batavia, N.Y.: William Seaver and Son, 1842), p. 30; and [Edwin James], A Narrative of the Captivity and Adventures of John Tanner (1830, rpt. Minneapolis: Ross and Haines, 1956).

[47]Kinnan, p. 323.

[48]Edward S. Ellis, Seth Jones: or, The Captives of the Frontier, (London: Beadle & Co., 1861) p. 97.

[49]Kelly, p. 73.

[50]Scott, pp. 14-16.

[51]Brown, p. 99.

[52]Plummer, pp. 342-43.

[53]Plummer, pp. 345-46.

[54]Plummer, p. 347.

[55]Kelly, pp. 159-60, 70-71.

[56]Panther, pp. 2-3.

[57]Bleecker, p. 32.

[58]Scott, p. 18.

[59]Kinnan, in VanDerBeets, p. 277.

[60]Jemison, p. 44.

[61]Johnston, in VanDerBeets, p. 277.

[62]Filson, 563-66; Morrow, 386-87.

[63]Plummer, in VanDerBeets, 339.

[64]Kelly, p. 51

[65]Kelly, pp. 62-63.

[66]Jemison, vii, xi.

THOREAU: WALKING TOWARD ENGLAND

by Robert Glenn Deamer

In the address which he made at Thoreau's funeral, Emerson spoke of his friend's preference for America and the American West, saying:

> No truer American existed than Thoreau. His preference of his country and condition was genuine, and his aversation from English and European manners and tastes almost reached contempt. He listened impatiently to news or bonmots gleaned from London circles; and though he tried to be civil, these anecdotes fatigued him. The men were all imitating each other, and on a small mold. Why can they not live as far apart as possible, and each be a man by himself? What he sought was the most energetic nature; and he wished to go to Oregon, not to London. [1]

Emerson, of all people, should have been aware of the immense irony in these remarks--as indeed he probably was, secretly. For whatever Thoreau may have thought of England in contrast to America, Emerson had been there, twice, had written a brilliant analysis (English Traits) of English society and character, and knew that if there was any place where "men were all imitating each other" it was America, not England--that if one sought "the most energetic nature" he should go to London, not Oregon. And--irony of ironies--Emerson undoubtedly was also aware that if ever an American existed who--in his self-sufficiency, eccentricity, independence, bluntness, manliness, and love of nature and vitality--resembled the Englishman, it was Henry David Thoreau. Yet as important and revealing as these ironies are, no student of Thoreau or of Thoreau's relation to American culture has taken note of them. Instead of examining the astonishing evidence in Emerson's book that Thoreau's traits were, after all, English Traits, scholars have been content to accept the stereotype of Thoreau as the quintessential, westward-looking American which Emerson presented in his funeral oration. Needless to say, the acceptance of this stereotype is a severe hindrance to any understanding of the real significance that Thoreau's life and writings have within the general context of American history and culture, and within the specific context of the American myth of the West. For if we persist in ignoring the fact that, whatever he may have thought, Thoreau was really an archetypal Englishman rather than an archetypal American frontiersman, we will continue to miss one of the most important ironies of the entire American westering experience: the fact that the virtues of the legendary heroes (Frontiersmen, Mountain Men, Cowboys) in America's Western myth are --as a long line of famous American observers (including such major American writers as Irving, Cooper, Emerson, Hawthorne, and Henry James) discovered[2] --actually embodied in that Old World social ideal, the English gentleman.

This is all the more important because, as Emerson suggested and as Edwin Fussell has definitively shown,[3] Thoreau was obsessed with the metaphorical and mythical meanings of the American West. "Let me live where I will," he announced in "Walking," "on this side is the city, on that the wilderness, and ever I am leaving the city more and more, and withdrawing into the wilderness. I should not lay so much stress on this fact, if I did not believe that something like this is the prevailing tendency of my countrymen. I must walk toward Oregon, and not toward Europe. And that way the nation is moving, and I may say that mankind progress from east to west" (W, V, 218).[4] Yet however literally true this may have been for his countrymen, we know that taking to the woods--walking, that is, "toward Oregon, and not toward Europe"-- was a metaphor rather than a fact for Henry Thoreau. He was, in reality, contemptuous of America's Westward Movement--its blatantly pecuniary motives were, he felt, epitomized by the California Gold Rush ("What a comment, what a satire, on our institutions!" [W, IV, 464]) --and in a personal letter of the same period as "Walking" he bluntly asserted that "The whole enterprise of this nation, which is not an upward, but a westward one, toward Oregon, California, Japan, etc., is totally devoid of interest to me. . . . It is not illustrated by a thought; it is not warmed by a sentiment; there is nothing in it which one should lay down his life for, nor even his gloves. . . . It is perfectly heathenish, --a filibustering toward heaven by the great western route. No; they may go their way to their manifest destiny, which I trust is not mine" (W, VI, 210). We know, too, that when, near the end of his life and in an attempt to regain his health and save his life, Thoreau really did travel West he was in no way invigorated or inspired by his actual westering experience. All of which is to say that Thoreau was in search of a West, all right, but that it was his West,[5] the West of an inner rather than a literal geography. Indeed, one of the most striking features of Thoreau's genius is unquestionably his perception, long before the frontier had actually closed, that if Americans were ever to realize the American dream of the West they would have to recognize that--whatever Frederick Jackson Turner later may have thought--the dream is not inherent in the literal frontier. This is a point worth stressing because most American writers, especially American novelists, have to this day felt a typically American need to define the mythic West spatially, geographically, in terms of a literal place. Thus, for example, we witness Ernest Hemingway taking off for the Green Hills of Africa, and explaining that his journey was necessary because

A continent ages quickly once we come. The natives live in harmony with it. But the foreigner destroys . . . . A country was made to be as we found it. . . . Our people went to America because that was the place to go then. It had been a good country and we had made a bloody mess of it and I would go, now, somewhere else as we had always had the right to go somewhere else and as we had always gone. . . . Let the others come to America

86

who did not know that they had come too late. . . . Now I would go
somewhere else. We always went in the old days and there were
still good places to go.[6]

Perhaps "we had always had the right to go somewhere else" (and certainly "we
had always gone"), but Thoreau, at least, knew, and knew at the very time that
Americans were most excitedly and energetically pushing westward, that the
frantic American search for "good places," for new frontiers and fresh starts,
is not an act of freedom, but its opposite. As he explained in A Week on the
Concord and Merrimack Rivers,

The frontiers are not east or west, north or south; but wherever
a man fronts a fact, though that fact be his neighbor, there is an
unsettled wilderness between him and Canada, between him and
the setting sun, or, farther still, between him and it. Let him
build himself a log house with the bark on where he is, fronting
IT, and wage there an Old French war for seven or seventy years,
with Indians and Rangers, or whatever else may come between
him and the reality, and save his scalp if he can [W, I, 323-324].

And once he had made his own brave, fructifying decision to "front only the essential facts of life" (W, II, 100), Henry Thoreau went, as the world knows, not
at all to Oregon, but to Walden Pond, one mile from venerable Concord.
This is clear enough. Yet we should not overlook the fact that--however
challenging was Thoreau's gleeful demonstration that the ideal man, the man of
courage, discipline, and integrity, is not the actual frontiersman but the man
who "fronts a fact"; and however appropriate were his caustic reminders to his
countrymen that the only travel of real value is inward rather than westward
("I have travelled a good deal in Concord")--the joke was still (as Emerson
knew, or should have known) to a considerable extent upon Thoreau himself.
For if Thoreau succeeded in showing Americans (those with the courage to read
him, at least) how small-minded and timid they were in their attitude toward the
geographic West, he did not thereby free himself from a rather severe paroch-
ialism of his own when it came to his understanding and evaluating of American
character and culture. If, as I have suggested, he had travelled to England with
Emerson, he would have found that ideal man--the man in whom wildness and
refinement are united--for whom he had searched in vain in American society
and history.[7] Since the ideal man was not to be found in American society or
history, Thoreau, with his usual self-sufficiency, wisely decided, we know, to
create such a man in himself (pre-eminently, of course, in the idealized, poetic
self which speaks in Walden). However, what better characterizes Thoreau's
essential attitude toward life, for example, than Santayana's description of the
Englishman as one who lives "in and by his inner man" and who "thinks the prize
of life worth winning, but not worth snatching"? Certainly Thoreau lived and
wrote out of a belief, like the Englishman's, that "if you snatch it, as . . .
Americans seem inclined to do, you abdicate the sovereignty of your inner man,

87

you miss delight, dignity, and peace; and in that case the prize of life has escaped you."[8] And as for those precise English Traits--practical ability, candor, unsentimentality, integrity, independence, learning, courage, love of privacy and nature and health--which Emerson, Irving, Cooper, James, Santayana, and other Americans found in the Englishman, what do they add up to but a portrait of Thoreau himself? Emerson habitually referred to his friend Thoreau as "the man of Concord," but note that in his praise of the English he seems to be defining "man" in a particular way:

> I find the Englishman to be him of all men who stands firmest in his shoes. They have in themselves what they value in their horses--mettle and bottom. . . .
> They dare to displease, nay, they will let you break all the commandments, if you do it natively and with spirit. You must be somebody; then you may do this or that, as you will.
> . . . .
> Every man in this polished country consults only his convenience, as much as a solitary pioneer in Wisconsin. . . . .
> Of absolute stoutness no nation has more or better examples. They are good at . . . any desperate service which has daylight and honor in it . . . .
> Their culture is not an outside varnish, but is thorough and secular in families and the race. They are oppressive with their temperament, and all the more that they are refined. I have sometimes seen them walk with my countrymen when I was forced to allow them every advantage, and their companions seemed bags of bones.[9]

Nor were Emerson's impressions unique. Irving, for example, affirms that he does "not know of a finer race of men than the English gentlemen. Instead of the softness and effeminacy which characterize the men of rank in most countries, they exhibit a union of elegance and strength. . . ."[10]

In all, the American observers from Irving to Santayana were vividly impressed by the fact that what governs the Englishman is, in Santayana's words, "the love of a certain quality of life, to be maintained manfully."[11] The same, it hardly need be said, is true of Thoreau--his aim in life always being to "have my immortality now, that it be in the quality of my daily life" (J, III, 351). But what, exactly, is meant by the "quality of life" which Thoreau and the Englishman love and manfully maintain? For Thoreau, "Life consists with wildness. The most alive is the wildest" (W, V, 226); and after a meditation, in "Walking," on the American West, he abruptly announces that "The West of which I speak is but another name for the Wild; and what I have been preparing to say is, that in Wildness is the preservation of the World" (W, V, 224). ("Walking" itself was originally entitled "The Wild.") This is immensely important; for it reveals that the West became meaningful for Thoreau only when he spoke of it in terms of the Wild--as a symbol, that is, for a disciplined, intense way of living. And this particular Wild West--Thoreau's West--was not to be found in the actual American West, but in England--as Thoreau himself might have realized had he been a little less smugly parochial in his preference for Concord ("the most estimable place in all the world" [J, IX, 160]). For if the West of which Thoreau spoke is but another name for the Wild, it can also be shown that the Wild of which he spoke is but another name for the quality of life loved and maintained by the English gentleman. Of course, Thoreau did not refer, usually, to a literal wilderness or a literal wildness when he spoke of the Wild any more than he referred to a geographical place when he spoke of the West (like his journey to the actual West, his journeys to an actual wilderness, to The Maine Woods and to Canada, were disappointing rather than fructifying experiences); nevertheless what he meant by wildness was something very definite indeed. Primarily, as I have indicated, Thoreau had in mind an ideal of conduct--an ideal emphasizing such values as independence, originality, intensity, and vitality-- when he spoke of wildness. "It is in vain," he stressed, "to dream of a wildness distant from ourselves. There is none such . . . . A little more manhood or virtue will make the surface of the globe anywhere thrillingly novel and wild" (J, IX, 43). He also noted that "original and independent men are wild, -- not tamed and broken by society" (J, II, 448). As for himself, he wrote in his Journal in 1841 that "It does seem as if mine were a peculiarly wild nature, which so yearns toward all wildness. I know of no redeeming qualities in me but a sincere love for some things, and when I am reproved I have to fall back on to this ground" (J, I, 296). And by "a sincere love for some things" Thoreau meant his love for the world of nature as it presented itself to his senses--a religious outlook, in fact ("Therein I am God-propped" [J, I, 296]), which stressed, always, the unspeakable importance of preserving health and vitality, of living "a purely sensuous life" (W, I, 408). In other words, Thoreau's mysticism was not at all Emersonian or Transcendental; rather, it was Oriental, a belief in the divinity of the immediate, sensuously and aesthetically apprehended world.[12] "Are we to be put off and amused in this life," he asked rhetorically and impatiently, "as it were with a mere allegory? Is not Nature, rightly read, that of which she is commonly taken to be the symbol merely? . . . What is it, then, to educate but to develop these divine germs called the senses?" (W, I, 408). Even more to the point, Thoreau was--unlike, say, Emerson or Melville--essentially uninterested in metaphysics, in God or in another world.[13] "One world at a time," he exclaimed in his famous deathbed remark; and in his first book he insisted that "Here or nowhere is our heaven" (W, I, 405). Thus, in the simplest terms, if the West equals the Wild, the Wild equals a love of the actual, natural world--of life itself. For Thoreau it is always the way one lives that counts; "To be a philosopher," as he cogently put it in Walden, "is not merely to have subtle thoughts . . . but to so love wisdom as to live according to its dictates, a life of simplicity, independence, magnanimity, and trust." And "it is admirable to profess because it was once admirable to live" (W, II, 16).

Thus it is that Thoreau's search for a real philosopher, for a real believer in the doctrine of wildness, for that ideal man whom he found neither in the frontier West nor in the civilized East, should have taken him to England. For what the American observers discovered in the English character--energy, independence, freedom of action, etc.--was precisely that cluster of attitudes, virtues, and values which Thoreau referred to as Wildness. Specifically, the observers found that what distinguished the Englishman above all things was, simply, the way he lived, what Santayana calls his "distinction in the way of living. The Englishman does in a distinguished way the simple things that other men might slur over as unimportant or essentially gross or irremediable; he is distinguished--he is disciplined, skillful, and calm--in eating, in public gatherings, in hardship, in danger, in extremities. It is in physical and rudimentary behaviour that the Englishman is an artist."[14] ("To affect the quality of the day," said Thoreau, "that is the highest of arts. Every man is tasked to make his life, even in its details, worthy of the contemplation of his most elevated and critical hour" [W, II, 100].) (In English Traits Emerson states, categorically enough, that the English are "some ages ahead of the rest of the world in the art of living," while in his address at Thoreau's funeral he explained that Thoreau declined "any narrow craft or profession, aiming at a much more comprehensive calling, the art of living well."[15]) Consequently, too, the Englishman, like Thoreau, is resolutely this-worldly and untranscendental: it is this life that counts. ("Even here," said Thoreau in the "Sunday" chapter of his first book, "we have a sort of living to get. . . . There are various tough problems yet to solve, and we must make shift to live, betwixt spirit and matter, such a human life as we can" [W, V, 74].) This attitude is epitomized for Santayana in the "Death-Bed Manners" (how like Thoreau's own conduct during his last long illness![16]) of the English: their absolute refusal to make any fuss about death. "English manners are sensible and conducive to comfort even at a deathbed. . . . Death, it is felt, is not important. What matters is the part we have played in the world, or may still play there by our influence. . . . We have tried to do right here. If there is any Beyond, we shall try to do right there also."[17] "One world at a time," said Thoreau.

Finally, it should be stressed that the life to which both Thoreau and the Englishman are first and last devoted is necessarily a vital, healthy, robust life. This is of course evident in Thoreau's ever-present commitment to his doctrine of Wildness ("The whole duty of man," he declared early in his career, "may be expressed in one line,--Make to yourself a perfect body" [J, I, 147]); as for the English, American observers from Irving to Santayana were simply awe-stricken by the energy and vitality of that people. Emerson, for example, was so conscious of the "impressive energy" of the English that in his lectures to them he "hesitated to read and threw out for its impertinence many a disparaging phrase which I had been accustomed to spin about poor, thin, unable mortals; so much had the fine physique and the personal vigor of this robust race worked on my imagination."[18] In spite of America's celebrated frontier tradition, that is to say, the prominent Americans who actually went to England were forced to admit that the country was, in Santayana's words, "a beautifully healthy England" ("domestic, sporting, gallant, boyish, of a sure and delicate heart") in a way that America was not.[19]

90

Thoreau's achievement as a writer grew, essentially and crucially, from his original, creative use of the frontier metaphor and the Western myth. If at times he tended toward chauvinism in asserting that "Adam in paradise was not so favorably situated on the whole as is the backwoodsman in America," he was more often tough-minded and to the point in remarking that it "remains to be seen how the western Adam in the wilderness will turn out" (J, II, 152-153). And in Walden he showed, classically, that this western Adam in the wilderness was not turning out so well after all; that Americans would have to return to first principles if they wished to realize the American dream of the West; that the West itself will remain illusive as long as it is identified with a geographical region rather than with a state of mind and a disciplined, intense way of life. Yet as Wright Morris has pointed out,[20] Thoreau himself was an archetypal American in his preference for taking to the woods rather than staying in the village--in his insistence that the "essential facts of life" (emphasis mine) are to be found in the woods rather than in the village. In preferring the woods Thoreau was, as he said, only following the prevailing tendency of his country-men to leave the city and withdraw into the wilderness. But why do Americans have such an urge to flee the city? Because, as Morris explains, "Each of these cultural centers, each of these established towns, became a fragment of Europe and a past to get away from--the prevailing tendency of Americans being what it was. Thoreau did not expose this tendency to examination--he accepted it."[21]

All of which is to say that Thoreau's life and writings classically drama-tize a central question inherent in any attempt to understand the American west-ering experience: what value and importance, comparatively, should be placed upon our frontier and our European--especially our English--traditions? Like most Americans, I am not at all unsympathetic to the Western myth, and it is obvious that no true account of America can ignore this myth. Yet the fact that Thoreau's ideal man was not (as he knew) the historic American westerner who sought geographic rather than inner frontiers, but (as he did not know) the his-toric English gentleman who stayed at home and sought to maintain a certain distinguished quality of life, is a striking reminder of the one-sidedness to which the Western myth can lead. And it reminds us, too, that Santayana may well have been right when he said that "English liberty"--by which he meant the English belief that true freedom is created by responsibility, manliness, and respect for privacy--"is the best heritage of America, richer than its virgin continents."[22] Perhaps more than any other American, Thoreau embodied the English view of life and liberty. If his quest for wildness, for a truly westering experience, took him to the woods, it also took him, unknowingly, to England.

Thiel College

NOTES

[1]Ralph Waldo Emerson, The Complete Works of Ralph Waldo Emerson (Boston: Houghton Mifflin, 1903), X, 459.

[2]Besides Emerson, the following famous American observers in England

offered, from 1820 to 1920, strikingly similar reports on the Englishman's vigor, independence, and manliness: Washington Irving (The Sketch Book), James Fenimore Cooper (Gleanings in Europe: England), Nathaniel Hawthorne (Our Old Home), Oliver Wendell Holmes (Our Hundred Days in Europe), Henry James (English Hours), and George Santayana (Soliloquies in England).

[3] Edwin Fussell, Frontier: American Literature and the American West (Princeton: Princeton University Press, 1965), pp. 175-231. See also Lawrence Willson, "The Transcendentalist View of the West," The Western Humanities Review, 14 (1960), 183-191; and C. A. Tillinghast, "The West of Thoreau's Imagination: The Development of a Symbol," Thoth, 6 (Winter 1964), 42-50.

[4] References to the first six volumes of the Walden Edition of The Writings of Henry David Thoreau (Boston: Houghton Mifflin, 1906) are indicated in my text by a "W" followed by volume and page. Volumes VII-XX of this edition are The Journal of Henry David Thoreau. References to the Journal are indicated by a "J," with the Journal followed by volume and page.

[5] Cf. Fussell, p. 189.

[6] Ernest Hemingway, Green Hills of Africa (New York: Scribner's, 1935), pp. 284-285.

[7] Cf. Walter Harding, A Thoreau Handbook (New York: New York University Press, 1959), pp. 154-155; Roderick Nash, Wilderness and the American Mind (New Haven: Yale University Press, 1967), pp. 91-95; and Charles Roberts Anderson, The Magic Circle of Walden (New York: Holt, Rinehart and Winston, 1968), pp. 151-178, and passim.

[8] George Santayana, Soliloquies in England and Later Soliloquies (Ann Arbor: The University of Michigan Press, 1967), pp. 37, 86.

[9] Emerson, Works, V, 102-103, 105, 131, 304-305.

[10] Washington Irving, The Sketch Book of Geoffrey Crayon, Gent. (New York: Dutton, 1963), p. 58.

[11] Santayana, p. 31.

[12] "In short, the Oriental uses the purely aesthetic to constitute the nature of the divine . . . instead of using the aesthetic merely as an analogical symbol to convey a divinity which is defined in some other way." F. S. C. Northrop, The Meeting of East and West: An Inquiry Concerning World Understanding (New York: Collier, 1966), p. 404. Cf., too, Stephen Railton, "Thoreau's 'Resurrection of Virtue!'," American Quarterly, 24 (May 1972), 210-227, esp. 210-211.

[13] Cf. Jonathan Fairbanks, "Thoreau: Speaker for Wildness," The South Atlantic Quarterly, 70 (Autumn 1971), 499.

[14] Santayana, p. 53.

[15] Emerson, Works, V, 101; and X, 452.

[16] See Walter Harding, The Days of Henry Thoreau (New York: Alfred A. Knopf, 1965), pp. 450-468.

[17] Santayana, pp. 91, 92.

[18] Emerson, Works, V, 106.

[19] Santayana, pp. 3, 2, 5.

[20] Wright Morris, The Territory Ahead: Critical Interpretations in American Literature (New York: Atheneum, 1963), pp. 39-50, esp. p. 43.

[21] Morris, p. 42.

[22] George Santayana, "English Liberty in America," in Santayana, Character and Opinion in the United States (New York: Scribner's, 1921), p. 232.

HAMLIN GARLAND'S NORTHWEST TRAVELS: "CAMP" WESTERING

by Robert Gish

> Each traveler... saw the West through his own limited experience—
> but he did see it. Our garnered knowledge will not be complete, our
> conclusions may not always be sound, but from the travelers we can
> eventually discover what the western world was like.
>
> —John Francis McDermott, Travellers on the
> Western Frontier

Called a reformer, a regionalist, a realist, and a romantic, Hamlin Garland is seldom thought of as a roamer—a traveler. Admittedly, such categories are not mutually exclusive and certainly travel writing may result from diverse impulses. Indeed, Garland incorporates a bit of all of these, usually ambivalently, into his work throughout the early, middle, and late phases of his career. A central assumption in this paper, however, is that to one degree or another, one might best view Garland in the context of his travels and the writing done in relationship to his travel—in the context which Michel Butor calls "Iterology," "a new science..., strictly tied to literature, concerned with human travel."[1]

Despite Butor's rather recent coinage of the term and his detailed proposal in Mosaic for founding such a new science, the context of travel is a broad and not so new one. The history of the genre of travel books runs from the beginnings to the present and there are major authors and works in all national literatures and periods. American literature and especially Western American literature are, by their very nature and process, literatures of travel. Iterological consideration of Western American literature is inevitable since the westering movement from Lewis and Clark to Thoreau and beyond directs feet to earth as well as words to paper. And the various purposes for heading West, fortune, fame, knowledge, religious exodus or pilgrimage, escape, pursuit, exploration, etc.,—all these purposes contribute to sub-genres that also extend the boundaries of travel writing past autobiography into fiction.

Papers like those resulting from the Edwardsville Conference on Travelers on the Western Frontier, February 22-23, 1968, and published by the University of Illinois Press, 1970, bring to mind with some excitement the vast amount of travel writing still in need of critical exploration. Paul Shepard's Man in the Landscape provocatively demonstrates some truly significant ecological and aesthetic ramifications of man's movements in the American West. And if we grant R. D. Laing his due, travel as experience and story, literature and myth, may well be one of the most significant of all "facts of life." When one thinks

94

about the pre-natal, intrauterine journeys of sperm and ovum down the Fallopian tube; thinks about the trips of implantation and fetal growth, as not only previews but programs of post natal travel, or as Laing says, "Some myths fit better than others but enough do to...consider seriously the possibility that conception to implantation, and subsequent prenatal adventures, are represented mythologically in postnatal imagery"[2]--when one thinks of this, then it becomes probable that all literature, and not just the purest forms of travel books, is iterologically based. The old cliches of life's journey then come to hold more than commonly realized. When Emily Dickinson says, "There is no frigate like a book," and when Keats, as traveler-explorer, stares at the Pacific, "Silent, upon a peak in Darien," they are on to something.

Hamlin Garland is not the same order of artist-traveler as Dickinson and Keats and to be overly serious about much of his travel writing risks the ridiculous. But his preoccupation with roads and trails, trailing and backtrailing, is obvious when one looks at the titles of his books--in fact, the trail and trips are key structures in all his work; and in his own life, travel seems both his modus vivendi and modus operandi as he goes East and West and Farther West. As Butor suggests, writing is often travel just as travel is often writing. So it seems for Garland. The reasons for his travels farther and farther West have long interested critics--some seeing these journeys and their resultant books, written during the twenty or so years between Rose of Dutcher's Coolly (1895) and A Son of the Middle Border (1917), as a fall or retreat from his realistic birthright; others seeing them as a continuation of romantic, westering motives beginning when, as a boy, Garland's father moved his family West to Iowa and Dakota.

Falling within the middle period of his interest in the Far West, Garland's trip by pack train through British Columbia, from Ashcroft to Glenora, at the time of the 1898 Yukon gold rush, can be regarded as representing the zenith of his search for the wilderness perimeters (real and imagined) of the Far West. In terms of how he dramatizes himself and his place in the landscape, his Northwest travels may also be viewed as representing a zany and unconscious parody of the ideal, heroic trailer and man of the wilderness which Garland never authentically and convincingly becomes; and thus his Northwest travels become the ultimate betrayal of the kind of traveler, something of an anti-self, he never really was and thus could only imitate in a most theatrical and stylized way. Garland can only narcissistically go through the motions of the rush for gold, can only observe and report the deeds of others and his projected, idealized self on the trail, trying to prove to himself as much as to the reader that he is part of the plot. One cannot help but feel, too, that Garland's Canadian junket serves as a sublimated version of the Spanish-American War, so that his travel is narrated as a heroic and virtuous journey into a war not with Cuba and the Spanish fleet, but with the Canadian wilderness and various and sundry depraved and greedy souls (i.e., the enemy)--Garland's alliance being with clean-living, but rough-riding, wholesome American types out for a romp in the wilds much like T. R. and his boys were out for "a splendid little war."

Garland's Northwest travels resulted in the publication of "The Trail to the Golden North" (<u>McClure's</u> <u>Magazine</u> XII-XIII, April-May 1889), pp. 505-507, 65-67, a six part sequence of doggerel poems; <u>The</u> <u>Trail</u> <u>of the</u> <u>Goldseekers:</u> <u>A</u> <u>Record</u> <u>of</u> <u>Travel</u> <u>in</u> <u>Prose</u> <u>and</u> <u>Verse</u> (New York: The Macmillan Company, 1899); "Hitting the Trail" (<u>McClure's</u> <u>Magazine,</u> 12, February 1899), pp. 298-304; and <u>The</u> <u>Long</u> <u>Trail</u> (New York: Harper & Brothers, 1907), a fictionalized version of <u>The</u> <u>Trail</u> <u>of the</u> <u>Goldseekers</u> intended for young readers. In March, 1898, in preparation for his trip, Garland published "Ho! for the Klondike!" in <u>McClure's</u> (X, No. 5, pp. 443-454), a tour guide which attempts to report by means of interviews with official surveyors and the Hon. Clifford Sifton, then Canadian Minister of the Interior, on "The Various Ways In--Where the Gold is Found and How it is Got--What New Settlers May Hope For."

Usually mentioned only in passing by critics interested in Garland's Far-Western phase,[3] or completely ignored by readers of his more accessible fiction, the literary products of Garland's Northwest travel bring to the surface, in both unique and typical ways, some of the concerns expressed in <u>American</u> <u>Literary</u> <u>Realism</u> by Warren French, i.e., "What Shall We Do About Hamlin Garland?" <u>ALR,</u> 3: No. 4 (Fall 1970), 283-289, in response to Donald Pizer, "Hamlin Garland," <u>ALR</u> (Fall 1967), 45-51, regarding the extent to which Garland really matters in American literary history. French sees Garland as important only as an example of an American type--"The man who made it too quickly and then hung around too long" (French, p. 283). Garland, says French, is to American literature what William Jennings Bryan is to politics, both being about as sincere as P. T. Barnum, and masters of "Me-tooism" (p. 285).

One way of getting at the problem of Garland's sincerity, in rhetorical terms, is a consideration of ethos and voice. And my interest in this paper is in the disparity between what Garland says or seems to intend to say and how he actually sounds; in the relationships between ethos and travel book, and why in the name of nostalgia, or whatever, such explicitly stated high-mindedness and moral intent comes off sounding like sanctimonious, pompous pap.

One explanation for such reader response comes under the heading of "Camp," a sensibility which at least allows Garland a way out of being thought good because he is so awful. A sensibility, Camp especially, as Susan Sontag points out in <u>Against</u> <u>Interpretation</u> "is one of the hardest things to talk about."[4] With Garland it is especially difficult to sort out what is going on in terms of reader response since Camp sensibility runs head on against the aesthetics of the Picturesque and the Sublime. I suspect it is precisely here, however, in finding out how Garland's Camp and Sublime sensibilities interact, that insight is gained into Garland's identity, ethos, and voice as a traveler. There is, I hold, a relationship between Garland's Camp performance and the "sublimation" of his Middlewest or "plains" self, a more realistic self, into his Farwestern or "mountain" ("romantic") self, which is reflected in the imagery, themes and plot structures of his travel writing--particularly in the sublime extremes of his Northwest travel writing.

To Sontag, Camp can be both naive and deliberate and includes such things as stag movies seen without lust--an observation only ironically applicable to Garland. Moreover, as far as nature and landscape is concerned, "A great deal of Camp suggests Empson's phrase, 'urban pastoral'" (Sontag, p. 279), a phenomenon less obliquely pertinent to Garland. Even less obliquely applicable to Garland is the idea that "To perceive Camp in objects and persons is to understand Being-as-Playing-a-Role. It is the farthest extension, in sensibility, of the metaphor of life as theater" (Sontag, p. 280). Two more Camp considerations help in considering Garland as traveler: (1) "In naive, or pure Camp, the essential element is seriousness, a seriousness that fails. Of course, not all seriousness that fails can be redeemed as Camp. Only that which has the proper mixture of the exaggerated, the fantastic, the passionate, and the naive" (Sontag, p. 283); and (2) "Camp is art that proposes itself seriously but cannot be taken altogether seriously because it is 'too much'" (Sontag, p. 284).

A definition capturing the full psychological and aesthetic complexity of the Sublime is impossible here. It is perhaps sufficient to repeat Edmund Burke's statement that "Whatever is fitted in any sort to excite the ideas of pain, and danger, that is to say, whatever is in any sort terrible, or is conversant about terrible objects, or operates in a manner analogous to terror, is a source of the sublime."[5] Because of Garland's campiness it is more fitting to speak of the "mock sublime" or the "ersatz sublime" in that throughout his travel narratives pain, danger, and terror--along with numerous other conditions like comfort or peace--register as affectation, seem feigned, insincere projections of what some ideal personage should feel under the circumstances. The expression of the more comfortable, peaceful, charming conditions, though admittedly oversimplified, can be called the picturesque; however, here again a term like "mock picturesque" seems more suitable.

The Trail of the Goldseekers is the center of Garland's Northwest travel writing. In it, he is "camping out" in more ways than one. This can be sensed even in Garland's diaries where he stresses his need for manliness--a machismo stance dramatized throughout the Goldseekers but ironically and unconsciously undercut at just about every turn (e.g., Garland purchases a new rifle and plenty of shells for the outing but never does any shooting; one senses he carries it like a prop, for when shooting must be done in the form of killing an injured pack horse, he turns his head and hands the gun and bullets to his trail companion, Burton Babcock.)[6] In the tradition of medieval travel, Garland, in his diary, readies himself for a pilgrimage that will bring self improvement, or as he puts it in educational terms, "It is my last chance to do a bit of real mountaineering, of going to school to the valiant wilderness...and I can not afford to miss the opportunity of winning a master's degree in hardihood."[7] In his "secret heart"--though it is not kept much of a secret--he is acting out the epic of the forty-niners. But he is not authentically questing for gold. He is posturing. In presumably sincere terms he confesses this in his diary (public diary though it is):

The truth is, with all my trailing about in the Rocky Mountains I have never been in a satisfying wilderness. It is impossible, even in Wyoming, to get fifty miles from settlement. I long to undertake a journey which demands hardihood, and so, after careful investigation, I have decided to go into the Yukon Valley by pack train over the British Columbian Mountains, a route which offers a fine and characteristic New World adventure. (Hamlin Garland, A Daughter of the Middle Border, pp. 53-54).

At the end of the trip, disgusted with what the "Long Trail" turned out to be, and attributing his frustration and disillusionment to the false advertising about the abundance of wildlife, and clearly marked directions left by surveying crews--none of which he found (and not exactly what could be expected of an advanced degree in hardihood), he walks out on the point of a mesa a few miles from Livingston and muses:

> It was plain to me that goldseeking in the Rocky Mountains was
> marvellously simple and easy compared to even the best sections
> of the Northwest, and the long journey of the Forty-Niners was
> not only incredibly more splendid and dramatic, but had the allure-
> ment of a land of eternal summer beyond the final great range. The
> long trail I had just passed was not only grim and monotonous, but
> led toward an ever increasing ferocity of cold and darkness to the
> arctic circle and the silence of death. (The Goldseekers, pp. 252-
> 253).

The paradox is haunting: Garland sought the wilderness and hardihood but found it too wild and hard, allowing him to sublimate his hopes back to his romanticized view of the Forty-Niners and in his mind the picturesque "urban-pastoral" Rocky Mountains. And despite his most flamboyant efforts in recording the terrors and disappointments of his trip, one is not all that convinced just how hard it was on Garland or how much of a failure it was not to continue all the way to the Yukon gold fields as his partner Burton Babcock and other trailers do. (One of the salient ironies of The Goldseekers is that Garland intends to make Babcock appear less experienced and a weaker trailer than Garland is; however, Babcock constantly upstages him.) Garland would keep his bedroll and his horse, Ladrone, and refer to them again and again like diplomas or medals. Especially in his subsequent volumes of memoirs he never let his reader fail in knowing what an expert trailer he was; that he earned his degree in manliness, and had lived and was qualified to write romances based on the life of the trailer hero. But in his fiction, too, his credibility does not authentically ring true.

Intending in The Goldseekers to sound tough and up to the test, a clean liver, a leader of men and horses, a noted author (and hailed as such at the most unexpected times and by the most unlikely goldseekers), Garland reveals himself in outlandish, hysterical and unintentionally humorous voices of priggish condescension and gothic garrulity. In the days of Mel Brooks' Blazing Saddles it is difficult to keep a straight face while reading The Goldseekers when Garland, for example, heads a chapter, "The Passing of the Beans," meaning the sharing of food with his trail companions. One senses the oblivious ambiguity of the phrase and is half embarrassed and half pleased that the self-proclaimed great trailer is so humorlessly naive. And in his exuberant and obsessive love affair with his horse, a relationship which takes precedence over men, women, landscape, food, and gold, Garland vies for effect with Thomas McGuane's and Marlon Brando's version of the lonesome cowboy and his faithful horse in Missouri Breaks.

Samples of Garland's poetizing speak for themselves. Here's one of his shorter outbursts in celebration of manliness which he entitles "Do You Fear the Wind?":

> Do you fear the force of the wind,
> The slash of the rain?
> Go face them and fight them,
> Be savage again.
> Go hungry and cold like the wolf,
>   Go wade like the crane.
> The palms of your hands will thicken,
> The skin of your cheek will tan,
> You'll grow ragged and weary and swarthy,
>   But you'll walk like a man.
>
> (The Trail of the Goldseekers, p. 95)

Wading like a crane is not your ordinary idea of manliness--though "ragged and weary and swarthy" probably comes closer to describing it in some minds.

Garland, in one way, sees the trip as warfare, a northern version of the southerly trouble, the Spanish-American War, which kept his friend, Assistant Secretary of the Navy, Theodore Roosevelt, from hitting the Northwest trail with him. Canada isn't Cuba but Rough Riders are needed, even so. "Ho! for the Klondike" is Garland's call to arms as he almost shouts:

> The Yukon country is a grim and terrible country, and the
> man who goes there to spend a year is likely to earn with
> the ache of his bones and the blood of his heart every dollar
> he finds in gold. He should go like a man enlisting for a
> war. He should be able to pass the examination which is
> required of a soldier in the German army, or of an officer
> in the mounted police of the Canadian government. It is no
> place for weak men, lazy men, or cowards.[8]

In The Goldseekers Garland acts like a drill sergeant yelling mostly to his horses every morning, "Line up, boys! Line up! Heke! Heke!"; but sometimes he comments on his trail companions and miscellaneous Indians with even less decorum and concern than that expressed in addressing his horses.

Most of the people Garland meets on the trail do not live up to his projected ideal of the hearty male, or for that matter the wholesome female. Most

99

of his utterances of piety and purity are intended for genteel, exemplary living and the ethical uplift of his readers--and to insure his reader that the trail has not and will not corrupt the likes of him. In this regard, he patriotically finds the Siwash Indians he encounters less reserved than the Cheyenne and Sioux back home, for "These little people chattered and whooped at each other like monkeys" (The Goldseekers, p. 98). One traveler who, out of supplies, asks for food is assessed this way: "He accepted our aid as a matter of course. No perfectly reasonable man would ever take such frightful chances as this absurd little ass set his face to without fear" (The Goldseekers, p. 165). Another traveler who lacks the moral fiber to keep himself from suicide is met with this obituary by Garland: "He seemed not to be a man of deep feeling. And one of the last things he uttered in my hearing was a coarse jest which I did not like and to which I made no reply" (The Goldseekers, p. 189).

As for women, meeting a pack train returning from Bennet Lake, he sees a "bold-faced handsome white woman followed by a huge negress. The white woman had made her pile by dancing a shameless dance in the dissolute dens of Dawson City, and was on her way to Paris or New York for a 'good time.' The reports of the hotel keepers made her out to be unspeakably vile" (The Goldseekers, p. 211). In the name of virtue Garland sounds almost lascivious. But Garland saves his full volley of moral indignation for matters involving his horse. When asked by "impertinent" railway hands if it paid to take his horse all the way back to Wisconsin, he proudly relates his hysterical response: "'Pay!', I shouted, thoroughly disgusted, 'does it pay to feed a dog for ten years? Does it pay to ride a bicycle? Does it pay to bring up a child? Pay-- no; it does not pay. I'm amusing myself. You drink beer because you like to, you use tobacco--I squander my money on a horse'" (The Trail of the Goldseekers, pp. 255-256). On the way back to Seattle, he sums up the Northwest's ship of fools like this: "None of them interested me very greatly. I was worn out with the filth and greed and foolishness.... They were commonplace citizens, turned into stampeders without experience or skill" (The Goldseekers, p. 241).

Garland's reaction to landscape and to nature occupies a major portion of The Goldseekers; however, even here, in his narcissistic way, he appears his own main attraction. His response changes from enjoyment of the picturesque to fear of the sublime. And these reactions parallel an almost archetypal narrative sequence of expectancy and quest to trial and disillusionment to emergence and deliverance. Basically he stresses the discrepancy between glorious advertising promises and the inglorious realities of the trail. Reaching Hazleton, midway on the long trail, Garland says, "As I now reread all the advance literature of this 'prairie route,' I perceived how skillfully every detail with regard to the last half of the trail had been slurred over. We had been led into a sort of sack, and the string was tied behind us" (The Goldseekers, p. 100). Such a discrepancy between expectation and reality parallels the Camp discrepancy between intended and understood statement, as well as the schism between Garland's urban and pastoral selves. The extent of his disappointment in the land as experience is seen in these words:

The trail was a disappointment to me, not because it was long and
crossed mountains, but because it ran through a barren, mono-
tonous, silent, gloomy, and rainy country. It ceased to interest
me. It had almost no wild animal life, which I love to hear and
see. Its lakes and rivers were for the most part cold and sullen,
and its forests sombre and depressing. The only pleasant places
after leaving Hazleton were the high valleys and timber line. They
were magnificent, although wet and marshy to traverse.

As a route to reach the gold fields of Teslin Lake and the Yukon it
is absurd and foolish. It will never be used again for that purpose.
Should mines develop on the high divides between the Skeena, Iskoot,
and Stikeen, it may possibly be used again from Hazleton; otherwise
it will be given back to the Indians and the dogs (The Goldseekers,
pp. 180-181).

The very trees Garland sees militarily as the enemy: "I began to dread
the dark green dripping firs which seemed to encompass us like some vast
army" (The Goldseekers, p. 121). And from the battle there was no retreat--
"There were no returning footsteps on this trail," as Garland hyperbolically
states.
At the start, the trail holds a picturesque beauty for Garland as he describes, with the excessive zeal of a would-be naturalist, his first encampment
around a small lake. He glories in the sight not of moose, elk, or bear, but
two cranes:

As we threw our tent and started our fire, I heard two cranes
bugling magnificently from across the marsh, and with my field-
glass I could see them striding along in the edge of the water.
The sun was getting well toward the west. All around stood the
dark and mysterious forest, out of which strange noises broke
(The Goldseekers, p. 49).

Certainly he anticipates a more sublime confrontation with nature here. And
in The Long Trail his youthful hero, Jack Anderson, will meet and kill a bear,
something that could only happen fictively to a man who carried a running argument, by his account, with Theodore Roosevelt who was not opposed to shooting
game as Garland was.
Still early in his trip, Fraser Lake elicits a picturesque response from
Garland: "Fraser Lake was also very charming, romantic enough to be the
scene of Cooper's best novels. The water was deliciously clear and cool, and
from the farther shore great mountains rose in successive sweeps of dark
green foothills" (Goldseekers, pp. 69-70). Hawthorne was reportedly more ex-
cited about the prospect of Niagara Falls than he was when he actually saw them,
because he had built them up in his mind into something more sublime than they
were to him on sight. Garland's reader feels a somewhat similar anticlimax

101

as Garland travels from picturesque to sublime, from periphery to center in emotionally exaggerated ways so that one cannot really accept either picturesque or sublime descriptions as authentic, leaving the reader to feel that the whole landscape must be both more and less beautiful or horrible than described. We see Garland, not the land.

Certainly Garland tries to impress upon the reader the contrasts between the presence of early, picturesque spots on the journey and distant, vast, more mysterious, unknown scenes soon to be experienced; and, in this sense, scenery is plot in The Goldseekers. Structurally, the first half of the trail and the narrative is picturesque, is happy expectation; the second half is fearful, horrible, sublime, unknown, ultimately disappointing. Garland's description of the divide between the Fraser and Skeena rivers reflects some of this:

> On the first of June we topped the divide between the two mighty watersheds. Behind us lay the Fraser, before us the Skeena. The majestic coast range rose like a wall of snow far away to the northwest, while a near-by lake, filling the foreground, reflected the blue ridges of the middle distance--a magnificent spread of wild landscape (The Goldseekers, pp. 74-75).

Perhaps the epitome of the picturesque is Garland's description of a large camp of goldseekers met while crossing the divide:

> Early in the afternoon we passed some five or six outfits camped on a beautiful grassy bank overlooking the river, and forming a most satisfying picture. The bells on the grazing horses were tinkling, and from sparkling fires, thin columns of smoke arose. Some of the young men were bathing, while others were washing their shirts in the sunny streams. There was a cheerful sound of whistling and rattling of tinware mingled with the sound of axes. Nothing could be more jocund, more typical, of the young men and the trail. It was one of the few pleasant camps of the long journey (The Goldseekers, p. 109).

As beautify and good cheer yield to fear and disappointment, towns like Telegraph Creek and Glenora are viewed as "ratty" collections of tents and shacks--dens of greed, exploitation, and wretchedness. At Glenora, Garland gives up on his plans to reach the Yukon, because, identifying himself now as a literary man (his urban rather than his pastoral self), he is disgusted with the experiences and people found on the trail of gold; certainly a turnabout for someone wanting a "M.A. in hardihood," Garland concludes to leave his friend Babcock, head home, and "push down toward the coast to go in by way of Skagway" (The Goldseekers, pp. 186-187).

This climactic "escape" via Lake Bennett to Skagway and then down the Lynn Canal offers a more truly sublime vista to Garland--assuming Burke's definition of the Sublime and Addison's observation that the Sublime is essentially "the echo of true danger and awe." But insofar as the truth of Garland's descriptions of danger are not altogether convincing and Camp responses subvert things, the term "mock-sublime" is perhaps better.

On the overland walk of thirty miles from Bennett to Dyea, Garland joins up with a prospector from Winnipeg, an anonymous Doctor G., who seems more guide than companion, and in a storm they climb "sharply over slippery ledges, along banks of ancient snows in which carcasses of horses lay embedded," as Garland's gothicism has it (The Goldseekers, p. 233). Because of the heavy mist, Garland says, "Nothing could be seen...but a desolate, flat expanse of barren sands over which gray-green streams wandered in confusion, coming from darkness and vanishing in obscurity. Strange shapes showed in the gray dusk of [Crater Lake]. It was like a landscape in hell. It seemed to be the end of the earth, where no life had ever been or could long exist" (The Goldseekers, p. 234). Thoughts of earlier picturesque scenes of Cooper turn to darker, more sublime thoughts of Poe: "The pinnacles around us were like those which top the Valley of Desolation. We seemed each moment about to plunge into ladderless abysses. Nothing ever imagined by Poe...could be more singular, more sinister, than these summits in such a light, in such a storm" (The Goldseekers, p. 134).

As for Garland's response to travel on the Lynn Canal: "Vast glaciers came sweeping down from the dread mystery of the upper heights. Lower still lines of running water white as silver came leaping down from cliff to cliff--slender, broken of line, nearly perpendicular--to fall at last into the gray hell of the sea" (The Goldseekers, p. 242). Against such a deliberately stylized sublime background Garland's poetic farewell to the Northwest invites Camp response through bathos, as in his deliverance he utters:

> I hate this cold, bleak northern land,
> I fear its snow-flecked harborless strand--
> I fly to the south as a homing dove,
> Back to the land of corn I love.
> And never again shall I set my feet
> Where the snow and the sea and the mountains meet.

That Garland succeeded in seriously and straightly impressing one reviewer with the account of his travels is seen in these words printed in The Nation in 1899: "We recall few books of travel which are so graphic in their portrayal of nature; and if the aspects chosen are mainly from the side of wretchedness...it can only be regretted that, in the region traversed by our author, the sterner aspects of nature are more often found."[9] Coming closer to recognizing the Camp elements involved in Garland's account of his Northwest travels is the reaction of the New York Times' reviewer who said of The Goldseekers in 1899 that the quality of descriptive writing is not much above average daily newspaper correspondence; that though the book is readable, Garland's sense of humor is obviously deficient, and that the poetry leaves the uninitiated reader puzzled and amused.[10]

Garland is notoriously puzzling and amusing, a curious mixture of contradictory and ambivalent voices which alienate and attract. As traveler he attempts to stage himself as a man of sophistication, fame, prestige, sterling morality, and "All American" hardihood; but he has the effect of naivety, narrowness, and boorishness. Had he been able to allow the truly picturesque and sublime aspects of the Canadian Northwest and American Far West to transport him outside of his loquacious narcissism to a more authentic level of self discovery, expression, and High Romanticism, this would have been a journey worth traveling--for both Garland and his reader. About all we can say now is that he tried, but the effect is more simulated than sincere.

University of Northern Iowa

NOTES

[1] Michel Butor, "Travel and Writing," Mosaic, 8: No. 1 (Fall, 1974), p. 5.

[2] R. D. Laing, The Facts of Life: An Essay in Feelings, Facts, and Fantasy (New York: Pantheon Books, 1976), p. 36.

[3] See Jean Holloway, Hamlin Garland: A Biography (Austin: University of Texas Press, 1960), pp. 146-147; Ruth M. Raw, "Hamlin Garland, the Romanticist," Sewanee Review, 36, No. 2 (April 1928), p. 209, neglects any detailed analysis of Garland's travel writing but does relate his attraction to romance formulas, to regionalism, and wanderlust. Three dissertations turn more directly to Garland and the North American West but are specific in varying ways about his travels: Edwin J. Neumann, "Hamlin Garland and the Mountain West," unpublished doctoral dissertation, Northwestern University, 1957; Joseph L. Carter, "Hamlin Garland and the Western Myth," unpublished doctoral dissertation, Kent State University, 1973; and George Howard Savage, "'Synthetic Evolution' and the American West: The Influence of Herbert Spencer ᴏn the Later Novels of Hamlin Garland," unpublished doctoral dissertation, the University of Tulsa, 1974.

[4] Susan Sontag, "Notes on 'Camp,'" Against Interpretation (New York: Dell Publishing Co., 1966), p. 275.

[5] Edmund Burke, A Philosophical Enquiry into the Origin of our Ideas of the Sublime and Beautiful (London: Routledge and Kegan Paul, 1958), p. 39.

[6] Hamlin Garland, The Trail of the Goldseekers: A Record of Travel in Prose and Verse (New York: The Macmillan Co., 1899), pp. 167-169.

[7] Hamlin Garland, A Daughter of the Middle Border (New York: The Macmillan Co., 1921), p. 60.

[8] Hamlin Garland, "Ho! for the Klondike!," McClure's Magazine, 10 (March 1898), p. 444.

[9]"Three Books of the Klondike," The Nation, 69: No. 1782 (August 24, 1899), p. 156.

[10]See Jackson R. Bryer and Eugene Harding, Hamlin Garland and the Critics: An Annotated Bibliography (New York: The Whitson Publishing Co., 1973), p. 19. Also, "Garland's Journey to the Klondike," New York Times Saturday Review of Books (June 10, 1899), p. 384.

THE EAST-WEST THEME IN DREISER'S AN AMERICAN TRAGEDY

by Martin Bucco

Westering in literature suggests a more or less continuous movement. Whatever hardships or obstacles stand in the way, the westering individual or group presses on. Often in serious fiction the travelers finally realize that a higher value adheres to the journey rather than to the journey's end. To make this outcome tenable the writer develops his plot and selects his details in the light of process instead of progress. But such is not the case in Theodore Dreiser's pessimistic An American Tragedy (1925).

Dreiser's massive Naturalistic triumph consists of three unsymmetrical books of 19, 47, and 34 chapters--a classic one hundred in all. The first chapter opens:

> Dusk--of a summer night.
> And the tall walls of the commercial heart of an American city of perhaps 400,000 inhabitants--such walls as in time may linger as a mere fable.[1]

The Souvenir section of the last chapter opens:

> Dusk--of a summer night.
> And the tall walls of the commercial heart of the city of San Francisco--tall and gray in the evening shade (II, 406).

During the long course of this narrative a discontinuous, yet relentless, westering impresses itself upon us.

The westward movement of the evangelical Griffiths family has begun long before the novel opens in Kansas City. The brooding narrator informs us that the Griffiths family had conducted missions or preached in the streets of Chicago. Before that in Milwaukee--before that in Detroit--and before that in Grand Rapids. Asa and Elvira Griffiths, in fact, had begun their fitful journey across America in New England. Back in Bertwick, Vermont, Asa's father had willed his two other sons fifteen thousand dollars each; Asa had received only one thousand dollars. Poverty is the force behind the Griffiths' westering. Even now, in Kansas City, Asa and Elvira and their four children live in a decrepit backwash, for the commercial life of this Western city has moved on, further south and west.

The early chapters of Book I treat the successive boyhood jobs of the pathetic hero, Clyde Griffiths, the eldest son: newsboy, department-store worker, drugstore clerk. Secretly he attends picture theaters and searches for a better job. When his sister runs away with a traveling actor, Clyde's parents, after five years in Kansas City, consider moving further west--to Denver, "for want," says the narrator, "of a better idea..." (I, 27). But Clyde, now sixteen, sees the move as futile: "There would be just another mission there, the same as this one" (I, 27). A better life in Kansas City seems possible--Western failure not inevitable--when Clyde secures a job as a bellhop in the Green-Davidson Hotel. Oscar Hegglund, a bellhop from New Jersey, explains how he himself has worked his way west: Buffalo, Cleveland, Detroit, St. Louis, and now Kansas City. The vain Easterner confides to the naive Westerner that in Kansas City the tips are big and the bellhops sporty. "And now more than ever," the narrator tells us, "Clyde was insisting that he did not want to leave Kansas City" (I, 40).

Yearning for money and girls, Clyde lies to his mother about his real wages and allows his bellhop friends to initiate him into the world of dinners, parties, and brothels. While his mother desperately seeks money for her daughter Esta (now pregnant, deserted, and unwed), Clyde spends his money on fickle, flirtatious Hortense Briggs. On a trip in a "borrowed" automobile with four other couples, to a roadhouse called the Wigwam, Clyde quarrels with Hortense, plays crack-the-whip on a frozen lake nearby, experiences the terror of a hit-and-run accident, pursuit by the law, and an automobile crash. Book I closes with Clyde fleeing on foot, "always," says the narrator, "toward some of those distant streets which, lamplit and faintly glowing, he saw to the southwest..." (I, 147).

While Clyde's family will continue in stages further West, Clyde's destiny lies not in that direction, but in a return to the East. As a discontented boy growing up in Kansas City, he finds only one family connection interesting: "the existence somewhere in the east--in a small city called Lycurgus, near Utica, he understood--of an uncle, a brother of his father's, who was plainly different from all this" (I, 13). We first see Samuel Griffiths through Clyde's motion-picture daydreams, daydreams based on news brought West by people who knew the Griffiths back East:

> As Clyde pictured this uncle, he must be a kind of Croesus, living
> in ease and luxury there in the east, while here in the west--Kansas
> City--he and his parents and his brother and sisters were living
> in the same wretched and hum-drum, hand-to-mouth state that had
> characterized their lives (I, 14).

While the westward movement halts in Denver, Clyde's eastward back-trailing halts in Chicago for three years. As a bellhop at the conservative Union League Club, he finally meets his fabulous uncle who is there on business. Clyde at last gets to Lycurgus, New York. The eastward movement in An American Tragedy concludes with Samuel Griffiths who, to escape the notoriety of his nephew's trial and execution for the murder of his pregnant sweetheart, moves his factory and his family to Boston.

Though this ponderous novel is saturated with all manner of detail,

Dreiser documents only the places, certain points, of the novel's sweeping criss-cross movements: never the act of going to the next place, but always the condition of being in the next place. Thus Kansas City, Denver, San Francisco on the one hand; Kansas City, Chicago, Lycurgus on the other. When Clyde in Chicago receives a letter from his mother, a letter postmarked Denver, the narrator tells us that it surprised Clyde, "for he had expected to hear from her as still in Kansas City" (I, 168). When Clyde decides to go to New York State, the narrator transports him there in the space between two sentences: "And so, after having notified his uncle as he had requested, Clyde finally took his departure for Lycurgus. But on his arrival there..." (I, 181-2). And when Elvira Griffiths in Denver learns of her son's indictment for murder (as reported in The Rocky Mountain News), she thinks: "They would have to give up and go somewhere else again" (II, 214). This "somewhere else" we discover in the Souvenir section is San Francisco, a fait accompli. Nothing derives from or attaches to the opposing journeys--one to the Promised Land in the West, the other to the Dream of Success in the East--except a dim structural chiasmus. [2]

That the characters in An American Tragedy leave one place only to be in another place without the usual Dreiserian ado is as significant as the many conspicuous contrasts which Dreiser sets up between the West and the East. The Eastern opening of Book II, for example, is a sharp contrast to the Western opening of Book I. But the contrast -- Samuel Griffiths' grand Lycurgus home contrasted with Clyde's little grey home in the West--is not merely tacit. For the past four days, the narrator informs us, Samuel Griffiths "had been absent attending a conference of shirt and collar manufacturers in Chicago, price-cutting by upstart rivals in the west having necessitated compromise and adjustment by those who manufactured in the east" (I, 151).

Next, the narrator tells us that Samuel Griffiths' son Gilbert "very much in face and build, if not in manner or lack of force, resembled Clyde, his western cousin..." (I, 155), and that Samuel Griffiths, unlike his shorter and more confused brother out West, is "a little above the average in height" and "incisive both as to manner and speech" (I, 158). As we saw the Eastern uncle first through the imagination of the Western nephew, so now--three years after the automobile accident in Kansas City--we see Clyde as a bellhop in Chicago first through the recollection of Samuel Griffiths. Sensing the early injustice done his brother Asa back in Vermont, Samuel now wants to help his well-mannered nephew. That Clyde has deceived his uncle is clear when Samuel Griffiths reports to his family that his brother Asa now is "connected with something in Denver--a hotel, I think" (I, 161). Samuel's young daughter Bella wonders about Clyde: "The son of a western hotel proprietor!" (I, 161).

But her aggressive brother instinctively dislikes this other Griffiths-- seeing him, we infer, as an upstart rival in the West for whom adjustment must be made by the Griffiths in the East. In Lycurgus Clyde is full of wonder: "For consider who the Griffiths were here, as opposed to 'who' the Griffiths were in Kansas City, say--or Denver. The enormous difference! A thing to be as carefully concealed as possible" (I, 194). Clyde falls in with a fun-seeking trio and discovers that it is as easy for a Griffiths to kiss a Rita in Lycurgus as it was difficult for a Griffiths to kiss a Hortense in Kansas City. Out West Hortense deceived Clyde, but in the East Clyde deceives Roberta. Clyde's dream of sexual conquest in the West is realized in the East. At parties thrown by Ivy Leaguers, Clyde, like Fitzgerald's Jay Gatsby, invents a usable past: "In Kansas City he had heard of the State University of Kansas. Also the University of Missouri. And in Chicago of the University of Chicago. Could he say that he had been to one of these--that Kansas one, for a little while any way" (I, 326).

Essentially the two sections of the country, we come to see, are comparable, the contrasts superficial. As Clyde looked in awe upon the Green-Davidson out West, so he looks in awe upon his uncle's house in the East. As for a time he toiled in a department store basement out West, so for a time he toils in the shrinking room of his uncle's shirt and collar factory. As Clyde felt superior to the Western bellhops, so he feels superior to the Eastern workers. As the drugstore manager checked his advancement in the West, so his cousin Gilbert checks his advancement in the East. As he was forbidden to fraternize with the hotel guests in the West, so he is forbidden to fraternize with the factory girls in the East. As Clyde yearns for Hortense Briggs in the West, so he yearns for Sondra Finchley in the East. As Clyde met Hortense clandestinely in the West, so he meets Roberta Alden in the East. As Esta Griffiths submitted to the traveling actor in the West, so Roberta submits to the role-playing Clyde in the East. Clyde's failure to secure advancement in the Western drugstore anticipates his failure to procure an aborticide for Roberta in the Eastern drugstores.

The dynamic East-West theme in this novel springs not from genuine divergence, but from ironic parallels between the two sections of the country. Like Clyde's city-bound father in the West, Roberta's land-bound father in the East is a portrait of failure. Dreiser's description of Biltz resembles a scene out of Western Realism, out of a novel by E. W. Howe or Hamlin Garland. Clyde thinks: "How far he had traveled away from just such a beginning as this" (II, 12). As Clyde quarreled with Hortense at the Wigwam, so he quarrels with Roberta at Big Bittern. As out West the game of crack-the-whip on the frozen Wigwam Lake anticipated the accidental collision with the little girl and the overturning of the automobile, so in the East Book II closes with the accidental upsetting of the rowboat and the drowning of Roberta Alden. As before, the deserter Clyde heads in a southwesterly direction.

Besides contributing to artistic unity, Dreiser's web of East-West tensions evokes the sense of an American tragedy. The bright flotilla of canoes on Bear Lake in Book III is a manifestation of the floral parade in Book II, where Sondra represents a Mohawk Indian legend--Eastern versions of the trip to the Wigwam in Book I, where Clyde and his Western friends also sought a bright and primitive dream. Waiting trial for murder, the former Western newsboy becomes himself a feature of the Eastern press. Clyde fears what the Eastern papers will reveal about his past--"and after all his bluffing about his rich connections here and in the west" (II, 227); and in dramatically effective

109

chiasmic design, he fears what the Western papers will reveal about his life in the East.

When Clyde's lawyers urge him to attend Sunday jail services, we sense Book III turning back on Book I. Though Samuel Griffiths procures Clyde legal counsel, the rich man fears that the yellow press would exploit the great social gap between the Lycurgus Griffiths and the Denver Griffiths, and thus he deeply objects "to bringing on any member of this western branch of the family" (II, 211). Elvira Griffiths traces the cause of her son's trouble in the East to Western influences--to the plush Green-Davidson Hotel and to Clyde's bad companions there.

Clyde, the Western movie-goer and Eastern picture-taker, watches Mason, the dynamic prosecuting district attorney, "as if some one had suddenly shouted: 'Lights! Camera!'"--symbolic of Clyde's dream-picture world of illusion. Though aware that Clyde really is not a bona fide member of the idle rich, Mason refers to Clyde's upbringing as more advantageous than most upbringings, and the old Kansas City accident now belies other testimony to Clyde's good character. After the press seeks out Clyde's family in Denver, "there was circulated in all the papers east and west a more or less complete account of the present state of Clyde's family"--and of Clyde's past--"a revelation which shocked Lycurgus and Twelfth Lake Society about as much as it did him" (II, 217).

Book III turns further onto Book I when Elvira, who helped her daughter in the West, now helps her son in the East. Connecting herself to a Western newspaper, she carries her organizational and oratorical skills to the East, telling Clyde's lawyers of her faith in God: "It was his voice there in Denver that directed me to that paper" (II, 344). But in time readers and orthodox congregations grow indifferent to the shabby woman's struggle for appeal money. Returning to Denver to nurse her ailing husband, Elvira--the noblest sufferer of them all--pleads with an Eastern churchman, the Reverend Duncan McMillan, to save Clyde's soul, at least.

In a triumph of mechanical formalism the opening dusky walls of Kansas City fuse with the closing dusky walls of San Francisco into an image of dusky American metropolitanism. On a higher level of abstraction America itself is but a place, a stage of life's journey where, without exalted suffering, most of us witness for a time "the pathos of helpless humanity in the face of the relentless and inexplicable and indifferent forces of Life!" (II, 102-3). How far, the narrator seems to ask, has any of us traveled? In Dreiser's circular geometry natural law and material limitation permit change of position but not of posture. Like chess pieces, the manner of movement from one position to another is incidental. To change position in the world of An American Tragedy is to change nothing. As the boy Clyde remarked when told of the plans to move to Denver: "There would be just another mission, the same as this one" (I, 27).

Thus geographic change, the implied journey, is mechanical, devoid of value. At what point in life's journey does Clyde lose all sense of value? That moment is before his mother's last appeal to the governor. The last vestige of

Clyde's dream-picture world of illusion vanishes when he reads Sondra Finchley's typewritten, anonymous, third-person letter, a letter expressing her remembrance, suffering, bewilderment, sorrow, sympathy, and good wishes. The envelope bears no return address, only a postmark: New York City. For Clyde the moment of lost hope is "as when night at last falls upon the faintest remaining gleam of dusk in the west" (II, 383). The mythic directions are as devoid of value as the journey's mysterious end.

Colorado State University

NOTES

[1] An American Tragedy (New York: Boni and Liveright, 1925), p. 3. Further references to this two-volume first edition will be cited in the text.

[2] Dreiser also used the chiasmic structure in the earlier Sister Carrie (1900). The Western Carrie Meeber moves upward toward material success in the East while her lover Frank Hurstwood moves downward toward material failure.

W. GILMORE SIMMS' "OAKATIBBE" AND THE FAILURE OF THE WESTERING IMAGINATION

by Jack L. Davis

A principal tragedy in the westering experience of European peoples in North America, as elsewhere, has been their inability to learn from native inhabitants. For four centuries, from the founding of Raleigh's abortive Roanoke colony to the Wounded Knee massacre of 1890, American history and literature depicted Indians as little more than physical obstacles to the manifest destiny of white people. With few exceptions, this writing dismissed aboriginal experience as irrelevant to the European task of conquering and adapting to the New World environment.[1] There is a profound irony here, for the wisdom and knowledge of Indian nations were solidly based upon their own coming to terms with this continent, a process beginning perhaps twenty thousand years before the dawn of European civilization. How that accumulated native heritage, based upon intimate understanding of the American environment, was so steadfastly ignored by our pioneering predecessors remains a relatively unexamined chapter in our westering experience.

The very idea that white people might go to the Indian for instruction in other than the rudiments of survival was clearly abhorrent if not outrageous. In the minds of most settlers, Indians were demonstrably savages, relics of a much earlier, primitive period through which Europeans had already successfully passed. Fundamentally, underlying a great contempt for Indian culture was an intense fear of going native, of adopting any Indian behavior beyond that necessary for sheer survival. Such attitudes long prevented pioneers from discovering that America was no hostile wilderness but a hospitable home for those who dealt with her sympathetically and imaginatively. But imbued with confidence in their materialistic technology, they sought to impose European patterns of living, land use, and agriculture upon the often recalcitrant land. If that failed, they temporarily borrowed useful Indian practices such as methods of planting and hunting. But virtually no pioneers seemed able to comprehend that native peoples had invested their energies in developing advanced social technologies and sophisticated approaches to living with the land and other peoples. They had already found solutions to problems Europeans had not resolved, problems of land utilization, resource allocation, political freedom, democratic government, and religious toleration, to name a few. Felix Cohen, a prominent philosopher and authority on Indian legal affairs, pointed out that native societies were more advanced in many respects than the white ones which conquered them. According to him, political and social democracy, old-age pensions, and unemployment insurance all appeared west of the Atlantic before they did on its eastern shore.[2] Thus, while westward moving whites were confidently trying to Europeanize Indians, they were subtly being Americanized by natives.

But since the move westward was predicated upon the assumption that native modes would have to yield to civilized progress, white people had a vested interest in ignoring the carefully wrought design behind native adaptation to the wilderness landscape. However, missionaries and other harbingers of civilization quickly found that hardly any Indians were willing to abandon their ancient values, despite their appreciation of selected civilized artifacts like rifles, iron utensils, and the like. In the face of such resistance, a conscious plan for cultural genocide was begun. If Indians did not relinquish their inferior culture, they would have to be exterminated or shut away upon reservations until they assimilated enough to function as civilized human beings.[3]

While many sympathsizers, especially people in areas from which Indians had been ousted, objected to this national policy of discrimination or outright genocide, few understood that the welfare of Euro-American civilization itself was at stake. And it was a writer of Western literature in the 1840s who first glimpsed that truth. He was not Fenimore Cooper, but his now almost forgotten near contemporary, William Gilmore Simms, who protested that obliteration of native culture would deny to the developing nation the benefits of Indian experience, gifts, and blood.

In the short story "Oakatibbe, or the Choctaw Sampson" appearing in his collection Wigwam and Cabin (1845),[4] Simms launched a two-fold attack on the popular myth that Indians had nothing to contribute to the westward movement. In a surprising indictment, he charged that the friends of the Indian, who urged assimilation, were no better than his enemies, who demanded extermination or impoundment on reservations. The former were cultural bigots; the latter racial ones. Neither were capable of seeing the inescapable logic in the Indian's vision of living harmoniously in this magnificent land with freedom for peoples of all races and persuasions. "Oakatibbe" indicates that Simms was perhaps the only early writer of Western literature who clearly understood that the success of the westering experiment ultimately depended upon learning the ancient truths about this land. Transplanted Europeans needed to see the land through the Indian's eyes, to gain understanding and respect for the delicate ecology of nature, and to become humanized from the corruptiveness of old world societies.[5] In his view, assimilation of Indian vision was the single imaginative act that could justify the American claim of bringing forth a new nation, free from the tyrannical usages of the European past.

Simms did not come by such heretical views easily and that has confused many readers. He has been accused, with perfect justice, for his racist treatment of blacks.[6] But the same charge does not hold, though it has been often made, for his depiction of Indians in The Yamassee (1835), The Wigwam and the Cabin (1845), and The Cassique of Kiawah (1859). In fact, Simms gradually dissociated himself from the major beliefs which had helped consign Indian culture to primitive superstition. By the mid-nineteenth century, those concepts had become popularized and explicit. According to Brian V. Street: "Primitive peoples are considered to be the slaves of custom and thus unable to break the despotism of their own 'collective conscience.' Any custom 'discovered' among a 'primitive' people is assumed to dominate their whole lives; they are unconscious of it and will never change it themselves. This provides the basis for the analysis of many customs being reported back to nineteenth-century England by the growing number of travelers."[7] Since these were precisely the views held by his countrymen, Simms took it upon himself to dramatize their falsity specifically in "Oakatibbe." By undercutting stereotypes of the Indian as an unthinking slave to primitive superstition, Simms hoped to awaken white Americans to the positive strengths of aboriginal cultures.

But because the subject was so touchy, Simms decided to work obliquely in "Oakatibbe." That tactic unfortunately caused most readers to miss his real intentions. A common mistake in interpreting the tale is assuming that the two white characters actually speak for the author. But a close examination reveals that Simms was in reality caricaturing racism, and proposing that assimilation would be as disastrous to the white as the red population. Thus, "Oakatibbe" is well worth examination by students of Western literature as a landmark cultural and literary masterpiece. It is a highly wrought, two-level drama in which the reader must discard the narrator's continual misinterpretations to see the significance of a Choctaw's decision to affirm the moral values of his own people rather than the competing ones of white civilization. Through this dramatization, Simms exposes the racial and cultural biases underlying most attempts to assimilate our native peoples. The failure of the westering imagination to appropriate the moral and poetic vision of our native people is, thereby, made painfully clear.

On the surface, the story seems simple enough. Perhaps this too has misled many readers. Colonel Harris, a pioneer to Mississippi Choctaw territory in the 1820s, has hired over forty neighboring Indians to help his slaves pick the first year's bumper cotton crop. He hopes this employment will induce the Choctaw nation to give up its barbaric ways. He is visited by the youthful narrator, who is skeptical about the colonel's cultural experiment. For the first two chapters the white men debate the possibility that Indians can be assimilated into white culture without undergoing a protracted period of enslavement as the Hebrews did under the Egyptians or the Britons under the Romans. The colonel is especially optimistic about rapid acculturation because the sole Choctaw warrior who has signed on his work force is the magnificent Oakatibbe, familiarly known as Slim Sampson, who has leanings toward white culture. Unfortunately, in defense of that alien civilization against a belligerent tribesman, Oakatibbe is forced to kill his opponent. Rather than leave him to face the death penalty dictated by Choctaw law, the colonel and narrator persuade Oakatibbe to flee because he is too valuable to be destroyed by slavish deference to barbaric custom. He can cross the Mississippi, there to establish an enlightened movement among the western Choctaw. But the warrior's conscience inevitably forces him to return and accept execution under tribal justice. Thus, the colonel's noble experiment barely fails. From the view of the two white spectators, Oakatibbe nearly transcends the barrier separating barbarism and civilization as he struggles to choose between two oppositional value systems.

However, this surface reading does not stand up under careful examination

114

of the text. First, it assumes that the narrator and Colonel Harris represent the author in interpreting the meaning of Oakatibbe's drama. There is plenty of internal and external evidence that they do not. Internally, the action of the story continually contradicts the analyses offered by the white men, suggesting that the reality lies elsewhere. On the matter of external evidence, the same year as this tale appeared, Simms published in the Southern and Western Magazine an extensive essay, "Literature and Art among the American Aborigine."[8] The detailed views expressed there ultimately contradict both those of the narrator and Colonel Harris. In this essay Simms appears to be working out his position on the complex questions of what Indian values might be assimilated into white culture and whether Indians themselves could or should be induced to give up any of their traditions. Indeed, one could make the case that thematically "Oakatibbe" dramatizes precisely the arguments advanced in the essay, for the tale pits the two views Simms considered at length in the latter but finally rejected. In the tale, those positions are embodied respectively in the conservative narrator and in the liberal Colonel Harris. Significantly, both positions are invalidated dramatically in the story just as they are rhetorically in the essay. But since the purpose of the story is to present rather than explain the case against forced assimilation, Simms lets the reader arrive inductively at the perspective he spelled out in his essay. To this end, numerous clues distributed throughout the tale dissociate the author from the romanticized and self-deceiving interpretations offered by the narrator. The real meaning emerges when the reader ponders for himself the significance to westering America of Oakatibbe's resolution to the conflicting claims of white and native culture.

Simms early calls into question the narrator's perspective. The tale's dramatic issue is raised when the latter, upon noting Indians at work on the colonel's plantation, comments that "this struck [me] with considerable surprise and disturbed, in some degree, certain preconceived opinions in my mind" (192). A hard-core Southern traditionalist, he cannot believe Indians, whom he stereotypes as "proud," "wandering" barbarians, can ever be weaned without force from "the wild satisfaction afforded by their desultory and unconstrained modes of life" to become a tame working class. Of course he is right, but for the wrong reasons. An irrepressible social evolutionist, he argues they must be forced into slavery and gradually win their right to participate in civilized society. Out on the frontier, this was undoubtedly a rather benign view.

At the other end of the spectrum stands Colonel Harris, who is cast in the role of liberal reformer, a friend of the Indians who believes the proper example of civilized conduct will effect voluntary assimilation by credulous natives, who regard whites as their superiors in all respects. Surely Simms has deliberately located these men so that their views span the range of national opinion on the solution of the Indian problem, from rigid segregationist to liberal assimilationist. By the tale's conclusion, we discover that both men are incurable elitists and that the racial and cultural bigotry underpinning the westward movement are the ultimate targets of Simms' caustic wit.

The perceptions of the narrator and the colonel hardly put the Choctaws, with the exception of Oakatibbe, in a flattering light. The narrator reports how the colonel "conceived the idea of turning to account the lazy Choctaws," for example. His condescending attitude is seconded by the narrator and even by the colonel's slaves. At the scene of the first weekly payment to Indian cotton pickers, the narrator describes black slaves looking on curiously: "a contemptuous grin might be seen on nearly all their countenances, as they felt their superiority in nearly every physical and intellectual respect over the untutored savages" (141). Since the action of the story finally vindicates Oakatibbe's moral superiority and the narrator depicts the young Choctaw's Herculean build with frank envy, we can be sure Simms is already being playfully ironic. The fatuous racism of black slaves aping their white masters leaves an unforgettable image, and the reader is thereby alerted to future distortions.

Colonel Harris, in the opening two-chapter dialectic with the narrator, supports his hope that Indians can be attracted into voluntary assimilation by arguing that "Money, the popular god, is as potent with them as with our own people. They will do anything for money" (196). This assertion is palpably untrue, for Simms has let us discover that the colonel cannot persuade any warrior but Oakatibbe to work. And when we reexamine the Indians who do, they are found to be outcasts from the main tribe generally. Since they are not typical Choctaws, the colonel's experiment, should it appear to succeed, would be invalidated anyway. The reliability of the colonel's judgment on things Indian is continually undercut in this fashion.

Neither are the narrator's opinions based upon sound understanding of Choctaw psychology. Typically, the narrator fantasizes that if our Indians had been invaded en masse and captured as the Britons were by the Romans, they would have been brought to a similarly high level of civilization. In his confused perspective, wherein racism is overlaid with romanticism, he can hold that Indians are "decidedly the noblest race of aborigines that the world has ever known." Yet he can brook no resistance to white manifest destiny. Referring to the Spanish-Indian people's resistance to invasion by Texans in the ongoing war with Mexico, he asserts vehemently: "Let the vain, capricious, ignorant, and dastardly wretches who occupy and spoil the face and fortunes of the former country, persevere in pressing war upon those sturdy adventurers, and their doom is written. I fear it may be the sword--I hope it may be the milder fate of bondage and subjection. Such a fate would save, and raise them finally to a far higher condition than they have ever before enjoyed" (202). Here is enunciated that now familiar principle that it is necessary to destroy the village to save it. It was the rationale in Simms' time for imposing genocidal war and reservation impoundment upon native Americans. The hysterical harshness of the narrator's language serves as ample notice of the author's disgust with America's obsession for violent conquest and his suspicion that such hysteria masked uncertainties about the moral basis of white civilization itself.

Colonel Harris, however, is skeptical about the need for force. He relates the example of a white-educated Indian who returns to his people after compulsory university schooling and chooses "the bucshin [sic] leggins, the moccasins, the bow and arrows, and the wide, wild forest, where his people dwelt" (197). The narrator responds that such a graduate gone native will not "fling away all the lessons of wisdom, all the knowledge of facts, which he will have acquired for [sic] the tuition of the superior race" (204). When he compares the moral and economic condition of his people to the advanced whites, the returnee will be impelled to oppose barbaric customs and laws. Even if murdered by irate tribesmen, he will be a success "if he has overthrown only one of their false gods--if he has smitten off the snaky head of only one of their superstious [sic] prejudices" (201). But despite his dislike of forced submission, the colonel finally assents to the narrator's tough-minded arguments. The two men are not really in disagreement. The latter concludes of the long dialogue that "our dispute, if any, was rather verbal than philosophical" (107). In effect, Simms cleverly telescopes into a unitary position the entire range of opinion on the Indian question, from encouraging voluntary assimilation to imposing virtual slavery. As some Indian spokesmen have observed, the difference between a racist bigot who wants to kill you and a liberal bigot who wants to destroy your culture is hardly worth discussion.

The stage is now set for Oakatibbe's drama. He is that model Indian, susceptible to white influence, who has the prestige and power to effect a change in his people's ways--or that is how the white men see him. But his flirtation with whites is challenged when another powerful warrior, Loblolly Jack, resentful of the colonel's meddling experiment and under the stimulus of alcohol, interferes. Oakatibbe defends the colonel's enterprise and later mortally wounds Loblolly. He goes in great distress to the colonel's cabin where he tells the two whites he is "one dog fool." The issue is fully joined at this dramatic point. On one side is ranged Choctaw code as Simms chose to represent it for this story.[9] According to the narrator, it is "like that of the Hebrews, eye for eye, tooth for tooth, life for life" (214). On the other is the individualist ethics of these enterprising whites who believe that morality is defined by what one can get away with. Oakatibbe accepts the forfeiture of his life on the morrow and is permitted by the chief to stay the night unguarded in Colonel Harris' cabin. That is the measure of the respect even Loblolly's relatives have for this splendid young man. It is a powerful symbol of the moral strength developed by native life. Yet the narrator, in his inimitably imperceptive way, comments "what an eulogy was this on Indian inflexibility! What confidence in the passive obedience of the warrior!" (215).

Both Colonel Harris and the narrator contrive to undermine Oakatibbe's deep regard for tribal codes, which they speciously deem savage superstition. First they appeal to his sense of self-worth, arguing that a man in his youthful prime should not be destroyed: "it's very hard to die for what you didn't wish to do" (217). In other words, he should unilaterally absolve himself from responsibility for the effects of his acts, though Loblolly's family will be left without a provider. The whites touch on every man's propensity to opportunism, telling Oakatibbe that all the Choctaws are drunk tonight. He can escape to the western Choctaws who live over the Mississippi. They urge him: "Go to them-- they will take you by the hand--they will give you one of their daughters to wife--they will love you--they will make you a chief. Fly, Sampson, fly to them" (218). Of course their motive is totally self-serving, for it is Oakatibbe's potential as a subverter of native culture they value.

At these appeals to save his life, the warrior is visibly moved. He admits "I love the whites--I was always a friend to the whites--I believe I love their laws better than my own" (218). But he cannot run. The narrator attributes his stubbornness to "that habitual deference to those laws to which he had given implicit reverence from the beginning." And he concludes smugly that "custom is the superior tyrant of all savage nations" (219). But the truth Simms shows us is that Choctaw society, like most native ones, depended primarily upon voluntarism supported by a deep respect for the individual and a strong sense of individual responsibility for one's actions.[10] Though the individual's tie to his people is purely voluntary, it is in no wise weak, as we soon discover.

Colonel Harris joins the narrator, leaving no stone unturned in the effort to persuade Oakatibbe to escape. Their trump card is that, in his case, they "were assisted by his own inclinations in favour of those customs of the whites, which he had already begun to adopt. We discussed for his benefit that which may be considered one of the leading elements in civilization--the duty of saving and keeping life as long as we can--insisted upon the morality of flying from any punishment which would deprive us of it" (219). The narrator's espousal of what today we dub Watergate morality shows Simms at his sardonic best.

Oakatibbe succumbs to advice, leaving surreptitiously on the colonel's best horse, which he promises to have returned. Naturally, the champions of white morality are exultant. They sleep late into the next morning, confident they have put one over on the Indians who opposed progress. However, their victory shortly becomes Pyrrhic, for Loblolly Jack's relatives discover Oakatibbe has fled and are prepared to attack his relatives. Here Simms slyly forces the chagrined narrator to confess that "we had not foreseen the effects of our interposition and advice. We did not know, or recollect, that the nearest connection of the criminal...would be required to suffer in his place" (220). We suspect they understood full well the consequences, but valued Oakatibbe's life over those of his unregenerate kinsmen.

The crisis is averted when Oakatibbe charges up on horseback between the warring camps. His heart had smitten him for his cowardice and "he remembered the penalties which, in consequence of his flight, must fall heavily upon his people. Life was sweet to him--very sweet" (222). This the narrator tells us in a moment of insight. But he erroneously concludes that though Oakatibbe "had taken one large step in resistance to the tyranneous usages of customs, in order to introduce the elements of civilization among his people[,] he could not withstand the reproaches of a conscience formed upon principles which his own genius was not equal to overthrow" (222). Such sophistry very nearly equates genius with unprincipled conduct. Fortunately, Oakatibbe's subsequent actions show the reader why the Choctaws, in Simm's opinion, have little to learn about morality from these whites.

Naturally the colonel and the narrator are "both mortified and disappointed" by the return of their protégé. Again Simms slyly casts their reactions in monstrous terms the reader must reject. The narrator muses "though the return of Slim Sampson, had obviously prevented a combat á outrance, in which a dozen or more might have been slain, still we could not but regret the event. The life of such a fellow seemed to both of us, to be worth the lives of any hundred of his people" (222).

The frustrated narrator acknowledges that "never did man carry himself with more simple nobleness" than Oakatibbe upon his return. He comforts his mother and uncle at length, then signals his willingness to be executed. He turns to the white men in a supremely ironic scene and says "with a smile: 'Ah, kurnel, you see Injun man ain't strong like white man.'" And the colonel, who misses this grim gem of Indian humor, answers with emotion, "I would have saved you, Sampson." But the Choctaw warrior knows such salvation is too costly, for it profits a man nothing to save his life if thereby he loses his soul.

The remainder of the story demonstrates beyond question the superior moral strength afforded by traditional Choctaw values. The narrator says of Oakatibbe that "his firmness [accepting execution] was unabated." He adds after a lengthy description of Oakatibbe's unshakably noble demeanor that "his look was like that of a strong man, conscious of his inevitable doom, and prepared, as it is inevitable, to meet it with corresponding indifference" (222). We well understand, though the narrator and Colonel Harris do not, that his strength derives from his voluntary choice--only in that sense is it inevitable. Oakatibbe thereby affirms the cornerstone of tribal morality, the concept that all people are interrelated. One cannot act without affecting others and therefore one must assume the full responsibility for the consequences of his deeds. This is the foundation of Choctaw morality which Simms ultimately erects into a referent for judging the opportunistic values of white men who presume to impose their vision of civilization upon ignorant barbarians. Simms makes it clear who are the barbarians and who needs to learn moral integrity.

How would Simms approach the problem of integrating native people and their values into the national society? I think he believed it was already too late by 1845. He wrote in his essay that English settlers were at fault for not sending into the hinterland colonists in the spirit of "such as issued from the fruitful ports of Carthage" (138). Then through cultural and racial mixing a new kind of American would have arisen, for "properly diluted, there was no better blood than that of the Cherokee and Natchez. It would have been a good infusion into the paler fountain of Quaker and Puritan--the very infusion which would put our national vanity into subjection to our pride, and contribute to keep us thoroughly independent of the mother country, in intellectual, as we fondly believe ourselves to be in political respects" (138). The word intellectual is stunning. Unmistakably Simms means that failure to incorporate the moral and intellectual traditions of Indian people marks the most crucial failure of the westering imagination. He concluded it "is only to be accounted for by reference to our blinding prejudice against the race--prejudices which seem to have been fostered as necessary to justify the reckless and unsparing hand with which we have smitten them in their habitations, and expelled them from their country. We must prove them unreasoning beings, to sustain our pretensions as human ones--show them to have been irreclaimable, to maintain our own claims to the regards and respects of civilization" (142).

It would be many years before another writer would penetrate so deeply to the source of those feelings, suppressed within the white consciousness, that dictated our policy of genocide and forced assimilation, and thereby corrupted the American dream of westering toward a purified vision of man and his world. And despite his somewhat patronizing attitudes in the essay quoted, William Gilmore Simms understood far more about the essential issues in our failure to respect native people and their values than his critics have yet given him credit. Finally, despite a rather cumbersome beginning, the tale "Oakatibbe" demonstrates Simms could be a gifted craftsman, showing the human heart, be it red or white, in conflict with itself. The framework of competing cultural values gives this tale an added density of meaning that places it at the well-spring of Western literature. And it suggests that a reassessment of Simms' work on the confrontation between Euro-American and native people is in order.

University of Idaho

NOTES

[1] There is a considerable body of exploration, travel, biographical, and speculative literature in which Indian culture is treated with some respect; but it is distinctly in the minority. Early examples are Sir Thomas More's Utopia (1516) and Roger Williams' A Key into the Language of America (1643). For commentary on the latter, see my "Roger Williams among the Narragansett Indians," New England Quarterly, 43 (December 1970), 593-604.

[2] "Americanizing the White Man," The American Scholar, XXI, 2, (Spring 1952), 177-91. Reprinted in Roger L. Nichols and George R. Adams, eds., The American Indian: Past and Present (Waltham, Mass.: Xerox College Publishing, 1971), pp. 29-41.

[3] In The Savages of America (Baltimore: Johns Hopkins Press, 1953), Roy Harvey Pearce discusses how the stereotypes of the savage precluded any real recognition of the nature of Indian culture and behavior.

[4] This volume was republished in 1968 by the Gregg Press, Inc., of Ridgewood, New Jersey. All future references indicate pagination in this republication.

[5] These are themes that can be found in the writings of More, Williams, Thomas Morton, William Byrd, the Bartrams, and many others. A useful source is Richard Slotkin, Regeneration through Violence (Middletown, Conn.: Wesleyan University Press, 1973).

[6]See Austin J. Sheldon, "African Realistic Commentary on Cultural Hierarchy and Racistic Sentimentalism in The Yamassee," XXV, 1, Phylon (Spring 1964), 72-78. A less severe, but still prejudicial, assessment, is J. V. Ridgeley's William Gilmore Simms (New York: Twayne Publishers, Inc., 1962).

[7]The Savage in Literature (Boston: Routledge and Paul, 1975), p. 6.

[8]This essay is included in C. Hugh Holman's edition of William Gilmore Simms, Views and Reviews in American Literature, History and Fiction (Cambridge, Mass.: Harvard University Press, 1962), pp. 128-147. Future reference in the text will be to this source.

[9]In another story collected in Wigwam and Cabin, "The Arm-Chair of Tustenuggee, A Tradition of the Catawba," Simms shows the far more common consequence of killing a fellow tribesman. The aggressor (in this story the mistaken culprit) is expected to take the victim's place literally. In this case, he was to marry the fearsome wife of the alleged victim, an action more dreaded than death itself.

[10]In the early sections of The Lost Universe: The Way of Life of the Pawnee (New York: Ballantine Books, Inc., 1971), anthropologist Gene Weltfish cogently explains how voluntarism is the key to Pawnee social organizations, as it was for most tribal groups in North America.

THE MISADVENTURES OF IRVING'S BONNEVILLE: TRAPPING AND BEING TRAPPED IN THE ROCKY MOUNTAINS

by Wayne Franklin

When confronted with a book like Washington Irving's The Rocky Mountains (published in 1837, and reissued later as The Adventures of Captain Bonneville), the critic of Western literature may feel constrained to react to its prose in an utterly "historical" manner. Even if composed by a man of letters, the narrative is based, after all, on the account which Benjamin Bonneville himself wrote, and which Irving purchased from him for a thousand dollars. The claim which Irving's book seems to exert on our attention is more active than contemplative, more literal than literary.

Yet we encounter problems almost immediately when we approach the work from this viewpoint. For one thing, Bonneville's manuscript is lost, and unless it should be discovered in the future, any assumptions about the closeness between Irving's narrative and Bonneville's remain tenuous at best. One can speculate, on the basis of Irving's practice in writing Astoria (published in 1836), that he followed his source here as closely as he followed his many sources in the earlier book. But to think of his role in either work as that of a mere scribe, a copyist whose boldest sallies aim at touching up rough frontier narratives for an Eastern audience, is to indulge in presumptions founded on the cliché́s of literary history rather than on the substance of Irving's own prose.

Ironically, the reputation of Irving's book has followed a path directly opposite to that which I would urge his readers to pursue. He clearly intended Bonneville to present, as Astoria had presented, a factual account of experiences parallel, for the recent age, to those which he had chronicled in his history of Columbus and his followers, published in 1828 and 1831. The two books thus mark Irving's firm commitment to a kind of writing which had its personal roots in his first literary success--A History of New-York (1809)--but which lay dormant during his period of renewed creativity in the early twenties. The books which he wrote in that period never ignore the kind of awareness which one might call "historical"--but they take as their primary concern the interplay between a limited narrator and his various "fields" of experience. One such "field" is that created by the confrontation with artifacts of the past--Westminster Abbey in The Sketch-Book (1819-1820), or the Moorish palace in The Alhambra (1832), a work which carries on Irving's older mode after his turn toward formal history in the Columbian books--but this field, like the others, has importance only insofar as it triggers ideas and feelings within the observer. One might say that the themes of all these "personal" works center on the question of confrontation itself; regardless of the form taken by this question in any particular instance--historical, folkloristic, even literary--what remains significant is the persistent stress which Irving or his personae place

122

on the act of perception, and on the emotions and thoughts which that act calls into being.

The irony in the case of Bonneville, then, is that the book was attacked-- by H. H. Bancroft, most signally--for being, in effect, simply another instal- ment of this older Irvingesque programme. To this later historian, Irving's two forays into Western historiography reeked of despicably "Romantic" drives; compared with his own narratives, born in an age more assertively "critical" in its historiographical claims, Astoria and Bonneville were hopelessly --and intentionally--inaccurate. Irving's donning of the historian's robes was merely another instance of his fondness for "costume." This estimate has formed the basis--despite the warm support given Irving by Hiram Chittenden in the early twentieth century--for more recent literary assessments that seem scarcely more perceptive. The books are described quite naively as "hack-work"; they key us, we are told, to a marked decline in Irving's imaginative powers, his turn toward subjects which could shore up by their contemporary appeal his own failing energies as a writer. He appears, in such accounts, as a rank literary opportunist for whom his chosen themes had little intrinsic interest; he is thrown only the bone of shrewdness for guessing so accurately that his readers would buy his "Romantic" narratives about a region that conjured up in their own minds equally romantic, and equally false, images.

We owe to one modern reader, however, a great debt for revising this hackneyed interpretation, and thus recovering for our serious consideration some thousand pages of Irving's narrative prose. Edgeley W. Todd has argued eloquently--and with admirably firm historical detail--for the essential accur- acy of Irving's books as factual accounts, and for the high intentions which guided Irving in their composition. Taking recourse, especially in his edition of Astoria, to the sources which Irving is known to have used, he demonstrates not only how closely Irving reads and uses them, but also how consistently he aims at "mapping" the scenes of his reported action for his readers. His books on the West represent a sincere effort to grasp the essence of American exper- ience beyond the boundary of white settlement--an intellectual endeavor of large dimensions and of great significance for the future course of writing about the trans-Mississippi region. [1]

An anecdote related by Stanley T. Williams, one of those whose regard for Irving's Western books is modest to say the least, pinpoints nicely the pains- taking effort with which Astoria and Bonneville were written. One J. N. Barry, an inhabitant of a valley described in the earlier book, was sceptical of Irving's accuracy, for he had inherited from the critics of Astoria a belief that "a large portion" of it was "'fiction'"; yet when Barry took Irving's narrative in hand and followed its description of his own land as he walked across the valley, he soon was convinced that the book's faithfulness could not be questioned. [2] Though Irving himself never had seen this landscape--he had seen, in fact, only the smallest fraction of the vast regions which he renders in Astoria and Bonneville--he strives throughout both works to convey his readers and himself into the actual locale of the deeds which they record. Far from being satisfied with the sort of general scene-painting which one would expect a mere "romancer" to achieve, he aims at a full comprehension of the real terrain over which his disappointed travelers move with such difficulty. In this broader, more "philosophical" sense--as in his close reliance on the manuscripts and printed sources available to him--Irving reveals a consistently historical attitude. He believes wholeheartedly in the reality of what he describes; his task is not simply to juggle his authorities so as to produce the best possible artwork, but rather to employ his literary talent in the service of "truth."

If one pursues this line of argument too far, however, a new risk arises. One may lose sight of the large role which Irving's imagination--and the theme of imagination in general--plays in Astoria and in Bonneville. For these books, and Bonneville especially, aim at something beyond the truth of their nominal subjects; they embrace as well the question of what the "West" is, how it is perceived by the nation and by individuals, and how the experience of traveling through it--either as the nation was traveling in its gradual migration, or as Astor's men and Bonneville's party moved across it--inevitably involves one in the comparison of ideas and realities, presumptions and facts, romantic wishes and historical constraints. It is fair to say, I think, that Irving's narratives were written against the oral "book" of national fantasies about the West; that his own struggle to engross as much Western reality as possible within them has roots not only in his commitment to historical methodology but also in his sense of how far short of that reality the normal American's perception of the West fell; and, finally, that his writing aims at providing both a model for further books about the West and an ethical guide for the audience to which such books, like his own, might be addressed. In these various goals, the imagination is culprit and hero at once: for if the national failure of perception can be traced directly to an over-indulgence in fantasy, Irving's solution to this problem lies in the full exercise of an historical imagination to match his own--a habit of mind which is expansive only in its desire to penetrate and understand the unknown. The West of Bonneville stands as a challenge to our capacity for acute perception and for intellectual openness. In mapping this world, and the human deeds enacted in it, Irving is mapping out the larger history of Old World migrations to the New--as well as the spiritual themes contained in that larger movement. To tell this one small story as he tells it is to unfold in its minute details a vast legend of the American past and future.

The legend is a rather bleak one. Though he gives, in his second title for the book, a seemingly romantic clue to his readers, the "adventures" of Bonneville are evanescent in the text itself. Irving possessed, it should be made clear, a rather precise notion of what consitutes adventure; the term can be defined with some exactness from his own uses of it--as in his most personal Western book, A Tour on the Prairies (1835)--and one would be wrong to see in it merely a conventional catchall, a piece of lingua franca so commonly used in his age that he adopted it without thinking. In A Tour, we recall, the young Swiss Count actively pursues, in the prairie world of mid-America, an ideal of romantic adventure which he has defined in the Old World, and which proves ridiculously inadequate as a guide to his American experience. Like the persona through whom Irving writes The Sketch-Book, the young man has cast into the distance an image of future fulfilment; and like Crayon--who thinks of England as his ancestral home, but who lands in Liverpool to find himself an utter stranger--the Count is forced, in a moment of heightened perception, to assess the realities of his chosen environment, and to discard ideas now quite evidently mismatched with it. Significantly, Captain Bonneville is portrayed in Irving's "Introductory Notice" as a man of "excitable imagination" whose "vague daydream" of an exploring expedition in the Far West smacks of the same obliviousness displayed in the Count two years earlier (Todd's edition, pp. 1, li). What saves him from the risible fate of Pourtales is the combination of his previous experience beyond the Mississippi with the serious extremity of his later journeys. Pourtales spends one night alone on the prairie, riding his saddle on a tree limb, but Bonneville, pushing much farther into the realities of the West, undergoes severe sufferings. That a rumor of his death preceded his return to St. Louis, and caused his removal from the Army lists, suggests just how close to being permanently lost he came.

The initial parallel with Pourtales has meaning nonetheless. Both of these travelers offer us a concise definition of Irving's attitude toward adventure--his sense of its vaguely spiritual origins in the imagination--as well as an insight into his estimate of the adventurer's fate in what Thoreau, when he distinguishes our adventurous desires from the realm where they must seek expression, calls "this actual world."[3] Adventure is not a form of action or a state of being for Irving, but rather an ideal of action and of existence never truly discovered in reality. Since the American West had become, even in the 1830's, a presumed realm of adventure for those who did not know it, Irving's records of his own experience there, and of the experiences endured by others who penetrated farther into it than he, allow him to test this national hypothesis, and to bring his own matured thoughts on allied topics to bear on the emergent mythology of the American frontier.

Bonneville's expedition provides him with a perfect microcosm of the nation's fugitive past and its hopeful future. Abandoning the omniscient viewpoint which he used in Astoria, and which allowed him there to shuttle back and forth between the Columbia River and New York, or to treat simultaneous expeditions concurrently, he makes his prose in Bonneville accompany his main character point-by-point, adding to the central record of the Captain's journeys the auxiliary accounts of other expeditions only when Bonneville himself, reunited with the other parties, learns of their successes and failures. The prose thus acquires a curious trait: it is as "bound" to the Western scene as those whose life it narrates. And if one may explain this trait by pointing to Irving's presumed closeness to Bonneville's own narrative--perhaps his laziness?--the fact remains that the book adheres to the spirit of the explorer's experience, not simply to its lost letter. We find few panoramas, for instance, which seem to have their warrant only in the imagination of Irving; the sweeping scenes which build toward a sense of great expanse do so against the background of Bonneville's awareness--they emerge from his sense of uncertainty and his growing sense of composure, not from Irving's static organization of the terrain.

This confinement of Irving's prose to the awareness of his main character makes the Western scene uncomfortably close. And in this way the texture of his style enforces on us conclusions allied to those which we are led to make with regard to the work's substance. The shape of Bonneville's experience is singularly ironic: he bears the torch of romantic idealism out into the region where, according to the national fantasy, the clear pure air ought to aid in its combustion; but his accumulating disappointments, his failure to discover a world of true adventure, quickly extinguish his own hopes and those which Irving's audience might easily invest in him. Those disappointments, severe as they are, are not the sole misadventures in the narrative. On almost every front, the book presents ethical ideals which the full course of Western life radically undercuts. The main form of social intercourse in the trapper's West, for instance, is the "rendezvous," and on its surface this colorful variety of "community" life seems to offer a particularly bright image of the possibility for open-hearted and open-handed living in the wilderness. The rendezvous gives vent to hospitality and generosity, to courtesy and celebration. But, like Bonneville's private dream for adventure, this form of public interaction has its own bleak negative. Invidious rivalries underlie this cheerful social occasion, and no safe middle-ground exists between those rivalries and the manic festivities of the winter camp. If it weren't for the heavy snows in the mountains, the men who gather in such cordiality would be at each other's throats-- as, indeed, they are even at some points during the encampments. As trappers, they all draw on the same wealth, and this fact makes their true relationship into a small-scale version of those mindless competitions with which Irving opens, so somberly, his account of Astor's early failures. Trapping becomes, in this sense, a more nearly true image of their social ethic than the rendezvous. They try to trick and deceive each other, to lay traps and snares which aim less at increasing their own wealth than at denying any share of it to the rest of the trappers. As a result, they are impoverished in a literal and a spiritual sense. With all of Western nature looming around them, they crowd in on one another; the landscape is strangely cluttered, the resources of any one region quickly depleted by their suspicious herding.

The dichotomies thus exhibited in the social world, and in the Western experience of Bonneville himself, are mirrored in Irving's portrayal of nature. The same principle of contrast is found throughout: in mountain and plain, in the alternation of abundance and scarcity, in the promise of wealth and the production of death and poverty. But to say that Irving is blaming the wilderness for these contrasts, and for their reflection in the social world, would be to simplify his meaning. If anything, it is the other way around, for the severest trials of the trappers develop from their own expectations and their own values. If they suffer from exposure, it is because they have exposed themselves to the West, and done so in a wrong spirit. Their tiresome journeys through the Rockies, like their moments of rendezvous, allow them to express the flaws inherent in their outlooks on the world, and on the American continent in particular. For them, as for the nation, the journey West becomes a "trial" in the other sense--a test of the adequacy of their ideas, feelings, and beliefs. The wilderness passively reads them, and the nation through them.

What Irving gives us in <u>Bonneville</u>, then, is an anatomy, dense in its detail and bleak in its tone of Eastern interaction with the West. He is concerned less with the "romantic" aspects of his chosen subject than with its potential as a means of national self-knowledge. One often reads that Irving en-
dorsed, especially in this period, the mottoes of manifest destiny and the ethics of national expansion. On the contrary, his Western books take those mottoes and those ethics only as a starting point, and they test them against the
reality which they pretend to describe and govern. This fact may reflect Irving's "cultural federalism," his uneasiness about the rougher and cruder features of American life, especially as he had seen that life across the Mississippi. Yet the record of his own "Tour" suggests that he felt a positive attraction
to the vibrantly active world he had seen on the prairies, that he committed
himself in 1832 to a very different notion of travel from the one which had gov-
erned his European books prior to that time. <u>Space</u> became for him, as it had
not been before, an immensely present "field"; he ceased to be a "tourist"
(despite the title of his first Western book) and became instead a traveler. And
if space could be threatening to him in the <u>Tour</u>, it could also symbolize physical freedom and exultation--and even some better notion of social possibilities
in an unsettled landscape. We see him, in that book (and in other documents
describing the same experience), struggling to leave his European prejudices
behind and to take up in their stead a set of values, as a man and a writer, more
nearly matching his newfound sense of American "reality." His call for a "Western education" at the start of the <u>Tour</u>--offered as a substitute for the Eastern
habit of sending the young to Europe--is not an idle or conventional piece of
rhetoric. It signalizes his own fresh intentions, fleshed out in his next three
books--and it hints, too, at an ideal apprehension of his own about the frontier,
an apprehension which he thought the actual record of American expansion had
betrayed and still was betraying. In this sense, he is lamenting a failure of imagination in <u>Astoria</u> and in <u>Bonneville</u>, a failure to grasp the spiritual potential
of a truly New World. Given the freedom of a Western empire, he is asking,
what would the East do with it? And what <u>else</u> might it do?

His answers are not overly hopeful. He persists in the vague belief that
some great apotheosis may occur beyond the river; but he feels compelled to
report--and this compulsion explains his rhetorical stance in <u>Bonneville</u>--as
accurately as possible the evidence of his own experience and his own researches.
The evidence hardly bolsters his initial beliefs. The tensions which he perceived in the trapper's life allow him to hold up against Eastern assumptions
the hard facts of its previous incursions into the much-touted West. Certainly,
the trapper's life is colorful, and Irving recognizes the duty of preserving its
color from the fading power of oblivion. More than a wistful melancholy demands such acts of preservation, however. As the prime moment of Eastern
expansion, the period of trapping is a benchmark for measuring (and perhaps
for redefining) the future course of growth. Its bleak contrasts, its blindness
to the true richness of a wilderness condition: such facts and others offer dire
warnings to a nation already wrapping itself in pelts wrenched at such cost from
the West. So dire are the warnings, in fact, that their enunciation in <u>Bonneville</u>

pushes Irving off the ground of his first Western hopes--away from his sense of the great freedom held out to America by the territories beyond it, and yet contained already in its myths as in its economy. For how "free" is American society, Irving asks finally, if, once it moves into the landscape which supposedly expresses its freedom, it almost immediately adopts a way of life that is oppressive and even self-destructive? No, this is no story of romance, no pleasing tale out of the vague distance. It demands of Irving, as of his audience, a pause of recognition and reassessment. To write, or to read, a true Western history is to call into service all the powers of one's sane imagination; the extremities recounted in such a book are not faraway or obscure, but rather they impinge uncomfortably on the territory of every self-aware mind.

The University of Iowa

NOTES

[1] Astoria; or Anecdotes of an Enterprise Beyond the Rocky Mountains, ed. Edgeley W. Todd (Norman: Univ. of Oklahoma Press, 1964), pp. xv-xliii; The Adventures of Captain Bonneville, U.S.A., in the Rocky Mountains and the Far West, ed. Edgeley W. Todd (Norman: Univ. of Oklahoma Press, 1961), pp. xvii-xlviii.

[2] Stanley T. Williams, The Life of Washington Irving (New York: Oxford Univ. Press, 1935), II, 88.

[3] Thoreau makes this distinction in "Walking," first published in 1863, but dating from ca. 1850; see Excursions (Boston: Ticknor and Fields, 1863), p. 175: "We would fain take that walk, never yet taken by us through this actual world, which is perfectly symbolical of the path which we love to travel in the interior and ideal world...."

THE PRINCE AS FROG: JOHN C. FREMONT
AND YEAR OF DECISION: 1846

by Anthony Arthur

In 1943, Bernard DeVoto's Year of Decision: 1846 was published to near-ly unanimous acclaim as an important account of the westering experience, a unique narrative summary in which the author combined his talents as a his-torian with his skills as a novelist. It was, as Wallace Stegner wrote later, "romantic history in literary terms," employing the device of history by synec-doche and seeking not merely the reader's comprehension but his response.

The response DeVoto desired was essentially a positive one: Year of Decision is an affirmation, written in the dark early years of World War II, of American courage and initiative. Its pages are crowded with men and women whose virtues are as manifest as their destiny, including William Eddy of the Donner party, Susan Doniphan, Jim Clyman, Jim Bridger, and Stephen Kearny.

But heroes require antagonists to set off their virtues. Somewhat sur-prisingly, the chief antagonist in Year of Decision is none other than John C. Fremont, the celebrated explorer who at 33 had already become, in DeVoto's words, a "popular image of our western wayfaring ..., a hero of popular dra-ma." It is in fact one of DeVoto's main tasks in Year of Decision to revise the popular image of Fremont, to show that it is not only misleading but false and harmful.

Given the accuracy of Stegner's phrase for Year of Decision--"romantic history in literary terms"--it may seem anomalous that Fremont, a hero whose fame was spread by his own and other accounts of his adventures, arouses such hostility in DeVoto. I propose both to show how he discredits Fremont and to explain why he felt it necessary to do so.

I should stress that it is not my concern here whether DeVoto is "right" or "wrong" in his estimate of Fremont, whose exploits in California and through-out his controversial life have been the subject of vigorous debate. For although no-one packed more "facts" into his books than DeVoto, it was with history as romance, drama, and myth that he was primarily concerned; it seems clear to me that in his impressionistic tableau of American history, Fremont is a cari-cature: it is clearly not the man but the popular image of Fremont that DeVoto seeks to destroy, because the image, unlike the man, is still alive and well--and inaccurate.

The facts concerning Fremont are familiar and can be summarized brief-ly. He was ordered in the spring of 1845 to undertake his third exploring expe-dition, in particular to find a better route for the last leg of the Oregon trail. In December he crossed the Sierras into California and received permission from Mexican authorities to winter in the interior valleys; early the next year he was ordered out of the Salinas Valley by General Castro for exceeding the conditions of his permission. After sitting defiantly atop Gavilan Peak for three days with his force of 50 mountain men and surveyors, Fremont moved northward. In early May, camped near Klamath Lake in southern Oregon, he was visited by Marine Lt. Archibald Gillespie with news of instructions from Secretary of State Buchanan for Consul Larkin in Monterey: Larkin was to cooperate with the Californians, but also to encourage them to secede from Mexico and join the United States. Fremont also received from Gillespie, he said later, a coded communication from his influential father-in-law, Senator Thomas Hart Benton, which said he should seize any chance to act in the best interests of the country.

Fremont thereupon turned southward and led a group of American dissidents in what became known as the Bear Flag Revolt. By June, when the California Republic under William Ide had been declared, Commodore Stockton had arrived in Monterey to assume command of the Pacific Fleet and, he believed, of all American forces in California. He made Fremont his deputy and sent him shuttling back and forth between Los Angeles and Monterey. Later that year, General Kearny arrived with his forces in southern California and claimed that President Polk had given him jurisdiction over the American forces; Fremont refused to serve under Kearny, arguing that Stockton had the better claim to command. When hostilities ended early in 1847 and confirmation of Kearny's command arrived from the White House, Fremont was taken back to Washington to stand trial for mutiny. He was convicted, but President Polk set aside the conviction and offered to pardon him as well as on various lesser counts of disobedience. Fremont refused the pardon and resigned his commission. In future years he would be the Republican Party's first nominee for President, a Union General in Missouri, and Governor of the Territory of Arizona.

All of this is covered in some detail by DeVoto. It needs to be understood that DeVoto apparently accepts the Bancroft thesis that California in 1845-46 was a ripe orange about to fall peacefully into the outstretched hands of the United States. Unhappily, according to Bancroft, foolish idealism, greed, and political ambition marched together under the flag with the misshapen bear that looked like a pig, and thus was born the short-lived Bear Flag Republic, or Republic of California--midwifed by useless bloodshed and leaving a bitter heritage of injustice and racial prejudice.

Engaged, then, in a dubious cause to begin with, Fremont further excites DeVoto's ire in two ways: first, he lied when he said he had secret information from Benton which justified his returning south and taking up arms against a foreign government; and second, his quarrel with Kearny enhanced his own reputation, even though he was found guilty, at the expense of a man superior to him in every way.

The first objection is derived from Bancroft, with echoes of Josiah Royce, and is essentially a restatement of their quarrels with Fremont's account. DeVoto's acceptance of their appraisal of Fremont's character provides the essential premise for his attack and a clue to his method. That is, although there is a change, or a progression, in Fremont as a character by the end of DeVoto's story, there is no change in his character, which was set in its unfortunate mold to begin with. As for method, DeVoto is not so much a novelist as he is a satirist when he deals with Fremont, as well as with Stockton, Merritt, Ide, and the rest of the Bear Flaggers: they are all, in the best Swiftian tradition, fools or knaves. The only difference in Fremont at the end of the book is that he is now dangerous as well as contemptible.

Thus DeVoto's treatment of Fremont involves a pattern of derision which progresses from amused contempt to outrage. When first introduced, Fremont is "Childe Harold," imagined by Byron with a dash of Rousseau. He is later called Galahad, Destiny's Courtier, the Conqueror, and Major Jinks of the Horse Marines. His men are, variously, the Army of Hollywood, Caesar's Tenth Legion, the Tallapoosy Vollantares, and the Rover Boys in the Halls of Montezuma. More directly, Fremont is a barnstormer, a freebooter, and a filibuster; an opportunist, an adventurer, and "a blunderer on a truly dangerous scale"; a man--DeVoto is no longer amused--with an "instinct for self-aggrandizing treachery"; and finally, at the end of the book, one who though "technically" not a traitor did not lack for "the raw stuff of which treason is made."

Besides undercutting Fremont indirectly through satire and directly through invective, DeVoto also presses his indictment by opposing him to General Kearny, whom he admires as a bluff, competent soldier, and by associating him with Zachary Taylor, whom he detests as a soldier-politician angling for the Presidency.

The opposition to Kearny begins as both he and Fremont are introduced in consecutive paragraphs, Fremont the "son-in-law" of Senator Benton "roaming" about in California, and Kearny our "ablest frontier officer" setting forth with his "crack regiment, the First Dragoons," for the southwest. As will become clear in the course of DeVoto's narrative, he regards Senator Benton's influence on the fortunes of Fremont as crucial. Thus the operative words in these initial descriptions are "son-in-law" for Fremont and "able" for Kearny; the contest between influence and ability which Kearny will lose is DeVoto's chief concern in the final section of Year of Decision. In the meantime, no opportunity is lost to oppose Kearny's competence with Fremont's posturing. When Kearny takes Santa Fe in an efficient and humane manner, for example, "without firing a shot," DeVoto praises him for having followed "Mr. Polk's instructions." This noble feat, and the implicit rebuke of Fremont for having failed to do the same in California, is followed immediately by an account of "the Conqueror" swaggering into Monterey to meet "D'Artagnan" Stockton, another man who "knew his Hollywood."

Again, when Kearny is engaged in the only real battle of the war in California, on December 6 at San Pascual, he is in trouble because Fremont's mentor, Stockton, has assured Kearny that his soldiers would not be needed in California. Everything was under control, Stockton said, so Kearny sent two-thirds of his force back to New Mexico and was nearly wiped out. And where was the heroic, impetuous Fremont? Two pages back and three days late, moving southward "with a most strategic deliberation," DeVoto says, carefully maintaining his unblemished record of not having once met "armed opposition in California."

131

In similar fashion, though less extensively, Fremont is associated with General Taylor, who became President because he "wrote prose" to newspapers while better men kept him from destroying his army in Mexico. Ambitious, incompetent, and unintelligent, but blessed with a good press, Taylor and Fremont are two sides of the same debased coin for DeVoto; they are associated to their mutual discredit several times, most explicitly in the following passage: "And on May 9, at Klamath Lake in Oregon, Lt. Gillespie of the United States Marines caught up with Captain Fremont and Zachary Taylor fought the engagement known as the Battle of Reseca de la Palma." DeVoto then describes the battle, the successful conclusion of which prompts Taylor to begin "his campaign for the Presidency," and returns to Klamath Lake. There Fremont, like Taylor, the reader is to assume, also sees that "his cue had been spoken," that it was time to "seize California and wrap Old Glory around him," and to become a hero "from the moment until he died...."

The vehemence of DeVoto's unremitting attack on Fremont is such that one wonders at it. At least part of the reason is clear enough: Fremont is considered an unworthy hero, whom it does the nation no credit to honor. The true heroes of DeVoto's account are not romantic individualists; they are competent men who can take and give orders, like Kearny; stoic, humorous, and consistent men, like Jim Clyman; brave and selfless men, like William Eddy; and men, like John Wesley Powell, with visions of a new society in the west that would "correct folly and restore social health." Above all, they are serious men, concerned more with doing their jobs properly than with abstract ideals or personal ambition. The composite portrait of the hero to be set against that of Fremont is dutiful rather than dashing, and constitutes a rebuttal of more popular notions of a romantic hero.

For a fuller explanation of DeVoto's attack, however, we need to examine the implications of his introductory appraisal of Fremont. "[We] are to follow" Fremont, DeVoto says, "through knotty and hardly soluble controversies. They will be less obscure if it is kept in mind that Fremont was primarily a literary man...with a literary wife." Now for a man of letters like DeVoto to refer to someone as a literary man would not ordinarily be considered pejorative, but in Fremont's case it implies criticism in two ways. First, it characterizes Fremont as an amateur among professionals; and second, it ties in with the creation of Fremont as a hero by the popular press and with the perpetuation of his false image.

DeVoto's admiration for professionalism and distaste for amateurs were essential to his nature, as Stegner's recent biography shows. "I dislike amateurs, esthetes, dilettantes," he wrote to a friend in 1944. "I dislike literary attitudes and those who take them." In Year of Decision DeVoto never misses a chance to discredit Fremont as an explorer, soldier, and politician, to persuade the reader that The Pathfinder was a comparative amateur, if not an incompetent, in everything except writing about himself. Emerson was quite right, DeVoto implies, in recording his reservations about "'the stout Fremont'" who "'is continually remarking on "the group" or "the picture" etc. "which we make."'" Despite the excitement of the narrative, Emerson says, there is always present '"this eternal vanity of how we must look.'"

The appropriateness of DeVoto's initial characterization of Fremont as Childe Harold, a posturing adolescent dandy, now seems apparent.

Initially, as I suggested earlier, DeVoto is more amused than outraged by Fremont, and his objections seem to be more a matter of taste than substance. But in his account of Fremont's trial one senses a mounting disgust that such a patently false man could be passed off on an undiscriminating nation as a hero. It was bad enough, one gathers, that Fremont was a literary man, but now he has become a literary creation:

> Neither misuse of Senatorial power in the pursuit of adver-
> tising nor the creation in newsprint of a great public hero is an in-
> vention of our age, which has not seen any betterment of the tech-
> nique that erected Fremont into a martyr and a man designed by
> providential forethought to save the American people from their
> governors. Here, at a trial designed to assess his actions on the
> fringe of empire, was created a figure of pure advertising that
> cost the nation heavily from then on, a creature of oratory and
> newsprint. That creation was almost enough to wreck the Republic.
> It was enough to convince innumerable people born since the adver-
> tising stopped and its proprietors died, so that you will still find it
> in the instruction given our children. The report of that trial is a
> case study in the dynamics of reputation.

Written in 1943 about events in 1846, this passage is remarkably prescient for modern readers who are familiar with the seeming power of the media to manufacture heroes at will. It is also typical of DeVoto's method, which involves the creative use of hindsight to link past and present, and which is one of the reasons why his history has a vital sense of personal involvement lacking in more conventional accounts. Finally, it explains why DeVoto has gone to such pains to discredit the romantic personification of the westering experience: though the man is long since dead, his fraudulently achieved heroic image remains intact.

The true romance of American history for DeVoto, as opposed to the false romance of Fremont, is explained in a letter to Catherine Drinker Bowen. Our history, he said,

> began in myth and has developed through three centuries of fairy
> stories. Whatever the time is in America, it is always, at every
> moment, the mad and wayward hour when the prince is finding
> the little foot that alone fits into the slipper of glass. It is a little
> hard to know what romantic means to those who use the word um-
> brageously. But if the mad, impossible voyage of Columbus or
> Cartier or LaSalle or Coronado or John Ledyard is not romantic
> ...I don't know what romance is. Ours is a story mad with the
> impossible, it is by chaos out of dream, it began as dream and it

has continued as dream down to the last headline you read in a newspaper, and of our dream there are two things above all others to be said, that only madmen could have dreamed them or would have dared to--and that we have shown a considerable faculty for making them come true.

For DeVoto, Fremont was not a romantic hero at all in the sense of this quintessentially romantic passage. He was blessed with influential family connections and lucky in being at the right place at the right time. Far from being a "madman," he was ambitious, shrewd, and selfish, transformed by his own accounts and the press into a popular hero. He was in fact not the hero of American romance but an impostor--not a prince but a frog. DeVoto's account of Fremont is an amusing, vigorous, outraged caricature, a corrective concentrating on the frog's warts. Ultimately, to play on DeVoto's words, it is a case study in the dynamics of disreputation.

California State University, Northridge

HENRY ADAMS, WALLACE STEGNER, AND THE SEARCH FOR A SENSE OF PLACE IN THE WEST

by Jamie Robertson

> The Rough Rock Demonstration School strives to fit
> its students for life in a modern world while, at the
> same time, keeping the best of Navajo tradition and
> culture.
>
> Grandfather Stories of the Navajo
> (Phoenix: Navajo Curriculum Center Press)

This quotation is taken from a preface to a collection of traditional stories of the Navajo whose purpose is to keep in memory the tradition that conveys a people's identity. It presents a central problem of education in the modern world: Can we preserve the best of our cultural traditions and still fit ourselves for life in the modern world? Henry Adams defined the problem in The Education, and Wallace Stegner continues Adams' inquiry in Wolf Willow.[1] Adams and Stegner view education as the human process of resolving the problem. Both authors understand education in the broadest metaphorical sense as an active, imaginative process of establishing a human connection to the landscape and to the life that is lived in it. For Adams and Stegner, education is the activity of making a coherent symbolic statement about our cultural traditions and how those traditions explain our relationship to, or sense of, place.

In the early years of the 20th century, when Henry Adams began to write his Education, there was a fantastic increase in the quantity of knowledge that it was a student's duty to learn. While the educational system did an efficient job of requiring students to assimilate these facts, it had made little effort to teach them how to make sense of those facts in the light of their cultural heritage. Henry Adams found himself a victim of this failure of education. In The Education he creates the embodiment of such a failure in the persona of Henry Adams, a personality of fragmented sensibility disconnected from the world and from the traditions of the past by the forces of the 20th century.

The technological forces of progress cut Adams off from the traditions of the past, a separation that, from his viewpoint, fragmented the world:

> No such accident had ever happened before in human experi-
> ence. For him, alone, the old universe was thrown into the
> ash-heap and a new one created. He and his eighteenth-cen-
> tury, troglodytic Boston were suddenly cut apart--separated
> forever--in act if not in sentiment, by the opening of the Bos-
> ton and Albany Railroad; the appearance of the first Cunard

steamers in the bay; and the telegraphic messages which
carried from Baltimore to Washington the news that Henry
Clay and James K. Polk were nominated for the Presidency.
This was in May, 1844; he was six years old; his new world
was ready for use, and only fragments of the old met his
eyes (p. 5).

Education is for Adams the process of putting the pieces back together. Adams'
effort in The Education is to offer a coherent symbolic representation of the
meaning of the technological forces of the 20th century, but the symbol that he
creates is the dynamo, paradoxically one not of order but of chaos and fragmentation. Indeed, in Adams' view, the forces of progress seem to have ended
the possibility of seeing the world, humankind and nature, whole again. Adams'
concern is that the artistic or life process of bringing order to the chaos that
confronts humanity is becoming an impossibility in the modern world. The
force of the faith of the past that created Chartres Cathedral, he argues, has been
lost in the 20th century, and the force of the power of coal has become the sole
human reality. And this force is technological rather than cultural. Its force
has shaped human beings to its image rather than the other way around.

The 18th-century American dreamed that technology would provide access
to the natural world where all might live as artificers who could transform the
world into a realized ideal, into a new Garden of Eden that would be both
democratic and popular. But that dream became impossible for Adams to maintain. The farms that St. John de Crèvecoeur had envisioned lining the banks of
the Ohio were now obscured by coal smoke, the emblem of the industrial revolution. For Adams and his contemporaries there remained only one landscape
where the 18th-century dream of Crèvecoeur could be realized. The West offered at least the potentiality for a successful education, for a temporary escape from the power of technology to fragment and destroy humankind's poetic
sensibility. Perhaps here in an unspoiled landscape, Adams mused, education
might still be possible:

In the year 1871, the West was still fresh, and the Union
Pacific was young. Beyond the Missouri River, one felt
the atmosphere of Indians and buffaloes. One saw the last
vestiges of an old education, worth studying if one would;
but it was not that which Adams sought; rather, he came
out to spy on the land of the future. The Survey occasionally borrowed troopers from the nearest station in case of
happening on hostile Indians, but otherwise the topographers and geologists thought more about minerals than
about Sioux. They held under their hammers a thousand
miles of mineral country with all its riddles to solve, and
its stores of possible wealth to mark. They felt the future
in their hands (p. 309).

Topographers and geologists, Adams notes, went west not with the outdated intention of creating cultural visions such as the Virgin, but with the dream of building more railroads and mining the landscape. One of these men of the future was Clarence King, a man who Adams thought had educated himself in a way to deal effectively with the forces of the 20th century:

> ...King had moulded and directed his life logically, scientif-
> ically, as Adams thought life should be directed. He had
> given himself education all of a piece, yet broad (p. 312).

If anyone could exert any degree of control over his future, Clarence King could. For Adams, Clarence King was the embodiment of the myth of the perfect American, a man of Eastern talent and social grace and of Western will and energy. This was in 1871, and Adams was at his most optimistic point. Twenty years later he no longer held any illusions of King's success:

> Thus, in 1892, neither Hay, King, nor Adams knew whether
> they had attained success, or how to estimate it, or what to
> call it; and the American people seemed to have no clearer
> idea than they. Indeed, the American people had no idea at
> all; they were wandering in a wilderness much more sandy
> than the Hebrews had ever trodden about Sinai; they had
> neither serpents nor golden calves to worship....The Amer-
> ican mind...shunned, distrusted, disliked, the dangerous
> attraction of ideals, and stood alone in history for its ignor-
> ance of the past (p. 328).

The Anglo adventure in the West was soon over. The hope it had briefly provided for the fulfillment of the dream was lost. Not even King was able to unify the forces of technology which Adams saw gathered together at the Chicago exposition in 1893. That exposition asked the question, "Did the American People know where they were driving?" Adams' conclusion was that they did not, and neither did he. It was unquestionable that we were moving, but whether it was progress or change, directed movement or passive response to uncontrollable forces, was uncertain.

The power of modern America was a different kind from that embodied in art. As Adams argued, "All the steam in the world could not, like the Virgin, build Chartres." Adams' failure as he perceived it was that he could not resolve the dilemma of education. He could not bridge the gap between the 18th and 20th centuries, between tradition and technology, and his identity, like the world, remained fragmented:

> His identity, if one could call a bundle of disconnected mem-
> ories an identity, seemed to remain; but his life was once
> more broken into separate pieces; he was a spider and had to
> spin a new web in some place with a new attachment (p. 209).

137

But what to attach the web to? How to connect the pieces? Adams remained far less optimistic about such a possibility than the transcendentalists of 19th-century America had been.

Wallace Stegner's Wolf Willow: A History, a Story, and a Memory of the Last Plains Frontier is a contemporary western-American version of Adams' Education. Stegner sees his education--at least the institutionalized part of it--as hopelessly inadequate to the needs of a person growing up in his boyhood home of Whitemud, Saskatchewan, and Wolf Willow is, at least in part, intended to redress that inadequacy.

> Far more than Henry Adams, I have felt myself entitled
> to ask whether my needs and my education were not ludi-
> crously out of phase. Not because I was educated for the
> past instead of the future...but because I was educated for
> the wrong place. Education tried inadequately and hope-
> lessly to make a European out of me (p. 24).

While Adams thought himself irrevocably separated from the traditions of the European past, Stegner laments the inadequacy of that same European tradition taught in a place rich in regional history. Education in this last plains fron-tier, Stegner writes, tied "us into Western civilization, if it taught us little about who we were, it taught us something of what we had been" (p. 291). The assumption made by Stegner as he grew up was the assumption handed to him by his teachers. He was told that this land was an untouched wilderness, a place of no history or tradition out of which the activities of the people in the landscape grew. Stegner's world "had neither location nor time, geography nor history" (pp. 28-29). The people of Whitemud acted naively on the assump-tion that they were completely separate from the influence of the tradition of their home place; but Wolf Willow repudiates the belief that they were living in such a cultural vacuum.

Stegner argues that, whether people are aware of them or not, the his-torical traditions of a place affect their lives:

> ...history is a pontoon bridge. Every man walks and works
> at its building end, and has come as far as he has over the
> pontoons laid by others he may never have heard of. The
> history of the Cypress Hills had almost as definite effects
> on me as did their geography and weather, though I never
> knew a scrap of that history until a quarter-century after I
> left the place. However it may have seemed to the people
> who founded it, Whitemud was not a beginning, not a new
> thing, but a stage in a long historical process (p. 29).

But what does education matter if the outcome of a people's actions is the same whether they know their history or not? The implicit argument of Stegner's

<u>Wolf</u> <u>Willow</u> is that their actions might very well not have been the same had they known and understood the cultural traditions from which they came. Stegner's book is one attempt to provide a coherent statement about the cultural traditions of his home place. It is a symbolic attempt to connect himself and others, spider-like, to the traditions that grow from that place.

Once Henry Adams realized the inadequacy of the 18th-century European tradition which had been his education, he sought a new beginning in the landscape of the West, an enterprise that he later understood was also doomed to failure. Writing half a century later, Stegner, with a very different idea of history, sought to reestablish connections between himself and a place. Like Adams, he was presented with fragments out of which to construct a new whole. In Stegner's childhood, the site of those fragments was the town dump, the only source of history and poetry Whitemud had. Stegner worked as an amateur archeologist to discover the meaning of his place in the town dump, but it was only years later, after he and his family had left Whitemud for good, that he was able to tie together the history and fiction that would recreate the union of self and landscape he knew as a child. <u>Wolf</u> <u>Willow</u>, the result of that at least partially successful activity, conveys in history and fiction the meaning of the Cypress Hills present interpreted by the light of its regional past. As such, it is a symbolic reenactment of a state of human connection to the world.

The book covers a sixty-year span from the first European intrusion of Lewis and Clark in 1805, to the Métis (French and Indian) settlements of the 1860's, to the survey of the 1870's that politically divided a unified geographical area, to the brief reign of the cowboy from 1882 to 1906-07, the end of the plains frontier. What is most interesting about <u>Wolf</u> <u>Willow</u>'s mixture of history, autobiography, and fiction is the philosophical statement it implies about the truth of a people's connection to a place. Stegner argues implicitly through such a mixture of fact and fiction that a sense of place is a poetic creation, both real and imaginary, that explains our relationship to a place and to its past. It is the task of the artist-historian to convey the memory, to teach the tradition. The Cypress Hills country of Stegner's boyhood as recreated in <u>Wolf</u> <u>Willow</u> is not a dead material fact of the world but a symbolic cultural expression. That is, it reveals an ordered expression of the dynamic interplay between nature and the human imagination, and so overcomes the alienation of humanity from the world that Adams perceived to be our technological inheritance.

The railroad was the symbol of Adams' alienation from the world. For Stegner, the imposition of the 49th parallel on a unified landscape is symbolic of the same sort of separation. This artificial line "split a country that was topographically and climatically one" (p. 84), and did not follow the natural line of the Cypress Hills divide that "had been established by tradition, topography, and a balance of tribal force" (p. 85). The Medicine Line was one of the most significant manifestations of the civilizing forces of the modern world acting to fragment the natural order of the Cypress Hills country and to separate the human world from it. Stegner writes that

> While I lived on it [49th parallel], I accepted it as I accepted

139

Orion in the winter sky. I did not know that this line of
iron posts was one outward evidence of the coming of
history to the unhistoried plains, one of the strings by
which dead men and the unguessed past directed our
lives. In actual fact, the boundary which Joseph Kinsey
Howard has called artificial and ridiculous was more potent in the lives of people like us than the natural divide of
the Cypress Hills had ever been upon the tribes it held
apart. For the 49th parallel was an agreement, a rule,
a limitation, a fiction perhaps but a legal one, acknowledged
by both sides; and the coming of law, even such limited law
as this, was the beginning of civilization in what had been a
lawless wilderness. Civilization is built on a tripod of
geography, history, and law, and it is made up largely of
limitations (p. 85).

Wolf Willow is Stegner's means of transcending the limitations of civilization
for it unifies the human and natural landscape that was divided by the artificial
boundary of the 49th parallel.

As a boy in Whitemud Stegner was able to realize Emerson's directive to
establish an original relation to the universe. He feels

how the world still reduces me to a point and then measures
itself from me. Perhaps the meadowlark singing from a
fence post--a meadowlark whose dialect I recognize--feels
the same way. All points on the circumference are equi-
distant from his; in him all radii begin; all diameters run
through him; if he moves, a new geometry creates itself
around him (p. 19).

Wolf Willow is a reenactment of this human connectedness to the earth that
Stegner knew as a boy. The Cypress Hills become for Stegner and the reader
the symbolic center of the world they had been before the divisions and limitations of civilization. Stegner makes us aware of the natural centrality of the
Cypress Hills which are the watershed not only of the Atlantic and Pacific slopes
of the continental divide, but the division of the north and south slopes as well.
Stegner's symbolic landscape is real in a cultural sense, for it is the creation
of the human imagination interacting with the natural world. The Cypress Hills
become once again a place where "For the moment, reality is made equivalent
with memory, and a hunger is satisfied" (p. 19).

Though it is a poetic creation, Wolf Willow's vision of reality is not a
solipsistic dream. When Stegner returns to his boyhood home, he relates that
he is afraid to visit his family's homestead for fear that all trace of their contact with the land will have been erased. If his family's mark on the land is
gone, he fears, he will be convinced that his vision is only a dream disconnected from reality. But the small shrub named Wolf Willow allays that fear. Its

smell, like the odor of madeleine and tea to Proust, convinces him immediately of the reality of the vision. Stegner's family's impact on the Saskatchewan landscape had been puny and little evidence of their struggle on the Plains is left. His proof that they had truly been there, and that Wolf Willow is history as well as fiction, is the smell of this small shrub.

Stegner implies that that is all the proof of meaningful human activity that we should need. The chief argument of Stegner's poetic vision of place is that the result of human impact on the land ought to be short-lived. Our transient imprint on the world should define our tragic and frail humanity. For Stegner as for Adams, the modern technological world keeps us from learning this lesson. The simple notion of wearing paths in the earth's surface, Stegner's metaphor for meaningful human activity, is banished forever in the modern world:

> Wearing any such path in the earth's rind is an intimate act, an act like love, and it is denied to the dweller in cities. He lacks the proper mana for it, he is out of touch with the earth of which he is made.
> . . . .
> So we had an opportunity that few any longer can have: we printed an earth that seemed creation-new with the marks of our identity. And then the earth wiped them out again (p. 273).

Stegner's childhood experience was acted out in a landscape that "seemed creation-new" not because there had been no one before him, but because the impact of civilization had not ended the possibility of making tracks in the earth.

In the words of Ray Henry in Wolf Willow's chapter-story "Carrion Spring," we engage in a heroic human activity when we attempt to make the country say "uncle," not by pouring concrete over it, but by wearing transient footpaths in it. In "Carrion Spring," Molly and Ray are heroic in this sense. After the most severe winter in Saskatchewan history they see the wreckage and death which the birth of spring reveals. The meaning of this experience is discovered along with the discovery of a Crocus growing amongst the carnage:

> "Crocus?" Ray said, bending. "Don't take long, once the snow goes."
> It lay in her palm, a thing lucky as a four-leaf clover, and as if it had had some effect in clearing her sight, Molly looked down the south-facing slope and saw it tinged with faintest green. She put the Crocus to her nose, but smelled only a mild freshness, an odor no more showy than that of grass. But maybe enough to cover the scent of carrion (p. 237).

This passage does not indicate Ray and Molly's escape from the reality of their

141

experience, but brings us to the tragic realization of their puny human effort to wrest control of the landscape from nature. This is a fictional experience, but it is one that might well have occurred in this region after the winter of 1906-07, a winter that marked the death of the open range and the cowboy. Though fictional, it is as much a part of the symbolic historical tradition of southern Saskatchewan as the survey that separated Canada and the United States.

The symbolic statement of Stegner's book is important, but there is still something unsatisfactory in the education that Wolf Willow affords those who read it. Wolf Willow becomes, like Henry Adams' Education, a statement about the failure of education. Stegner's book teaches us that the European experience in the Garden of the West contained the seeds of its own destruction, and the cultural vision expressed in Wolf Willow is one that few, if any of us, can experience in our own lives today:

> One who has lived the dream, the temporary fulfill-ment, and the disappointment has had the full course. He may lack a thousand things that the rest of the world takes for granted, and because his experience is belated he may feel like an anachronism all his life. But he will know one thing about what it means to be an American, because he has known the raw continent, and not as tourist but as denizen. Some of the beauty, the innocence, and the cal-lousness must stick to him, and some of the regret. The vein of melancholy in the North American mind may be owing to many causes, but it is surely not weakened by the perception that the fulfillment of the American Dream means inevitably the death of the noble savagery and freedom of the wild. Anyone who has lived on a frontier knows the in-escapable ambivalence of the old-fashioned American con-science, for he has first renewed himself in Eden and then set about converting it into the lamentable modern world. And that is true even if the Eden is, as mine was, almost unmitigated discomfort and deprivation (p. 282).

Like The Education, Wolf Willow conveys the triumph of the technological dream over the poetic vision of place even as it recreates that poetic vision of an ear-lier time. But Adams' Education and Stegner's Wolf Willow are not simply nos-talgic remembrances of a lost golden world. Stegner's work makes us aware of the historical tradition of this American place. Too few of those who lived on the edge of the frontier had such an awareness, and too few of us even today have it. By connecting us to the cultural tradition of the Cypress Hills country Stegner does not solve the dilemma of education, but he illuminates the prob-lem. The historical memory that Wolf Willow brings to the reader should pro-vide what the town dump provided Stegner as a boy: "an aesthetic distance from which to know ourselves" (p. 35).

University of New Mexico

142

[1]Page references in the text are made to the following editions: Henry Adams, The Education of Henry Adams (Boston: Houghton Mifflin Company, Sentry Edition, 1961) and Wallace Stegner, Wolf Willow (New York: The Viking Press, 1966).

H. L. DAVIS' BEULAH LAND: A REVISIONIST'S NOVEL OF WESTERING

by George M. Armstrong

H. L. Davis' novel Beulah Land, published in 1949, [1] is the only one of his major works of fiction to show the process of westering directly. It is a unique description and treatment of the westering experience which criticises our traditional assumptions about it, rejecting its identification with economic and moral progress and expressing instead the bleak comedy and pathos of a "fool's errand" in the wilderness, tempered by the beauty of a protean nature, the joy and humor of human stories well told, and the dignity attained by men and women striving for goals unattainable in a world where illusion blurs even hindsight.

Davis' first historical novel, Harp of a Thousand Strings, [2] (1947) was a complex work composed of a tale of the French Revolution, set in a frontier American "frame" made up of intrusive historical judgements by the narrator, realistic stories and symbolic parables derived from tall tales, and detailed natural descriptions, all intended to destroy the myth of the uniqueness of the American frontier experience by stressing its unity with all human experience, however different in appearance. Harp, actually a story of "eastering," is Beulah Land's intellectual near-relative.

Harp is about history and its "subtle confusions," as its opening quotation from T. S. Eliot's "Gerontion" warns. [3] It expresses a lack of faith in history as the explicable product of rational human agency, echoing Eliot in its attempt to instill a faith "outside" human will and yet dependent upon it; upon acts of faith which can "still count for much" even in their failure to achieve their actors' ends. What Davis valued was the ability to live in spite of the knowledge of failure at the end; to balance the wisdom that says all effort is vain against foolish pride in one's ends and the illusion that one can gain them. Harp tries to show that one can accept the paradox of a "disillusionment" which accepts both love and ambition as illusory and necessary.

Beulah Land was longer aborning than Harp, simpler and better controlled, and, as H. L. Mencken's praise of it insisted, "more authentic Davis," [4] that is, more clearly related in both subject and structure to Davis' previous work than Harp. Actually the two historical novels are rather closely related in their attitude toward history and the problems of historical fiction, and the fictions it expresses. Harp was an experiment to see if Davis' beliefs could stand the test of a setting unlike the American West, the story of the weaving of certain threads of "story" that includes both "westering" and "eastering." Beulah Land brings a few of those threads back to the West and ultimately "back home" to Oregon, making the same basic points about human experience and the proper "reading" of it on the way. Here as in Harp every apparent success brings on failure, and

144

no one ever gets a quid for his quo. In Beulah Land as in Harp "received" or traditional history is shown to be a foolish oversimplification of the real complexity of life, which Davis counters with sharp and skeptical comedy and supplants with a mass of specific detail that defeats traditional fictional stereotypes by being both more convincing, and more interesting.

Beulah Land, for example, spends a great deal of its effort confounding the established American myth of the necessary separation of the white and red races, and of the predestined "passing of the Redman." It is a novel of uncivilized whites and the Civilized Tribes, and their long and interesting relationship. In making an extended comparison between the two groups, Davis also sought to make the larger "anthropological" point that, while social "nurture" can alter the superficial aspects of humanity very greatly, it does not alter what he sees as basic human motivations. Needless to say, this was as much an issue in his time as it is in ours, and Davis expresses throughout the novel his belief that imposed cultural differences were relatively superficial and that "under" them you would find a man like other men--human--neither Creek nor cracker.

Both Beulah Land and Harp examine the nature of historical fictions and historical fiction, and in both novels Davis denounces the use of history for the "lower goods" of commerce and political gain, since he wished historical writing to seek for larger truths about life, while at the same time cautioning its readers about the elusive nature of such truths. He maintained a critical view of American historical writing, especially historical fiction, all his life, constantly smelling ulterior motives in the productions of his contemporaries, as well as in the classic writers of historical novels such as Cooper. Typical of his attitude is a letter to his friend and fellow historical novelist, George R. Stewart, in which he accuses the Pentagon of "pushing" Nevil Shute's "aggressively fourth-rate" On the Beach to help get "defense" appropriations passed; he further identifies the military historian S. L. A. Marshal as the chief "pusher." On the basis of this judgement of the state of "historical fiction," he further "encourages" Stewart to try to get Defense Department backing for his Earth Abides, also a kind of "historical novel" of a future apocalypse, "providing, of course, that you're willing to write badly."[5]

A related denunciation of ulterior motives in historical fiction led Davis to try to set the record straight in Beulah Land regarding a number of historical topics that he felt had been distorted by previous novelists. The main such topic is the relation of Indian to white on the frontier, specifically the history of the Cherokee Removals and their aftermath in the Indian Nations up to the end of the Civil War. Davis objected to both the denunciation of the Indian as subhuman in American historical fiction and the "fictionized weeping" for the plight of the Indian which is the literary reaction to it, seeing both views as self-interested distortions. The basis of the dichotomy that allows these distortions is the myth that the two races are indeed separate; that they are two different kinds of people, a basic assumption of white American culture, and one which is refuted in the first paragraph of Beulah Land, a refutation continued to the last.

Davis supports this refutation with a tremendous mass of detail drawn from historical sources, with characters whose personal makeup reflects the

145

mixture of "white" and "Indian" traits, and with a selection of apparent historical ironies. These ironies are ultimately seen by the reader to be ironic only
from the conventional fictional point of view which sees the histories of the red
and white races as exclusively separated by spilled blood, rather than partly
connected by shared blood.

Davis' treatment of the Civil War in the Indian Nations in Beulah Land is
an example of his use of historical events which complicate, and thus challenge,
fictional convention. Since history is important both in retrospect and in pro-
jection, because what we "make of" the past we then try to apply in making the
future, he also "spreads" the implications of that war "within the War" to make
a general statement about the nature of historical fictions. This continues a
generality first stated in Harp, man's chronic inability to "read" history and
learn from that experience:

> Experience is repetitious in its teachings because man too often
> carries them backward instead of forward, applying them merely
> to confirm what already happened, instead of holding them ready
> for contingencies still to arise. [6]

Davis, as the lives of his fictional characters show, is somewhat skeptical about
the possibility of using one's experience of the past to deal with the demands of
the future, but certainly there is no possibility of learning from history if a
historical period's assumptions about itself are simply projected backward on
the past in historical fiction to "confirm themselves" as an apologetic for its
problems and origins.

The prime example of this phenomenon in Beulah Land is Uncle Hoy Pay-
ton, the Cherokee patriarch with whom the protagonist, halfbreed Ruhama
Warne, lives after her flight with her white father from North Carolina to the
frontier. Uncle Hoy has an "addiction" to the Highland romances of Walter
Scott:

> ...his special favorites were the works recounting the wrongs and
> injuries the Highland clans had sustained at the hands of their Saxon
> oppressors...He had been in the Cherokee Removals, and such pas-
> sages always put him in mind of the treatment the Indians had under-
> gone from the invading and land-grabbing Americans in his own
> younger days. He never tired of having her read them over to him,
> though the removals he had actually witnessed were something he
> preferred not to be reminded of. [7]

There are multiple ironies here. Uncle Hoy, in spite of relishing the pathos of
"past history," and apparently somehow associating it with his own, also apparently successfully accepts or ignores Scott's overall effect as an Anglo-Saxon
apologist with motives and techniques similar to American political, and then
fictional, apologists' justifications for the "necessary" tragedy of the American
Indian. Uncle Hoy was apparently convinced enough of the justice of the Cherokee

past "which he preferred not to be reminded of" that he finally lost everything for his Union sympathies in the Civil War, and was left with only his love of his stricken people. He refused, furthermore, to join the "Confederate Indian" faction, in spite of being a slaveholder, apparently so that the semi-autonomous Indian Nations would not be destroyed politically through gaining the offered status of a Confederate state. That is, he chose "Union" precisely to avoid union with the people who had evicted his people from their sacred highland homes, even though to do so he had to lose everything but his dignity in the service of the very government which protected and tacitly directed the usurpers. "History has many cunning passages," as Davis' earlier quote from Eliot reminds us, and in Beulah Land Davis goes into some of them which simply don't get mentioned, much less explored, in conventional historical fiction.

A deeper irony is that even were Uncle Hoy to perceive all of the ironies brought to mind by his "fictional addiction," even were he to see the multiple implications of his relation to the subjects and intentions of Scott's fiction with its combined "denunciation" of, and "weeping" for, the Highland clans, he would presumably be no more fit to act in the service of his people than he was in his "illusioned" state. Any choice that he makes will lead to political and material disaster, and to the bleak triumph of his love for his people and dignity of endurance. The only gain which he could make at all is if he were to have the prerogative of Davis' reader of "understanding why he had been defeated," to Davis a heroic understanding because of its severity and rarity.

Formally, Beulah Land returns to the apparently linear, but actually circular, journey-structure used in Davis' first novel, Honey in the Horn (1935).[8] The journey is not a purposeful westering "Long March," but begins, like Honey, with a flight, and drifts westward to Oregon, Honey's setting. Originally impelled by hillbilly sex and bad shooting, the random westering has its causes and motives, but no Mover either secular or supernatural, neither a Jehovah nor a Thomas Hart Benton. Its apparent first cause is the selfish white landgrab, the Cherokee Removals. Its immediate cause in the plot of the novel, and the device which allows Davis to use a historical "fallow space" unworked by previous writers of historical fiction, is the story of Cherokee Sedaya Gallet's bargain with the white invaders which lets her tribelet stay in their North Carolina home, Crow Town, where the novel begins, after the main events of the Removals. Even that apparent sacrifice is shown by Davis' narrator to be actually motivated by simple jealousy and greed, the motives of the invaders themselves:[9] her "sacrifice" is thus "very white of her!"

Beulah Land continues the dialogue about the relation of humanity to nonhuman nature begun in Honey and Harp. Like both earlier works, and Davis' work in general, it is full of painstakingly accurate descriptions of natural scenes from our past history which emphasize the mutability of nature, scenes such as

...the vast chestnut forest that used to cover all the long sandshelf of the Alleghenies from North Carolina through Virginia and far up into Pennsylvania, beautiful in its time...[10]

147

which the protagonists encounter in the first few miles of their flight. That flight encounters many natural beauties, stressing the fecundity and variety of wild nature with a Whitmanian love of "naming." But Davis was not a "nature worshipper" in the simple sense of that term, and a negative view of the relationship of man to nature has to come sometime. When it does come, it is not as a dualistic dichotomy, a "dark and light side" to nature, but as a complex, a synthesis of elements in the "sea of blind energies," as he calls nature in Harp.[11]

The most important example of this treatment of man's relation to non-human nature comes in the second-to-last "leg" of the westering of Ruhama Warne, the half-Indian protagonist, and her companion Askwani, an Indian-raised white. This passage, which traverses the Great American Desert from Illinois to the Indian Nations, resembles a passage in Honey in the Horn[12] in several particulars. In both cases a man leaves a woman in gynecological difficulties. In Honey the male protagonist, Clay Calvert, leaves his lover Luce in the process of a miscarriage to seek help from anyone who can help. He returns to her with a Paiute woman, only to find that his mission has been aborted by her recovery and abandonment of him. In Beulah Land, Ruhama, the female protagonist, becomes weak and ill during her "period" and is left by Askwani, who goes to seek help, spurred on by his "Indian" fears of menstruation. In Beulah Land the situation is not seen from the male point of view as it is in Honey, but from the viewpoint of the passive female who is left behind. Instead of moving through a symbolic and surreal natural landscape as Clay does in Honey, Ruhama is the center of a series of natural cycles which complicate the "positive" views of nature and bounty that fill the book, at the same time that they reinforce them.

The meaning of Ruhama's menstruation in this sequence is quite conventional, however unusual a subject in historical fiction: it symbolizes the overall picture of nature Davis gives in the novel, a paradox of birth and decay, of fecundity and beauty giving rise to "obscene greed and gluttony and ferocity."[13] The plot's reason for her "interlude" alone in wild nature is that both she and the old draft horse have "broken down"; she from her "catamenial indisposition," as Davis too delicately puts it; the horse from eating poisoned plants at a water hole that was

> ...less water than thin mud, choked and stained by yellow pond-
> lilies, and ringed around with dry-stemmed spotted tulips, prairie
> gourd-vines, wild geraniums that smelled like almonds, and a
> pinkish flower with a peachlike odor that clung to everything and
> wouldn't wash off.[14]

The colors and smells in this place, combined with the imagery of reptiles, fungi, and birds of ill omen which precede it, are a very broad hint of its nature to the reader, but the protagonists miss the fact that it is a poison spring, and thus "bust" at the next water hole, also apparently a place of idyllic beauty. The horse and Ruhama take sick and Askwani leaves on his pony to get help.

Ruhama is left alone in her pastoral little world, which is immediately smashed to ugly pulp by a hailstorm. [15] The horse dies and Ruhama is left to watch it devoured by prairie wolves which seem to welcome her shooting at them so that the pack can devour the unlucky casualties, providing another of a series of the book's "contingencies in which firearms were useless," in itself a situation rather foreign to Western fiction. Then painted buzzards come and finish devouring the horse.

These three images--the heroine's "womanfilth" as Faulkner's Calvinistic Doc Hines puts it in Light in August, the poisoned flowers, and the painted buzzards--add up to a symbolic presentation of the paradox of the interdependence of beauty and ugliness, life and decay. The painted buzzard seemed to be Davis' favorite symbol for it: the paradox it represents is quite conventional except in traditional "Western" literature, where such complications are rather unusual. Davis knew that his symbols for the life-death paradox were conventional, and also that there is a difference between conventions which are still powerful, and those which are "dead," vestigial, and pro forma. A merely pro forma protestation of the paradox will simply heighten the impression of the beauty of the Garden of the West which his other natural description has created, and will not "stick." For this reason he pushes this element very hard in Beulah Land, adding for emphasis a symbolic surreal scene centered on a passenger pigeon nesting ground.

The passenger pigeon runs the Indian and the buffalo a close third as a major American symbol, first of the power of nature which it was our manifest destiny to overcome, and then, in our own time, of the burden of guilt caused by that conquest; in traditional historical fiction the two phases of that "fictionalized denunciation and weeping" which Davis deplores. In Beulah Land the pigeon is used, not as a symbol of man's reckless "pride of dominion," or as a challenge to exert dominion, but as a symbol of the correspondence of man and nature. The scene surrounding the nesting ground is an analogue of the Eastern Oregon dustbowl show in Honey:

> The country around them had been built from soil weathered down from the high mountains to the west. It was new, as countries go, and the various forms of animal life had not yet worked out of the space each was entitled to in it, or the rate of increase that it would support among all of them. Every few years, some species would take a spurt and threaten to overwhelm it: ricebirds, jackrabbits, grasshoppers, buffalo-gnats. Sometimes quail would cover the land, and, departing, leave behind them acres of famishing hawks that had overbred by preying on them. Sometimes there would be a migration of squirrels, or water-dogs, or snapping-turtles, or crawfish marching hopefully forth from their swamps in search of roomier territory and scaring settlers' children in the night with the dry clacking of their claws. Wild pigeons were a case of the same kind, though they behaved better. [16]

The implicit but clear analogy with human population explosions holds out some hope that, like the other members of the animal kingdom, man may at some time "work out the space" that he is entitled to. But at present the main effect of the analogy is to show that man, while he is a special thing in nature, is still part of it; even his booms and busts have their analogues among lower forms, and even the Anglo-Saxon "fighting man's" Long March from the swamps of Frisia searching for lebensraum, which Frank Norris and the first Western writers (Roosevelt, Emerson Hough, Wister) took as a unique and apocalyptic event, is no more special than "crawfish marching hopefully forth from their swamps in search of roomier territory." Even in our guilt we can find no special place apart from nature; just like the wild animals which prey on the passenger pigeons, we were "secure in the knowledge that there were enough pigeons to go around,"[17] until there were none.

The surreal swirl of colors, sounds, and smells that surrounds the nesting ground[18] is literally meant to be surreal--it is an intensified image of nature which points out basic truths which might otherwise not be registered. It is a massive illustration of the fact that man is a part of what Davis called that "constantly self-renewing mystery"[19] which is nature, and that even his ecological follies are largely ordained by that kinship. As with so many of the unavoidable negative truths about man that his fiction illustrates, Davis wouldn't see this as an excuse for ecological disasters--he wasn't engaged in apologetics, and he deplored man's waste of the land perhaps more than most men. Man's wasteful nature is simply one of the iron rules of life which we must struggle against to find any heroism, but a disillusioned view demands that we not expect any "final" victory.

Having passed through the intertwined bounty and gluttony of wild nature, the protagonists of Beulah Land pass into first the bounty, and then the gluttony, of man. The structure of the book doesn't take them all the way to Oregon in one stage, partly because that would miss too many connections along the way, and partly because such a conventional Westering structure implies that Oregon is an end, like Zion. Writing from Mexico City, Davis knew it wasn't.

The Indian Nations which are the second stage of the westering journey in Beulah Land are paradoxically, given the conventional Western implications of "Indian," the most civilized place in the book. Ruhama's situation with the Cherokee family, the Paytons, "could not have been pleasanter."[20] Actually it seems somewhat like a parody of an ante-bellum Southern plantation idyll, complete with the rather unbelievable myth of the slaves who are so spoiled that they tend to control their masters. The idyll, like the conventional Southern one, doesn't last--it is smashed in the Civil War disaster. Ruhama's idyll cracks up before the war hits, for personal reasons. Indeed, had Davis ever chosen to write about the destruction of the ante-bellum South, he would almost certainly have found base motives behind that, too: his explanation for the "Bloody Kansas" border preliminaries to the Civil War in Beulah Land is not states' rights nor abolitionist ideals, but simple greed and land hunger.

I find the tragedy of the marriage of Ruhama to the gambler Savacol the most facile part of the book, but it at least reinforces the emphasis Davis constantly puts on the insufficiency of human will to order its own affairs, and the destructive power of human pride. Ruhama marries Savacol apparently largely to spite Askwani, who in his campaign of vengeance against Ruhama's father's killers is temporarily connected with a "fancy woman" who later turns out to be Ruhama's half-sister. There is a sort of logic about his hunting up the girl who had caused the feud (in order to find her protectors, Warne's murderers) but the "chance meeting" of the four together is a bit thin.

The Ruhama-Savacol match is brief and ends in a miscarriage as a result of her shock at seeing him commit a murder which "would have ended it anyway." Savacol's paranoia about his origins as the son of a whorehouse madam, and his materialism, manifested in a desire for the bright lights and envious crowds of some Eastern city, make the miscarriage a too-easy symbol of their mistaken love. Their marriage, while it allows Davis to moralize on the power of spite in human affairs and to go into some fascinating details about early-day gambling and the early Civil War armies of the West, is clearly doomed from the start.

Askwani finally "gets her in the end," after they have reached Oregon, fleeing the defeat of the Union Indians at the Battle of Bird Creek; they go in company with a group of Delawares who, having been ousted from their Eastern seaboard homes centuries before, have made a virtue of necessity ever since and westered out of sheer joie de vivre:

> ...the Delawares felt reckless and uprooted and ready for anything.... They had no trouble all the way...except from cavalry-patrols trying to turn them back for fear of Indians and letting them go, on discovering that they were Indians themselves.[21]

Askwani and Ruhama are like many of Davis' pioneers in that they have come West fleeing the Civil War, not because they want to "save Oregon from the British," or even to get fertile land. They are not instruments of destiny, but human flotsam from its tides, yet they "still count for much in the end."

Askwani dies in a flu epidemic in the late 1880's, after a full life in Oregon with Ruhama, feeling a loss at leaving her which only the narrator can "look past":

> Love did hurt people. It punished them, maimed them sometimes, but in the end it reached down to things worth finding out, worth keeping. The important thing was to hold out to the end, to believe in love through the shifts and changes and cruelties. And the end was not an end at all, only a change. It shed, and sprouted again, and went on.[22]

The "end" of the novel takes Davis' fiction back home to Oregon, but he refuses to leave it there, ending it with the story of how Ruhama's daughter ultimately marries an English dude and turns up in a diplomatic receiving line in Washington. The story which "began" with the greed of the land speculators behind the Cherokee Removals and survived so many shifts and changes and cruelties thus ends up headed back to the Old World, toward the realm of Henry

James. Davis knew better than to try to follow it there, but he felt obliged to end his "westering novel" with a reminder that stories do not end even when they reach the promised land, for the only heaven in Oregon Territory is Horse Heaven. To end a Western whose "hero" is a half-breed woman, whose story shows many "contingencies in which firearms were useless" and whose companions on "the Way West" were civilized Indians newly come from fighting for the Union, with the conventional "Hurrah for Oregon!" would have been an irony that even Davis would not perpetrate. His next two novels, Winds of Morning and The Distant Music, were to be examinations of Oregon after the hurrahs died out, but the "eastering" ending of Beulah Land is meant to emphasize that every "end" is merely a threshhold, even if it is one that his particular genius was disinclined to cross: Ruhama Warne's quarter-breed daughter's "eastering" fate is left as ambiguous as Hawthorne's Pearl's; a fate as unfulfilled, threatening, and fascinating as America's own.

Washington State University

NOTES

[1] Harold Lenoir Davis, Beulah Land (New York: Morrow, 1949).

[2] Harold Lenoir Davis, Harp of a Thousand Strings (New York: Morrow, 1947).

[3] Davis' novel seems written almost specifically to prove the validity of the quote he chose for a "header":

> ...After such knowledge, what forgiveness? Think now
> History has many cunning passages, contrived corridors
> And issues, deceives with whispering ambitions,
> Guides us by vanities. Think now
> She gives when our attention is distracted
> And what she gives, gives with such supple confusions
> That the giving famishes the craving...
>
> Neither fear nor courage saves us...

[4] In an otherwise undated letter of 1947 which is in response to Davis' proposed outline of Beulah Land. This source and all other manuscript references are to be found in the H. L. Davis Collection of the Humanities Research Center at the University of Texas, Austin.

[5] In a letter to Stewart dated March 2, 1959, in the H. L. Davis Collection's "Ms. Letters" section.

[6] Harp, p. 181.

[7] Beulah Land, pp. 256-7.

[8] Harold Lenoir Davis, Honey in the Horn (New York and London: Harper Bros., 1935).

[9] Beulah Land, p. 4.

[10] Ibid., p. 27.

[11] Harp, pp. 264-7.

[12] Honey, pp. 304-11.

[13] Beulah Land, p. 239.

[14] Ibid., p. 225.

[15] Ibid., pp. 226-7.

[16] Ibid., p. 237.

[17] Ibid., p. 240.

[18] Ibid., p. 238.

[19] In a journal entry dated Feb. 13, 1960 collected in the H. L. Davis Collection's "Ms. Works Journal" section.

[20] Beulah Land, p. 255.

[21] Ibid., p. 310.

[22] Ibid., p. 312.

THE FRONTIER IN JACK SPICER'S "BILLY THE KID"

by Frank Sadler

> For the beginning is assuredly
> the end--since we know nothing, pure
> and simple, beyond
> our own complexities.
>
> WILLIAM CARLOS WILLIAMS

This quotation from Paterson suggests one of the basic themes of Jack Spicer's poem "Billy The Kid"--that a poem is the working out of its possibilities. It implicitly suggests that the significance of a poem does not lie in its meaning, as that term is traditionally understood, but rather that the significance of the poem lies in its act of self-creation. This proposition rests on the assertion that a poem is a form of experience in which the moral dimension of life finds its expression in the act of creation, and in no other place. Thus the proper concern of the poet and, consequently, the poem is with poetry itself. And, if, as Williams apparently understood, "the beginning is assuredly / the end" and our knowledge of that "beginning" lies within the recognition of "our own complexities, " then the poem becomes a search for the solution to the idea that creation itself may be endless. The exact expression of this concept is found in Spicer's poem "Psychoanalysis: An Elegy" in which the final line reads "I am thinking that a poem could go on forever. "[1] The emphasis here is placed on the process of thought as a type of continuing or ongoing genesis for which the poem provides the mechanism by which the creative act may consummate itself. This act of the mind, of thinking itself, finds its expression in this "place" of the poem--"Billy The Kid. "

The poem begins "Back where poetry is" in the complexities of the narrator's mind, for it is the mind of the narrator which orders and selects and makes subjective the world of the poem--the poem which we perceive. It is the background out of which all our acts are made known.

> The radio that told me about the death of Billy The Kid
> (And the day, a hot summer day, with birds in the sky)
> Let us fake out a frontier --a poem somebody could hide in
> with a sheriff's posse after him--a thousand miles of it if it is
> necessary for him to go a thousand miles--a poem with no hard
> corners, no houses to get lost in, no underwebbing of
> customary magic, no New York Jew salesmen of amethyst
> pajamas, only a place where Billy The Kid can hide when he
> shoots people.

154

We are immediately within a mythic dimension in the mind of the poem's narrator. The subject of the poem is poetry itself, the creative act. The persona sits ostensibly in a room in which a radio announces that Billy is dead. The obvious incongruity between fact and time is obliterated, that is, the present with its various realities--the radio, the summer day, the birds, the absence of New York Jew salesmen, etc.,--is effaced in a type of space-time relativity in which the possibilities of the present exist in the working out of the alternatives of the past. The "frontier" with all its potentialities, both historical and imaginative, as a thing to be explored and mapped out, is presented in terms of the poem, that is, not only in its physical existence as artifact but also in its descriptive process as a poem in which the frontier is a "poem somebody could hide in." Thus, in a sense, the poem becomes its own frontier, its own avant-garde, its own "house" without any "hard corners." The east--as suggested by "no New York Jew salesmen"--is contrasted against the west-- the frontier, the sheriff's posse, etc. Further, the east becomes symbolic of tradition in art, of imposed order and form, whereas the west suggests openness and freedom from the intellectual traditions of past art with all its limitations and restrictions on style, structure, theme, and idea.

The poem presents a subjective world in which the reader is faced with the appearance of a rational and logical frame--the radio, the poem as artifact --but which, in the final analysis, is only appearance. The radio serves as a background out of which the world's events impinge upon the consciousness of the narrator. Further, the radio suggests the impersonal and mechanical, the closed world of fact, and is contrasted with the openness of the mind, of the poem, of the imagination. It also suggests that the poem, in a limited sense, will take the form of a news report. Finally, the emphasis in these opening lines is on "Let us fake out a frontier." The word "Let" permits us to escape from the confinement of the objective world, the radio, and permits us to lay out, to devise, the alternate routes we may take to coming to know the frontier, the poem, and consequently, the creative act.

The mythic dimension of the poem, of the death of "Billy The Kid," serves as a device by which the narrator erects a "death notice"--the poem itself, which becomes, in one sense, the gravestone of the historical figure, but which, at the same time, leaves the possibilities for creation open. As Eliot noted in "The Love Song of J. Alfred Prufrock," "There will be time, there will be time / To prepare a face to meet the faces that you meet; / There will be time to murder and create," and, in a sense, the narrator of the poem murders Billy in order to create. The frontier of the poem, of Billy mythically resurrected from the grave--regardless of whether he bears any resemblance to his day-to-day existence in real life--is presented through an imaginative rendering of historical fact in order to preserve the idea, the fiction, of a poem which works toward creating and defining itself--its background out of which the alternatives for continuing creation may take place. Clearly, then, "the beginning is assuredly / the end" and all that remains is to see how the poet works out the poem's ending.

With the second part of the first division of the poem the poet presents us

155

with the possibilities, with the alternate routes, which he may take to render
past into a present that contains the solutions to the poem's complexities.

> Torture gardens and scenic railways. The radio
> That told me about the death of Billy The Kid
> the day a hot summer day. The roads dusty in the
> summer. The roads going somewhere. You can almost see
> where they are going beyond the dark purple of the horizon.
> Not even the birds know where they are going.
> The poem. In all that distance who could recognize
> his face.

The remaining parts of the poem each explore the alternate routes in turn
but are quickly rejected as the persona of the poem comes to realize that the
solution to the "roads going somewhere," to the direction of the poem, lies in
the imaginative rendering of the possibilities of things. The narrator's search
to try to "recognize his [Billy's] face" is an attempt to understand the face of
creation, to come to terms with the enigma of the "haze," of the summer day
and the meaning, to borrow from Marianne Moore's poem, of "all this fiddle."
The thing that fixes, that defines, from within the world of the poem, the significance of the search is that very search itself. It is, as Spicer wrote, "You can
almost / see where they [the roads] are going" but not quite, and the end of the
road will not come until the final line of the poem has been written. Spicer,
then, is aware that the success or failure of his poem lies in the way in which
he works out the various alternatives that he has set up. And, it is these alternatives or possibilities which will determine and control the shape of the rest
of the poem.

In the first part of the poem the emphasis on point-of-view is placed on
information being directed toward the narrator by the radio--"The radio that
told me . . . ." But with the second part of the poem we move from the "me"
of the first part--which establishes a type of controlling point-of-view or voice
--to the internalization of that information. The radio acts as a device which
links the world outside the room to the world within the room. This movement
is paralleled by a shift in the perspective of the narrator from an auditory knowledge of the death of Billy to a visual knowledge of his death provided by the objects of the room itself. These objects in their own turn visually impinge their
existence upon the consciousness of the narrator. Thus the movement of the
poem, from external distances toward internal realities, parallels the movement of the first stanza in the same sense as the frontier, the horizon, continually recedes from the narrator's vision. All is movement and impression
in the first part of the second stanza and the images of the room's objects are
presented in a visual potential which furthers the suggestive possibilities of the
radio's information. In short, we move from an auditory knowledge of the death
of Billy to a visual knowledge of that death.

156

A sprinkling of gold leaf looking like hell flowers
A flat piece of wrapping paper, already wrinkled,
   but wrinkled again by hand, smoothed into shape
   by an electric iron
A painting
Which told me about the death of Billy The Kid.

The movement in these lines allows us to trace the actual movement of narrator's eyes as they fall upon objects in the room. Again, things have been framed and given the appearance of a rational and logical structure--a background out of which the narrator's acts may be made to stand out. This movement parallels the earlier contrast between the narrator's auditory knowledge of Billy's death and the visual perspective of the birds in the sky. But unlike the birds in the first part of the poem who do "Not. . . know where they are going" the implication is that the narrator does. With the second part of the second stanza of the poem we are ostensibly told what "heroes / really come by."

Collage a binding together
Of the real
Which flat colors
Tell us what heroes
         really come by.
No, it is not a collage. Hell flowers
Fall from the hands of heroes
        fall from all our hands flat
As if we were not ever able quite to include them.

The idea here is that the narrator is not "ever able quite" to capture the creative vision of Billy that is suggested by the objects of the room. Something is missing and incomplete in the reality presented to the narrator's conscious mind as he sees those objects and that something which is missing is nothing less, at this point, than recognition on the part of the narrator that the objects themselves are not the poem but simply the perceptual field which will make his acts significant. In the final lines of this second part the narrator moves into a consideration of the significance of the historical outlaw Billy and concludes that his life in the real world is unimportant.

His gun
     does not shoot real bullets
               his death
Being done is unimportant.
Being done
In those flat colors
Not a collage
A binding together, a
Memory.

In this poem we are dealing with a reflective intellectual consciousness which contains an empowered imagination. We are informed that Billy's existence is not dependent upon a "memory" of the past or a "binding together" of external objects--"a collage"--in the poem but with the imaginative rendering of the mind as it makes itself known in its exploration of the poem.

With the beginning of the third part of the poem the narrator makes the final leap from having things imposed upon his consciousness from outside to the complete and total internalization of the idea of "Billy" as a poem about poetry. Obviously there are other interesting questions raised by these first two parts--questions which deal with the theological implications of Billy as an Americanized Christ figure, the obvious Freudian sexuality of "shooting," etc., but these questions are too lengthy to handle here other than briefly mentioning them. With the beginning of the third part, then, the narrator who has simply been referred to as "me," "us," or "our" becomes the fictive "I" of the poem and refers to himself thereafter in the poem as "I" with the exception of a certain technical shift in point-of-view which deals with the identity of the narrator.

The creative process as developed in "Billy" and as exemplified by Charles Olson's remark that "FORM IS NEVER MORE THAN EXTENSION OF CONTENT" is the opposite of the so-called "confessional" school of poetry represented by Robert Lowell, Anne Sexton, John Berryman, and others.[2] Lowell's poetry is the expression of personal experience in which certain historical facts of his ancestry and background are dragged from the past and given objective and mythic weight in his poems. As such, Lowell's poems continually try to universalize the unique experience of one individual, whereas Spicer's poem begins with a universal, a mythic figure which is already established in the American imagination, and makes it personal.

Thus in the first two stanzas of "Billy The Kid" we fluctuate between the world of external reality and the world of the imagination. Each swing inward moves us deeper and deeper into the life of the imagination until, in the third part, the narrator finds himself completely submerged in the creative process. With the opening lines of this stanza we are deep in the frontier with the narrator.

> There was nothing at the edge of the river
> But dry grass and cotton candy.
> "Alias," I said to him. "Alias,
> Somebody there makes us want to drink the river
> Somebody wants to thirst us."

It is within these lines and the ones which immediately follow that a shift in the point-of-view of the poem occurs. Theoretically we would expect the narrator of the first stanza, who is informed by the radio of Billy's death, to become the voice, the "I," who addresses himself to "Alias." And this view is reinforced by the fact that we think of Billy in terms of the possibilities that he used other names--aliases.

"Kid," he said. "No river
Wants to trap men. There ain't no malice in it. Try
To understand."

However, what does happen is that the "I" of these lines becomes Billy
speaking to someone else named "Alias." The significance of this switch in the
point-of-view of the poem is such that the narrator has become his myth. This
effacement of the narrator and his replacement by Billy in this stanza, however,
is only temporary, for the stanza concludes

> We stood there by that little river and Alias took
>   off his shirt and I took off my shirt
> I was never real. Alias was never real.
> Or that big cotton tree or the ground.
> Or the little river.

The fictive "I" which has become Billy admits that he "was never real,"
and if he was never real and "Alias was never real" the "they" must have been
the narrator submerged within his own consciousness. In one sense the act of
removing the shirts is a recognition by the narrator that in order to come to
an understanding of the heart of the creative process, of the life of the imagination, he must rid himself of the "clothing" of external objects, that is, he
must "see" through and into his own imagination. He must deny any significance for the objects of his physical and external world. In so doing he exposes
the structure and pattern of the poem, since the life of the imagination is his
world--the poem. The narrator explains in part four

> What I mean is
> I
> Will tell you about the pain
> It was a long pain
> About as wide as a curtain
> But long
> As the great outdoors.
> Stig-
>   mata
> Three bullet holes in the groin
> One in the head
>   dancing
> Right below the left eyebrow
> What I mean is I
> Will tell you about his
> Pain.

The pain which the narrator experiences is rightfully his own but in order
to come to the poem in its conclusion he must tell of Billy's pain. He must, in

essence, struggle with the discipline of completing his act--the poem as it presents itself. Thus the narrator is forced to explore the significance of Billy before he can come to understand the meaning of his own creative act.

The final stanza of the poem results in the unification of the various themes in the poem with the narrator having travelled the various routes presented at the beginning of the poem as the possibilities of things, and in so doing the narrator has looked back in time and become a reflective intellectual consciousness.

> Billy The Kid
> I love you
> Billy The Kid
> I back anything you say
> And there was the desert
> And the mouth of the river
> Billy The Kid
> (In spite of your death notices)
> There is honey in the groin
> Billy.

With these final lines the perspective of the poem has changed once again. The poem began in the present and presented the possibilities of the past as alternatives that must be worked out in order that the present may exist. The tense changes from the present to the past--"And there was the desert"--brings us to the understanding that the poem has set up a mechanism by which it, the poem, "could go on forever." Spicer's line "In spite of your death notices," which is given as a type of aside, suggests that though the poem comes to its end it contains the potential for endless growth, for endless creation. Thus the penultimate line "There is honey in the groin" asserts the mythic vitality of the poem as a source for creation itself.

Gainesville, Florida

NOTES

[1] Jack Spicer, "Psychoanalysis: An Elegy," Evergreen Review, I, no. 2 (New York: Grove Press, Inc., 1957), pp. 56-57.

[2] Charles Olson, "Projective Verse," The New American Poetry, ed. Donald M. Allen (New York: Grove Press, Inc., 1960), p. 387.

RICHARD HUGO'S RETURN TO THE PACIFIC NORTHWEST:
EARLY AND RECENT POEMS

by William J. Lockwood

I would approach Hugo's work directly, by suggesting that contrary interpretations of the role of Eros, as depicted in the lives of the men and women who inhabit the northwestern corner of North America, appear in his poems; and, that out of them two major conceptual outlooks emerge--the one involving the idea of a closed world, the other of an open world. This distinction between closed and open worlds becomes especially marked in some of the recent poems wherein Hugo seems to celebrate his discovery of an open-ended universe. But before exploring the shift that occurs between the early and the recent Pacific Northwest poems, I wish to define my terms. By "Eros" I mean that primary force in both the human and non-human realms which integrates and makes whole, which opposes itself to stasis, disintegration, and death. By a "closed world" I mean a world which defies human understanding and denies to man a sense of intellectual and emotional wholeness. And, finally, by an "open world" I mean the opposite, a world which, by virtue of the vital, continuous, and inclusive elements that visibly operate in it, seems to offer us relief from the otherwise overwhelming sense of our human limitations.

It is tempting to identify Hugo's closed world with inland places. Western Montana and Idaho may still, after all, be broadly conceived of as part of the original Northwest Territory and in the Montana poems we see Hugo steadily facing up to the almost unendurable suffering that seems required of the inhabitants of that inland region. Remarkably distinct from that inland scenario, on the other hand, one finds, as I have noted, other poems set in coastal areas of the Northwest which picture a world free from suffering confinement. By the terms of such a geographical opposition, Hugo's inland places would seem to define a physically closed-off world corresponding to stunted intellectual and emotional development; and coastal places whose open vistas correspond to a condition of intellectual and emotional wholeness. By such an opposition a kernel of truth is expressed; yet it is an oversimplification of the kind of truth-to-experience Hugo is most concerned with in his writing. It oversimplifies, first, because the drama that gets played out in Hugo's poems requires to be understood, finally, as an interior, personal drama, more firmly rooted in the personal experience of the poet than in the landforms of the places that provide his settings; and second, because the fact is that it is in the early poems, set in the environs of Seattle that that heavy stoical attitude, an attitude notably defining the pattern of Hugo's later, tough-minded Montana poems, gets first established. By this light we come to the more sophisticated awareness that Hugo's outlook is not after all defined by a fixed geography but a mutable mind,

161

by a mind which constantly re-evaluates people and places and works toward a re-assessment of the possibility of achieving wholeness of personality.

Between the early and the recent Northwest poems lie the informal "letter poems" Hugo published in the American Poetry Review in 1973, and we might turn briefly to them as an early expression of the new elements that distinguish the recent poems from the early ones. In the letter to "Denise Levertov from Butte" he summarizes that closed world with which Hugo's readers are most familiar, a world in which men and women are made to suffer more than they can understand or endure. It is an especially interesting piece of writing because we see Hugo here engaged in a kind of retrospective effort to face up to aspects of his personal history and to consider the connection between his own life and that which he sees persisting in the lives of those Montaneans who, like his grandparents, migrated West and who handed down as a legacy, the basic loneliness and self-denial required by the old Westering code. To one of the most gentle of living American poets, Hugo writes these lines portraying a world suffering the lack of gentleness:

> My way of knowing how people get hurt makes
> my (damn this next word) heart go out through the stinking air
> into the shacks of Walkerville, to the wife who has turned
> forever to the wall, the husband sobbing at the kitchen
> table and the unwashed children taking it in and in and in
> until they are the wall, the table.

In another of the letter poems, on the other hand--his "Letter to Wagoner from Port Townsend"--quite a different voice is heard, that of a man who seems to have broken through the lessoned restraint by which he has learned to survive in this hard region. Instead of denial, Hugo projects here a surprised sense of self-satisfaction and release from a life of constant facing-up to an adamantly passive reality.

> Rain five days and I love it. A relief
> from sandy arroyos, buzzards and buttes, and a growing season
> consisting strictly of June. Here, the grass explodes and trees
> rage black green deep as the distance they rage in. I suppose
> all said, this is my soul, the salmon rolling in the strait
> and salt air loaded with cream...

The celebrated lush "black green deep" country of the latter poem stands opposed to the relatively arid Montana landforms that Hugo had, himself, over the previous the years, adopted as a consequence of his move from Seattle to Missoula, Montana. Yet, again, I think that the areal contrast--between dry, inland and fertile, coastal areas--operates chiefly here as a metaphor, serving to articulate the speaker's sense of the renewed state of his soul. Thus the constant rain, he says, relieves him of the pressure of always making choices; and though he concedes that it may eventually get him down, he asks "what matter ?" since he plans to spend the rest of his life dependent upon moon and tide. And just as the tide washes the debris of the beach back into the ocean's source, so, he suggests, it is washing the detritus of his life back to a renewing source, leaving him the luxury of enjoying driftwood fires and stars and dreams of girls.

After years of hard reckoning with the resistances of a closed world, Hugo thus reveals in the extroverted form of the letter poems his discovery of openness, the congruence of sea and land in the scene having, apparently, triggered off, in the interior landscape of the self, a feeling that there is, after all, room--room for celebration and even for self-indulgence. Yet it seems doubtful that this discovery is an instance of ex nihilo fit. For beneath the surface of even his most demanding forms, and notably, in those early poems in which the reluctance to generalize is the most insistent principle of Hugo's sincerity, there lies a romantic energy that, however modified, subdued, or even denied, finally persists. A more discursive and lengthy examination than is permitted here would be required to trace the continuance of this romantic strain through the several volumes of Hugo's poems; but we may abstract that quality and trace its evolution by proceeding to an examination of those poems in the early volumes and in the recent ones which share common Pacific Northwest coastal settings.

The early Pacific Northwest poems I would like to consider are from A Run of Jacks (1961) and Death of the Kapowsin Tavern (1965). Hugo's use of Northwest landforms is here characterized by the technique of narrow focus and by an affinity for forlorn and derelict places. It is not a picture of new, open territory we get here but one of accelerated decay. "Duwamish" from A Run of Jacks, for example, is set in the once swampy south section of Seattle with its network of incoming railroad lines at that point where the Duwamish River flows into Eliot Bay. And curiously here, the reference is not to the landscape of the West but to that of the mid-West:

> Midwestern in the heat this river's
> curves are slow and sick.

The poem goes on then to create a mindform that corresponds to the sluggish immediacy of the scene. The poet's almost obsessive use of dissolute images underlies the poem's subsequent development: in images of salt and river water mixing, of mills and mill-crud waste, of molded kegs of nails, of abandoned brick yards.

This mood of sluggishness and dereliction persists even in the poem called "Port Townsend" (from Death of the Kapowsin Tavern) where the scene shifts away from the urban area to the stately Victorian port town. The town is here depicted as living in the past and barely hanging on in the present, subsisting on a kind of Victorian haughtiness enforced by its location upon coastal cliffs. But that claim to distinction is undercut by the speaker's observing that the local ferry carries no passengers and that the "pulp mill shoots bad odors at the sun." The speaker's confession, moreover, of his own "silly dream"--a dream

163

of a time of emotional integration and peaceful settling down--is likewise undercut in the second stanza. It begins:

> Arriving here is feeling some old love--
> half a memory--a silly dream of how
> a war would end, a world would settle down
> with time for hair to gray before you die.

But in the final line of the stanza, the speaker adds:

> The town is rotting every Sunday night.

The place is, after all, understood simply as another faded and closed world--
a place of dreamed-up memories, static and by-passed because it lacks vitality. Hence the final note of flat irony in the third (and final) stanza:

> Freighters never give this town a second look.
> The dead are buried as an afterthought
> and when the tide comes glittering with smelt
> the graves have gone to look for meaty ports.

"Duwamish Head," from Kapowsin would seem to offer a like picture of
a closed world. It begins by rendering a scene conveying a mood of dereliction,
empty possibility, and human dislocation. Of the river itself, first, the reader
learns that its original cascade quality has been lost, that it is colored like the
"crud" dredged up at the river's mouth where "salmon are gone and industry
moved in." The voice we hear crying out of the poem seems reminiscent of the
underlying voice in Eliot's The Waste Land:

> My vision started at this river's mouth, on a slack tide, trying
> to catch bullheads in a hopeless mud. The pier was caving from the
> weight of gulls.

And yet something else comes into view here, glimpsed in the named possibility of "vision" and heard in the lines' expressive energy. We see emerging in this long and complex poem a pattern that stems from an implicit but
powerful correspondence between the speaker's life, as projected outward in
his confession to the river of some obscure crime, and the motion of the tide
governing that river's life. And when, in section two of the poem, this correspondence becomes fully clear, the reader discovers a poem that is, quite unlike Eliot's, essentially romantic in its affinity for dereliction:

> River, I have loved, loved badly on your bank.
> On your out-tide drain I ride toward the seas
> so deep the blue cries out in pain from my weight.
> Loved badly you and years of misery
> in shacks along your bank.

Thus there emerges in the poem a sense that if the universe is closed, it encloses restless, energetic forces, forces imaged here in the tidal flow beneath the sluggish surface of the Duwamish and released in the tides of feeling in the speaker's own bowels. If the poem begins with the image of slack tide, the image of the ebb or out-tide drain on which the speaker indeed imagines himself riding to sea finally displaces it. Beginning with the morning newspaper's account of a horrible murder, the poem gradually opens out to a landscape peopled with old men dreaming of a river boiling with fish in the moonlight.

On second look, then, we come to perceive that the aesthetic quality of the poem is more precisely comparable to the opening chapters of Zola's Germinal than to The Waste Land. And just so, we come to discover running through most of these early Northwest poems the presence of what might be termed an attitude of romantic stoicism. It is the consequence of an at once sympathetic and resistant relationship between the scene at hand and the human consciousness that receives it; and we see that it involves on Hugo's part an insistent emphasis upon the courage and pathos of men who endure in the face of a baffling, hard, closed world. Those familiar with Hugo's best known volume of poems, The Lady of Kicking Horse Reservoir (1973) will I think recognize this quality of Hugo's work, and will recall too (and notably, in the initial group of poems entitled "Montana"), a strong orientation toward a mimetic idea of art as distinct from an expressive one. For it is Hugo's sense of reality--at least before his most recent poems--that a scene has the power of imposing itself upon a man greater than that man's power to impose himself upon it. Thus, as we saw in "Duwamish" and "Port Townsend," a mimetic technique and a stoic attitude seem appropriate to the poet's vision of closed-off worlds.

On the other hand, as the "Duwamish Head" poem and as "Plunking the Skagit" (which I want to take up next) make clear, an idea of poetry as an expressive art also begins to surface; and it seems to me that what catalyzes that idea is the poet's imaginative response to the dynamics of watery forces in nature--a response to the continuous power and motion of ocean waters, of streams, and of the fish that abound in them. Indeed, I would suggest that it was precisely the success of Richard Howard's pioneering essay on the early Hugo that that reader's sympathetic imagination was enabled to reach out and into the Pacific Northwest world in order to discover the vitality Hugo perceived in it: in the rose-apples that extend along the sides of rainbow trout, and within such precisely observed images the latent principle of Eros as a vital and integrating force.[1]

Thus in that marvellous early poem "Plunking the Skagit" from Kapowsin, we find within the poem's mimetic framework, a glimpse of that expressive energy that would emerge, fused with a new clarity of outline, beyond the Montana experience, in those poems that have issued out of Hugo's return to the Pacific Northwest. For in "Plunking the Skagit" Hugo seems to have perceived within the landform elements not only of resistance but also of release. Aspects of geography became correspondences to his own inner landscape, significant aspects of which he was thereby enabled to dramatize and project outward. The Skagit itself, one of ten or so rivers that flow into Puget Sound, empties into the Sound just below Anacortes, the small port-city, about fifty miles north of Seattle. The poem is set in December, in the heart of the chilly rainy season, on a coastal range that gets little sunshine. But despite the rain and the rawness, perhaps even because of it, the atmosphere becomes feverish as the big fish--varieties of trout and salmon between 10 and 20 pounds--make their annual run up the river to spawn. The tough men standing along the river banks, the poem tells us, are obsessed with the fish, they lose consciousness of the weather, and they love their obsession. By contrast with the grayness of their daily lives, they wait upon the mystery that impells the brown-speckled, hard-nosed trout, the silvery chinook salmon, and the rose-spotted rainbow trout to move back to their birthplace, upstream in the river's fresh waters, to lay and fertilize their eggs. Out of that contrast, then, the poem discovers and develops this passionate correspondence: between the vital journeying impulse of the fish, "when big rains bring him/roaring from the sea with fins on fire," and the active glands of the men who, impervious to cold and chill, wait along the river's banks:

> These men are never cold. Their faces
> burn with winter and their eyes
> are hot. They see, across the flat,
> the black day coming for them and
> the black sea. Good wind
> mixes with the bourbon in their bones.

Thus rooted in the Skagit River's vivid annual drama, the poem images the powerful recurrence of dreams--erotic visions prompted and colored by the water's life--in the minds of the men who fish it.

A fragment of unifying vision, then, one qualified by the sense of human limitations in the face of all there is to be endured, but a redemptive vision nevertheless, begins to emerge in Hugo's early Northwest poems. Old men dream; their dreams are sustained by an awareness of the mysterious life cycles that operate in this world; and for such men, who have learned how not to die inside, life renews itself. Thus Hugo himself, several years older and recovering from a physical and emotional breakdown, can celebrate with a new sense of open perspective the beauty of the Pacific Northwest.

It is in the Montana poems that the psychodramatic aspect of Hugo's art, as it struggles toward a conception of an open universe, is most evident. In them his personal history is most fully drawn upon. It is there that he is actively engaged in a process of looking back, of taking stock of who he is, of working out a new definition of the old Western code of manhood. Hugo's change of residence from Seattle to Missoula seems to have given the question of personal heritage, location, and values a new urgency and to have prompted the deliberate creation of those poems that elicited William Stafford's observation that "a part of the west belongs to Hugo...telling over and over again its places and people he reclaims it from the very bleakness he confronts."[2]

Hugo's consciousness of family history on his father's side appears to be, at best, incomplete, and all that is surely known is that his father was Frank Hogan, the son of Irish immigrants. That this gap in Hugo's consciousness of his past created in him a certain sense of emotional and social disconnection, and that he sought to supply in its place a detailed acquaintance with the woods and hills and water in the Seattle/Puget Sound area--an acquaintance Hugo himself stresses when speaking of his early childhood years--both the Northwest poems and the Montana poems seem to testify. Their speaker's attraction to forlorn and derelict places and his sympathy for the men who frequent bars and fish streams seem indeed to express a need not merely to live in the margins but to establish as well real human connections. But it was in his maternal grandparents' Seattle home that Hugo actually grew up, and so it is from his maternal grandparents that Hugo's knowledge of his family history was chiefly acquired. His grandmother and grandfather had been tenant farmers, in the Ann Arbor-Ypsilanti area of south-central Michigan and they, seeking the security of work in a city and a better climate, participated in the second great move of immigrants to the Northwest, moving in 1920 to Seattle, one of the two booming port cities and centers of supply and transportation for the Northwest. The grandmother, a daughter of German immigrants, and the grandfather, the son of immigrants from England, were 47 and 51 years old, respectively, at the time of their move; and from them Hugo would seem to have learned some of the stoical toughness, dignity, and patience required of the early homesteaders in the Midwest whom Carl Sauer describes in this way:

> These people who settled the prairies were farmers, born and reared, out of the Northeast or from overseas, first, and in largest number, German and thereafter Scandinavians. They knew how to plow, to work the soil to keep it in good tilth, how to care for livestock, how to arrange and fill their working time.... The hard pull was to get enough capital to improve and equip the homestead, and this was done by hard labor and iron thrift. This is a sufficient explanation of the work ethic and thrift habits of the Midwest, often stressed in disparagement of its farm life. In order to have and hold the good land, it was necessary to keep to a discipline of work and to defer the satisfactions of ease and comforts.[3]

One instance of Hugo's drawing upon the Midwest heritage may be found in What Thou Lovest Well Remains American (1975), in the poem "A Good Day for Seeing Your Limitations." In the dramatic situation of this poem a former student of Hugo's, a woman recently divorced, comes to him in a bad state of nerves, seeking his help; the moment triggers off a memory, and Hugo interpolates into the working out of the poem a story his grandmother once told him, of how, when she was a little girl, their house burned to the ground and how the neighbors pitched in and built them a new one. And all he had to give the woman who came to him now was the idea of courage he had received as a legacy of his own Midwest past, the courage to go on and build your life again out of the ruins:

167

Abandoned by her husband,
nerves near storm, words searching my hand.
I have little to give. Just that durable gift
from Michigan, a century old, where a home
burned down and men from neighboring farms
pitched in to build a new one free.
They said, 'Don't worry,' and the dispossessed
stopped weeping and danced to ringing mauls.

Turning to the personal past finally emerges in Hugo's work, then, as a source of strength and as a means of attaining freedom from the ever-present sense of a closed world. More precisely, Hugo's looking back takes the form of having the courage to face up to the mistakes of the past, to measure the precise truth of that past in order to be free to live in the present and so allow oneself a wider range of feelings. Indeed, the whole sequence of "A Snapshot of the Auxiliary" poems, in the opening section of <u>What</u> <u>Thou</u> <u>Lovest</u>, constitutes a deliberate return to the Seattle of Hugo's childhood. It mirrors the past in a kind of family picture album of faded snapshots, revealing, after all, a fairly ordinary mixture of grayness and sunshine; but it is also a form of indulgence. Indulgence was not permitted under the old "gray" code of enduring, but it is something Hugo allows himself now that old premises have been revised and incorporated into his new sense of an open universe, one that includes a broadened definition of manhood:

Today I am certain, for all my terrible mistakes,
I did the right thing to...receive like a woman the
world in its enduring decay and to tell the world like a
man that I am not afraid to weep at the sadness, the ongoing day.[4]

Hugo's language in the recent poems employing the Northwest scenario becomes more confident: "On this dishonored, this perverted globe/we go back to the sea and the sea opens for us." So begins the recent poem "Port Townsend, '74" published in the spring 1975 issue of the <u>Northwest</u> <u>Review</u>. And here Hugo dramatically employs as his conceptual field the open vista of the Pacific Northwest as seen from Port Townsend, the city lying on a peninsula, west of Seattle, which juts out into the Sound. In contrast to the deliberately limited focus of the early poems--and in contrast as well to his representation of the mindforms of the earlier "Port Townsend" poem--we enjoy a heightened point of view here, one which embraces the Pacific Ocean to the West and the inland mountains to the east. The sea opens up for us, the speaker declares, and spreads "a comforting green we knew when children" through the islands, and then a "fresh immediate blue beyond the world's edge." Imitating "sad grasses/on the inland plains," the sea now speaks for those who live inland as well as for those who live here. It releases rage and combines with the sky in answer to man's prayer to be relieved of a claustrophobic world, to become whole again:

The sea releases our rage. Logs fly over
the seawall and crush the homes of mean neighbors.
Our home too. The sea makes fun of what we are
and we laugh beside our fire, seeing our worst selves
amplified in space and wave. We are absurd.
And sea comes knocking again in six hours. The sea
comes knocking again. Out there, salmon batter
candlefish senseless for dinner. The troller flashes
his dodger through the salmon school. The sky widens
in answer to claustrophobic prayer. [italics mine]

This poem has a curious close. Ending with a coda-like tale of a man
frozen in the inland mountains, it seems, on first sight, to be an almost reflex-
ive motion toward that irony and ingrained stoicism that runs so heavily throughout Hugo's writing and is so dominant in The Lady of Kicking Horse Reservoir.
On reflection, however, the poem's final image appears to be an integrated part
of that pattern (established by the earlier comparison of the sea to the grasses
of inland plains) that makes this seascape an absolute point of reference for all
other places. The effect of Hugo's final introduction of the mountain man here,
then, is not to undercut the initial image of the sea's inclusiveness but rather,
I think, to amplify it by extending it into the inland consciousness of this man
who begs to be taken there:

          The sea believes us
when we sing: we knew no wrong high back in the mountains
where lost men shed their clothes the last days
of delirium and die from white exposure. We found one
sitting erect, his back to the stars, and even dead
he begged us to take him west to the shore of the sea.

Another recent poem and a chapbook, the latter a collection of early and
recent poems located in coastal Washington places, may serve to further illustrate the radical shift in Hugo's outlook away from a world closed to human
possibility to one that is open to it. The "Bay of Recovery," first published in
The New Yorker in the spring, 1975, deserves careful attention. "Bay of Recovery" begins by attributing to the northern sea the origin of the dream-like
experience that the poem goes on to relate:

     This water started it all, this sullen arm
     of gray wound loose about the islands
     whipped in patches by the north wind white.

The mention of cliffs, grayness, north wind, and islands suggests that Hugo's
scene is a point on the Georgia Strait of Washington in view of the San Juan Islands pointing toward Alaska. The poem thus seems to bear out Hugo's earlier
promise to live his life henceforth "dependent upon moon and tide"; only Hugo's

169

stance in this poem suggests poise more than dependence. Although the title implies a recovery from illness of some sort, and the speaker standing "awkward on.../his/bad leg" is clearly Hugo himself (who does in fact have a bad leg), the poem's persona is remarkably happy and self-possessed. The dazzle of light playing upon the waters creates an illusion that he gradually comes to understand, one which, through a play of mind, he turns into a vision of the entwined nature of truth in an open-ended universe:

> This water started it all, this sullen arm
> of gray wound loose about the islands
> whipped in patches by the north wind white.
> The girl on the cliff exposed her body
> to wind and whispered "whip me whip me."
> I was less than bird, awkward on my bad leg,
> half drunk from last night, and maybe
> you don't think I'm telling it all.
>
> All right.
> There was this sullen girl in tight pants
> on the shore who whispered "love me"
> at the stumps of broken pile.
>
> All right.
> There was this girl I could barely make out
> alone in moonlight on a passing ship.
> Sequins, I am sure. Even now I see the sparkle
> of her skin.
>
> No. No. Let me try it again.
> There was no girl and I was in good shape.
> This water started it all, the dazzling arm
> of blue blue promise and the dazzling gull.
> Gull. Not girl. And it was less than dazzle,
> it was more than being alone on the beach
> young under the moon started it all.

The correspondence between the man's "bad leg" and the landscape's "stumps of broken pile" will recall the immediacy of Hugo's use of local scenes in the early Northwest poems, and the establishing of a strongly rhetorical and confessional "I - you" relationship echoes the later letter poems. But a new combination of elements comes into play now--it is a sign of Hugo's new generous vision--elements of clarity, sophistication, and playfulness. They are not wholly new--the earlier poems "Dog Lake with Paula" and "With Kathy in Wisdom" from Kicking Horse certainly embody Hugo's capacity for wit--but, as combined here, these elements suggest that what has emerged from Hugo's return to the Pacific Northwest is a wholly self-accepting and self-forgiving Hugo

170

who has come to perceive a universe that is thus open to self-acceptance and self-forgiveness.

I would like to close this examination of the emergence of Hugo's new outlook with the following observations on Hugo's recent chapbook Rain Five Days and I Love It: in particular, on the book's publication and upon Hugo's arrangement of the eight early and recent Northwest poems it contains. Published in the fall, 1975, it is perhaps the most concrete evidence of Hugo's rediscovery of his native area. The title, borrowed from the opening lines of the "Letter to Wagoner," suggests that the frequent rains in this place are not to be resisted but celebrated: "Rain five days and I [actually] love it [!]" and the origin of the publication itself, the small Graywolf Press of Port Townsend, which takes its name from the local Graywolf River, expresses Hugo's love for the area. But we also find in the selection of poems included here a geographical orientation toward the North: that orientation is implicit in Hugo's choice and arrangement of poems; and it underscores his evident decision to be finished with the business of the immediately familiar past, to adopt new, more open vistas for his poetry, and to free himself from what he refers to in the "snapshot" poems as that "gray disease," the old provincial skill of stoic endurance. The first three poems, opening with "Port Townsend '74," involve scenes from the Port Townsend peninsula; and, together with the fifth and seventh poems, the Wagoner "letter" and "Port Townsend," they offer an extended "Map of the Peninsula" (the title of poem number three). Coupeville, Orcas Island, and Anacortes, place-names in the titles of poems number four, six, and eight are are all located in the San Juan Islands that lie to the north.

As Hugo's most recent collection of poems, Rain Five Days re-affirms his rediscovered love for the peculiar landforms of the Northwest--and especially for places on its northernmost coast. And yet it lends itself no less conveniently, I think, to a "regional" categorization than do the earlier poems. While celebrating the qualities of that place, Hugo's underlying concern persists: with human limitations and with the possibility of release from them in a universe that he finally discovers to be not so closed as he had once thought. It does not exclude the hard truth that suffering remains the basic substance of human experience. But it leaves room for periods of release from the claustrophobic effects of one's cultural history, and it allows time for enjoying the simplicities of driftwood fires and stars, and dreams of girls."

University of Michigan - Flint

NOTES

[1] Alone with America (New York, 1969), p. 332.

[2] As quoted on the dustjacket of The Lady of Kicking Horse Reservoir.

[3] "Homestead and Community on the Middle Border," originally published in the journal Landscape (1962), and reprinted in John Leighly, ed. Land and Life: A Selection from the Writings of C. O. Sauer (Berkeley, 1963), p. 36.

[4] "A Conversation with Richard Hugo," Madrona, Vol. III, no. 8 (1974), 42.

EDWARD ABBEY'S ANTI-HEROES

by Robert M. Benton

One of the persistent ideas of the American experience is that the frontier has been its structuring theme. The 1890 official declaration that the American frontier was closed prompted what has been called the most influential single piece of historical writing ever done in the United States, Frederick Jackson Turner's essay "The Significance of the Frontier in American History." It was Turner's thesis that American history and the new democracy were essentially the story of a westering frontier. What Turner suggested as true in American history has also been abundantly apparent in American literature where the frontier has long been a dominant theme, perhaps the dominant theme because of its potential for mythic development.

An American frontier attitude was first exemplified by the early colonists, especially the Puritans with their unique sense of mission. They did not simply take land in the name of conquest, for they viewed their "errand into the wilderness" as a divinely ordained period of trial which would make them worthy of entering into a new Promised Land and a New Jerusalem. Above all they desired a tabula rasa on which they could inscribe their dream. It is an anomaly that the arena for regeneration was also viewed as a place of temptation. Puritans conceived of the American wilderness as analogous to that land through which the Hebrews wandered for forty years or that where they believed Jesus had been tempted before his ministry. The "communities of the saints" who were engaged in a psychological and spiritual quest for salvation in the wilderness of the human mind and spirit saw the physical world of America simply as a type of this primary wilderness. It is consistent with their sense of a divine mission that they might condone any means which would achieve their preconceived end.

Since the necessary skills of frontier life were those of survival, our frontier heroes have always been characterized as men of strength, courage, and self-reliance. It is now also apparent that they were men of violence, individuals who often sought regeneration through violent attempts to subdue the natural world in which they found themselves. They maintained an antipathetic attitude toward the culture and institutions native to the aboriginal population of America. They also held an economic philosophy whose concept of private property gave an owner unlimited rights. Through the help of Ramistic logic, the Puritan proceeded to winnow the wheat from the chaff, the good from the evil, in an attempt to preserve the former and destroy the latter. The good was believed to be supernatural while evil was considered as of the world, of nature. Consequently, it was appropriate to destroy the natural wilderness in the name of a higher good. By only slight extension, it was also deemed proper to oppose, even destroy, anyone who would worship the natural world, as the Native Americans did.

The Puritans did not consider the reading or writing of novels to be "useful" activities, so that the early development of the novel in this country was inhibited. Once the novel became an accepted form, however, the characterization of the frontier hero generally incorporated the earlier Puritan attitudes. Charles Brockden Brown's Edgar Huntly is a hunter and a man who pursues violence, as much against himself as the Indians upon whom he takes revenge. The development of the Daniel Boone legend grows out of these Puritan attitudes, and the same may be said for Cooper's Natty Bumppo whom D. H. Lawrence described as the archetypal American frontier hero, "hard, isolate, stoic, and a killer." Through these and thousands of similar characterizations, such as Wister's Virginian, Americans have been given epic heroes who literally dominate their environments. For at least 300 years the basic structure of American frontier heroes has remained constant, and a perusal of paperback book racks will show that the traditional hero is still a saleable commodity.

But heroes do not make history, as Marshall Fishwick reminds us in American Heroes: Myth and Reality. "They are the products of historic times" (p. 230). Perhaps a change is in the wind and a new development in the fictional frontier hero is taking place, a development accompanied by a pronouncement similar to the one in 1890 which prompted Turner's essay. Not too long ago, Professor H. William Menard of the Scripps Institute of Oceanography wrote, "Once the whole world was a frontier challenging man. Now the land is explored, occupied, and bursting with people. Only the sea remains as Byron described it, 'dark--heaving--boundless--endless and sublime.'" Perhaps the fact that most all habitable land has been claimed, often in a violent and destructive manner, has caused thoughtful writers to question that traditional heroic figure in literature which they had been encouraged to emulate. Certainly, the past few years have brought an ecological consciousness which is increasingly being incorporated into all forms of literary endeavor. It may become apparent that we are witnessing the birth of a new type of frontier hero who will compete with the traditional model.

In increasing numbers, novelists are writing books with characters placed in rather typical frontier situations but who have a quite different relationship to the land than did their literary progenitors. In The Milagro Beanfield War, John Nichols's Jose Mondragon is an independent and courageous chicano who, because he refuses to be pushed off the land of his family and give up ancestral water rights, has leadership thrust upon him. Kentuckian Wendell Berry, through Mat Feltner in A Place On Earth, creates a hero who portrays a concept of stewardship toward the land.

Wendell Berry's hero may appear to be a contemporary characterization of Thoreau in a Kentucky farmer's clothing, and John Nichols told me last summer that he sees his reluctant hero, Jose Mondragon, as a traditional fictional figure. The same cannot be said for the work of Edward Abbey. In The Monkey Wrench Gang Abbey urges wilderness protection while utilizing anti-heroes who, like the early colonists, pursue a goal with missionary zeal, but in a manner

173

abhorrent even to their creator. The Monkey Wrench Gang has created a storm of controversy because its protagonists attempt to preserve southwestern wilderness by destroying the machines and the construction projects designed to bring industrial tourism to the area.

Abbey's novel, classified by one reviewer as a new fictional genre--the ecological caper--did not come entirely unannounced. Many had just not seen the rumblings in his earlier works. His 1956 publication of The Brave Cowboy, the story of a solitary and self-reliant wrangler unable to adjust to the modern, urban environment into which he is drawn, might have passed, generally unnoticed, if it had not been for the film adaptation, "Lonely Are The Brave," starring Kirk Douglas. Abbey's reputation has primarily been due to his 1968 publication of Desert Solitaire, a collection of polemical essays based on the author's three summer tours as a ranger in Arches National Monument in the early 1950's. It is a work which Joseph Wood Krutch praised as "a passionate celebration" and which A. B. Guthrie, Jr., said may help us "save something of the values that the bulldozers are costing us."

Since his desert book, Abbey has been primarily involved in attempting to save some of those values. Through a host of environmental essays, including several volumes in concert with photographers, Abbey has been doing what he passionately believes in doing--writing to tell the truth and to give pleasure. He sees himself as a tract writer who wants to influence people, and he calls himself not so much an environmentalist as "a wild preservative." But his primary instrument is fiction, and in The Monkey Wrench Gang he presents sabotage as a vehicle for the prevention of environmental degradation.

In the novel Abbey brings together four unlikely associates. Doc Sarvis is an Albuquerque surgeon who destroys highway billboards as a hobby. Bonnie Abzug is Doc's twenty-eight year old receptionist, mistress, and assistant in "his nighttime highway beautification projects." On a river trip through the Grand Canyon, these two join Seldom Seen Smith, a river guide and polygamous outdoorsman, and George Washington Hayduke, a former Green Beret and Viet Cong prisoner who has become infuriated with the industrial development of the desert he loves. The four decide to become a team and their first escapade is the immobilization of several million dollars' worth of road building equipment near Natural Bridges National Monument.

Fired by the success of their early endeavors, they move to bigger projects: destruction of the railroad line hauling coal from Black Mesa to the Navajo Power Plant and an attempt to blow up two bridges near Hite Marina on Lake Powell. Predictably, the gang is opposed by state and local authorities, and after incredible chases--including one in which Hayduke rappels his jeep down a one hundred foot vertical cliff using the jeep's winch--Hayduke is apparently killed and the remaining three captured.

Although the novel has a questionable--many say weak--ending in which Hayduke reappears at night on horseback, the book is much more than the outrage of a frustrated protectionist. As a young writer, Abbey saw life as a tragedy, but twenty years later he views it as comedy, a fact everywhere apparent in The Monkey Wrench Gang. This novel presents sabotage as a means

174

of achieving a political as well as an aesthetic goal, but that does not mean that it is simply a handbook for environmental saboteurs, despite the controversy which surrounds the work. Abbey's particular achievement can best be evaluated through specific attention to one of its elements: the utilization of anti-heroes.

Perhaps Ernest Hemingway was the literary father of the anti-heroes, those characters who, cut off from the traditional heroic meanings and attachments to families or communities, turned their backs on public values for personal rituals in refusing to play society's game. Such characters have dominated recent fiction, often ridiculing the old conceptions of the hero and forcing readers to see through their own out-of-date and absurd illusions of themselves. Abbey's heroes are not absurd, for they have purpose and pursue actions which may have ultimate sense. Because they are motivated by a deep concern for those few wild places yet left, they might attract admiration, but Abbey makes such traditional hero worship extremely difficult.

Doc Sarvis is a bald, fat, forty-nine year old with few friends. He has taken as a mistress a girl young enough to be his daughter, and he gets his kicks destroying billboards at night. George Hayduke is a twenty-five year old, hairy, beer guzzling, chauvinist whose penchant for violence is exceeded only by his incessant profanity. Seldom Seen Smith, perhaps the most likeable of the gang, is a jack Mormon with three wives in Utah, each a day's drive apart. Bonnie Abzug is an insult to women: a middle-aged man's mistress and a young man's conquest whose ample endowments receive much more attention than the quick mind the author claims for her. Abbey has made genuine attempts to dissuade readers from identifying too closely with his characters.

A careful reading of Abbey's earlier novels and his environmental essays will show, however, that his use of anti-heroes is not the only way in which he falls within the Hemingway tradition. The three men in The Monkey Wrench Gang all possess characteristics of Abbey as he sees himself or as he dreams of being. The Edward Abbey who twenty years earlier as a ranger in Arches National Monument pulled up five miles of surveyor's stakes for a proposed road into the park and who, with a chain saw "borrowed" from the National Park Service, cut down a billboard outside of Moab behind which the highway patrolman would hide to catch speeders has moved on to bigger and better things. He is now destroying earth moving equipment and blowing up trains and bridges, albeit vicariously.

Like Doc Sarvis, Abbey had an early history of nighttime minor sabotage. Abbey removed one billboard; Sarvis sometimes three in one night. Both acknowledge their actions to be of minor importance, and both dream and talk of attempting something which might significantly retard the industrialization of the desert. In their personal lives there are also comparisons which could be made. With Seldom Seen Smith, Abbey may share primarily admiration for Smith's ability to keep three wives modestly happy. But both are self-reliant men who prefer action rather than discourse.

A much closer comparison can be made between Abbey and George Hayduke. Both suffer quite severely from an allergy to tumbleweed. Both are

175

basically solitary men, finding life's great moments when they are alone in the wilderness and forced to utilize all of their resources to survive. When being pursued, Hayduke can do anything. He can scale impossible walls, winch jeeps down sheer cliffs, and overcome death itself. Although Abbey has performed no similar miracles, in <u>Desert Solitaire</u> he chronicles several dangerous adventures in the desert or on the river. His novel <u>Black Sun</u> also shows how Abbey's desert knowledge allows him to push his body to the limits of possibility, certainly a Hayduke characteristic. But it is not solely in physical abilities that the author and the character may be compared. Hayduke, like Abbey, believes in higher laws, and despite their rough exteriors both receive aesthetic satisfactions from their desert experiences. It seems obvious that beyond the real enjoyment he had in writing the novel, Abbey is so closely identified with the characters that he must have received vicarious dream fulfillment through it, as have several readers.

Abbey and <u>The Monkey Wrench Gang</u> are not criticized by those who fear the novel will promote the establishment of eco-raiders whose single-minded zeal will create untold waste and destruction. Such possibilities are slight. In fact, Abbey has said that he does not advocate illegal action--except maybe at night. The real danger, and the virtue of this novel, is that it will prod thinking about the strengths and weaknesses, the successes and failures, of the law to protect the country adequately against the plastic food chain stands and the power plant emissions, against damming our wild rivers and clear cutting our National Park forests. <u>The Monkey Wrench Gang</u> does not indicate a new direction for Ed Abbey. For years he has been developing heroes who are drawn into the fight against inhuman technology by their feelings against the overwhelming weight of industrial profit-centered rationality. <u>The Brave Cowboy</u> ends tragically when the hero, escaping urban frustration on his horse, tries to cross a modern freeway and is struck and killed by a loaded semi. Although his anti-heroes may fail, their failure does not change Abbey's polemical stance, a stance most specifically asserted in <u>The Monkey Wrench Gang</u>.

Central Washington State College

COMPARATIVE
VISIONS

"THE HISTORY OF THE FRONTIER LIKE A SAGA": PARKMAN, PRATT, AND THE JESUIT ENTERPRISE

by Kenneth Innis

In <u>O Canada</u>, Edmund Wilson's pioneer exploration of the undiscovered North American cultures beyond the Republic, the author confessed that in youth he had always thought of Canada as "an inconceivably limitless extension of the wilderness--the 'Northwoods'--of upstate New York." It was, he said, "a realm of huge forests, frozen lakes, large and dangerous animals";[1] and it is in a tone of mild surprise and distinct pleasure that the latter day Wilson, a connoisseur of literary cultures, reports the existence of two distinct North American ways of life, a Turgenev (Morley Callaghan) in Toronto, and a striking literary renaissance in Quebec.

Wilson, of course, did not arrive in Canada with nothing but youthful fantasies of limitless forests. He had, as usual, done a lot of homework; yet his viewpoint remained, perhaps inescapably, an American one, as in his suggestion that "the best way to lay a foundation for the understanding of Canada is to read Francis Parkman's great history <u>France and England in America</u>." He was surprised to find this "unrivalled, and fascinating work" conspicuous by its absence in Canadian bookstores and libraries, and that a serious, well-informed Canadian journalist he met had never even heard of Parkman. On reflection he noted Quebec's Roman Catholic hostility to a Protestant writer, and suggested that Anglophone Canada, within its own solitude, did not care to read so much about the French in Canada.[2]

This paper, as its title suggests, is concerned with an Anglo-Canadian vision of the Jesuit missionary enterprise of the 17th century as this is embodied in E. J. Pratt's documentary epic <u>Brébeuf and His Brethren</u>. By comparing the poem with the historical account that appears to be its major source I hope to bring out some Canadian-American differences in focus and emphasis, and to suggest some reservations an Anglophone Canada, for all its traditional indifference to "French" exploits, is likely to make when confronted with Parkman's historical perspective.

I should like, first, in raising some general historical considerations, to put forward a Canadian view of the Westering experience as this is expressed by the historian W. L. Morton in his essay "The Relevance of Canadian History."[3] Canada, he notes, has a separate and distinct history with "one narrative line" and "two variant responses," both imposed, in large measure, by the peculiarities of a Northern and austere land. Viking frontiersmen, Bristol traders, Norman fishermen, all participated in a medieval-modern movement across the Northern Latitudes, advancing what is in every way a frontier of Northern European civilization. French pioneers, who continued the process, exploited the hinterland from a narrow soil base in the St. Lawrence, the characteristic wilderness venture and the return to the family homestead in accordance with a seasonal rhythm. In Morton's view "The line which marks the frontier from the farmland . . . the hinterland from the metropolis, runs through every Canadian psyche. " Today the hinterland is exploited from the soil base of not only the St. Lawrence but also of the Saskatchewan valleys and the delta of the Fraser.

The British, then, became part of the same pattern of expansion as the French before them; and, as Hugh MacLennan has pointed out in "The Rivers that Made a Nation,"[4] Alexander MacKenzie's birch bark canoe, emerging on the Pacific coast in 1793, completes the series of canoe voyages begun by Champlain, the anonymous craft finding a Northwest Passage where more famous vessels had failed. If there is a true archetypal image of the Canadian movement West it is not a procession of covered wagons advancing towards a limitless frontier of opportunity (certainly not the prairie immigrants arriving by the national railroad to an order of things already laid out by the authority of the RCMP and the Royal Bank) but a birch canoe making its tentative way through the enveloping forest. This ancestral boat contains Indian and Jesuit, as well as pragmatic Scottish trader.

The Indian has to be included. We need to remember that the definitive Canadian frontier of heroic origins, the West of the explorer, fur trader, and (in the early French phase) missionary, is not the farming frontier which Turner saw as characteristic of the settlements to the warmer and richer south.[5] The natives were essential parts of the economic system, often allies, sometimes even Christian brethren. I would in no way wish to suggest that Canada is an Indian-loving country, yet we should be aware that Tecumseh--on the wrong side in American history--is something of a national hero in Canada and that the record of the Jesuit missions shows Indian heroes. Refugee Mohawks, too, are sometimes regarded as another species of United Empire Loyalists.

Another relevant factor in the historical consciousness of Canadians, in Morton's analysis[6] a basic orientation, is the strong monarchial bias of the country, monarchial government being seen, paradoxically, from a U.S. point of view, as a protector of the people's rights. United Empire Loyalists, the basis of English Canada, leave rather than cast their lot with republican rebels; Quebecois, conditioned by their religion and history, refuse the invitation to join the United States, and take up arms against their would-be liberators. In spite of contemporary suggestions that the Queen is irrelevant to modern Canada the monarchial bias is still felt, and there is hardly any great swell of public feeling for a republic.

These, then, are some primary historical and cultural facts which ensure that Parkman's history must have a somewhat different reception north of the 49th parallel. He operates from a set of assumptions that cannot automatically be shared there.

I am concerned in this paper primarily with the Parkman of Volume II, The Jesuits in North America in the Seventeenth Century, and, to a lesser extent, Volume I, Pioneers of France in the New World. I shall deal, first of all,

180

with some basic conceptions before making more detailed comparisons with Pratt's poem.

As is well known, Parkman considered the historian a man of letters; and he devoted considerable attention to the art of characterization, dramatic arrangement, and stylistic effectiveness. But history was also for him a moral judgment, the romantic literary conventions of Chateaubriand and Scott which he employed having ultimately a rhetorical function: Parkman, the son of an eminent Unitarian minister, perpetuates the Puritan interest in history as God's judgment, and inherits the old New England case against Rome.[7] For all his virtues as a narrative artist, he falls short of the trans-personal sympathy of Ranke's ideal historian who, neither prosecutor nor counsel for the defense, writes for the judgment of the court of history.[8] Parkman's heroic tale of the American forests becomes a cautionary and exemplary one with a predestined end: God is on the side of progress, liberty, and the ultimate expansion of the United States. How, really, could it have been otherwise?

In his introduction (V. 1) he speaks of "the vain attempt of Feudalism, Monarchy and Rome" to master a continent. What, for Parkman, is completely unnatural in New France was the attempt to crush, by way of feudal authority, "a people [frontier born] compassed by influences of the wildest freedom," a "brave, unthinking people" with soldier virtues and faults, "made independent by forest, sea, and savage conflict." But "the conflict between Liberty and Absolutism was never in doubt." Reflecting (V. II, XXXIV) on the close of the first act in the bloody drama of New France, the destruction of the Jesuit missions, Parkman sees the Iroquois as the providential and paradoxical agents of what, in effect, is the manifest destiny of the United States. Thus a moral and progressive law, immanent in history, worked ultimately against reactionary evil,[9] though in mysterious fashion indeed.

Parkman permits himself a shudder at the notion that the French enterprise, involving the conversion of the Indians, could have succeeded, at the thought that there might have been (XXIV) populations "formed in the ideas and habits of a feudal monarchy and controlled by a hierarchy profoundly hostile to freedom." The lesser breeds would have been "tamed, not civilized," for that, given their nature, was hardly possible. The salutary decline of the Indian population would have been stayed. A prosperous New France, extending over the Great Lakes and Mississippi valley, would have certainly slowed the march of Liberty, and remained "a great stumbling block" to the American experiment, even though in the end Liberty must ultimately have prevailed. From the Parkman perspective it does seem accidental and unfortunate that Canada, not part of the United States, still does not enjoy republican liberty, and that the Roman Church should have survived till now in Quebec. Undoubtedly there are some Anglo-Canadians, the spiritual children of Orange Lodgers calling for the death of Louis Riel and the elimination of Métis rights, who feel a certain sympathy with the second notion; but even these unreconstructed WASP supremists, the deadly foes of bilingualism in all its forms, do not normally see themselves as Americans cheated of their destiny. It is true that Pelham Edgar, the friend and mentor of Pratt, did edit The Romance of Canadian History from Parkman's writings,[10] yet I submit that Parkman does not provide, ready made for English Canadians, a useable version of the heroic origins of the country. The Canadian "matter of France" was to find its place in the literary imagination of the Anglais through Pratt's documentary poem.

Pratt himself has been called, accurately enough, "the last born literary child of frontier America."[11] Born in 1882 in Newfoundland, this poet, by virtue of a culture-lag and the harsh Atlantic environment of his upbringing, does seem like a survival from another age. His was recognizably a Victorian, Protestant, boyhood, --the Bible, Pilgrim's Progress, Shakespeare, Carlyle, Paradise Lost[12]--within a robust folk culture rich in song and oral tradition. An Evangelical by orientation, he was originally trained, like his father before him, for the Methodist ministry.

In Toronto, however, he was diverted from the study of Pauline eschatology to the study of psychology and to the production of Newfoundland Verses (1923). Switching his academic field to English Literature, he eventually settled down to a teaching career at the University of Toronto, achieving, long before his death in 1964, the status of unofficial poet-laureate of English Canada, popular in his own country as serious poets have rarely been in the 20th century. In Brébeuf and His Brethren (1940) "the values of the primitive epic are found again," in a way disconcerting to modernist critics in search of ambiguity.[13]

The poet seems instinctively to have grasped an underlying unity of Canadian experience, the single narrative line of Morton's historiography, transcending the celebrated solitudes. In his characteristic fashion he did thorough historical research, moving from Parkman, to the Jesuit Relations themselves, to Brébeuf's own spiritual journal. He visited the martyrs' shrine in Huronia. He studied (clearly with an imaginative sympathy) the liturgy and doctrine of the Roman Church.[14] According to E. K. Brown he went back to the national past not as an escape, but, with the outbreak of World War II heavy on his spirit, because he wished "to be re-assured as to qualities of Canadian life,"[15] of, we might say, the capacity for endurance and survival bred of the land and its history.

In penetrating his material a central image emerged in his mind's eye. As Brown reported, the twelve books of the epic actually began with a search, in Pratt's words, for "a simile for the Cross which would express alike shame and glory, something strongly vernacular set over against cultivated imagery and language."[16] Pratt may be nearer to a real concern with characterization in this poem than before, but the emphasis of the species of poetry here is upon the deed, not upon the complexities of character and motivation; the heart of the poem lies in its awesome conclusion, written first, in which the martyred saint becomes a type and symbol of Christian glory, the source of the strength that baffled the Iroquois torturers being ultimately

> . . . in the sound of invisible trumpets blowing
> Around two slabs of board, right angled hammered
> By Roman nails, hung on a Jewish hill.

It appears to me that subtle textual analyses of Brebeuf's psychology, and attempts to discover the poet's own theological stance (or his atheism) are mistaken exercises in ingenuity. [17]   The world plainly given by the omniscient narrative at the outset is a counter-Reformation world of miracle, mystery, and the incalculable power of God.   "The story of the frontier like a saga/Sang through the cells and cloisters of the nation."   New saints are called to leave the cloister for ". . . chartless seas and coasts/ And the vast blunders of the forest glooms."   Brébeuf the neophyte hears, in Normandy, of "Champlain, Brule, Viel,/Sagard, Le Caron. . . .

> The stories of those northern boundaries
> Where in the winter the white pines could brush
> The Pleiades, and at the equinoxes
> Under the gold and green of the auroras
> Wild geese drove wedges through the zodiac.

What draws him, however, is not the romance of the New World, but a true vision of the Via Dolorosa, ("Real Presence to the naked sense") that comes to him in contemplation at the altar at Bayeux.

The wealth and diversity of the historical material obviously presented organizational problems for Pratt in his concern for producing an aesthetic or - der while remaining faithful to available facts in their sequence.   The final re- sult was a discontinuous series of episodes, a loose chronicle of the corporate Jesuit enterprise, linked by theme, symbol, and   recurrent imagery (e.g. flame, altar, cross).   In addition to the majestic climax of the last book the other high points of the poem are located, symmetrically, in books three, six, and nine. [18]   The transcendent vision of the whole unites, in one world of won- der, such binary oppositions and contradictions as Normandy/the savage fron- tier; The cathedral/the pines and oaks of the Indian lodge; Peace / broken al- tars; Indian cruelty / Indian charity; Jesuit idealism / mercantile ambition.[19] It is, indeed, a very rich poem, but for present purposes I shall look only at two large matters: its presentations of the Jesuits, and of Indian life. Wherein and how, does Pratt vary from Parkman?

We are in no doubt as to where Parkman stands on the subject of Jesuits. In the prologue to his swelling scene, the close of this first volume, he paid grudging tribute to those politic promoters of superstition whose mission, in- deed, was "marvellous as a tale of chivalry or legends of the lives of saints." But "Who," he asks, "can define 'the Jesuit'?" a "systematized contradiction?" His Jesuits, for all their heroic virtues, are alien and other, their form of faith a pathetic fallacy, and their quixotic plan of embracing Indians as brothers in Christ and children of France a basic misreading of aboriginal nature and its possibilities.

In "Brébeuf and His Associates" (V. I, VI) he charges that the Jesuits, ex- pecting to conquer by the cross rather than sword, hoped to subdue the savages to a passive state "repugnant to manhood and averse to the invigorating and expansive spirit of modern civilization."   In "The Character of the Canadian

Jesuits" (V. I, IX), as elsewhere, he praises the masculine virtues of Brébeuf, "the Ajax of the mission"; but Brébeuf, like his valiant associates, is given to visions which, Parkman says with unmistakable cynicism, require the professional psychologist rather than the historian to explain. Parkman is often the amused, sometimes irritated spectator, inviting us to smile at the foolish Jesuits with their notion that the Devil has a stronghold in Huronia and taking alarm at the inroads made by the soldiers of Christ with their conversions.

For Pratt, Brébeuf and his associates are brethren and ancestral figures. Brébeuf has been called hard names: "rationalist technician," "Pelagian" optimist; "reverent" agnostic; "apostle of corporate man" (for even Brébeuf is not --American style--the story of an individual super-hero, but of an organized, collective action).[20] No one who knew him in the flesh detected any trace of mysticism in his genial, sociable personality; but the material with which Pratt worked, and the objectivity imposed by the genre of epic reportage, ruled out subversive skepticism. He could not be "true to the mystic heart of the poem," as one critic says, and make us, by subtle indirection, suspect that Brébeuf is deluded, or that this fashionably problematic hero did the right thing for the wrong reason.[21]

Pratt, it is true, does not overlook certain ironies about the Jesuits' mission and strategy built in to his material: the grotesque misunderstandings of the Hurons, or the fact that the Fathers have no scruple about using the most effective means of persuasion in the particular circumstances--many pictures of Hell, the magic of a superior technology. Yet Brébeuf, Garnier, Jogues, and the other priests remain types of human endurance, of heroic charity, paladins of faith who are finally beyond the range of tragedy and of critical irony. Theirs is a wonder story.

The Indians cannot infer self-gain or anything but simple courage in the way in which the priests minister to the sick and conduct baptisms at the risk of their lives (though in the later mission to the Petuns and Neutrals the black-robes themselves are taken to be symbols of plague and famine). And the Jesuits do not approach the Indians as great white gods. In Brébeuf's letter to priests who were to come out to Canada (1635, Bk. III), he advises them

> You must sincerely love the savages
> As brothers ransomed in the blood of Christ
> All things must be endured. To win their hearts
> You must perform the smallest services.
> * * * * * * * * * * * * * *
> ....Carry
> Your load on portages. Always appear
> Cheerful - their memories are good for faults.
> Constrain yourself to eat their sagamite
> The way that they prepare it, tasteless, dirty.

In the long run this love produces the Indian martyr Eustace who, in the fires, entreats his fellow Hurons to let no thought of vengeance injure French hopes

184

for an Iroquois peace. Native metal could, indeed, take the ultimate test of faith as truly as the French. There is, too, the case of the youthful captive Onnonhoarton, killed when, on seeing Father Jogues prepared for torture, he offers himself as substitute for the man who had brought him to Christ. And Totiri, a native of high rank, who emulates Jogues by plunging through the torture flames to apply the Holy Water to an Iroquois. In Parkman's larger and more crowded canvas, where strokes of caricature sometimes appear, such details get less proportional emphasis.

The image of the Indian in the poem, however, will not please doctrinaire cultural relativists, or anyone seeking an opportunity to indulge in moral indignation over white imperial crimes against the innocent. Quite predictably, Pratt has been accused of mistreating Indians[22] (as if he had invented the uncomfortable details of their way of life[23] and their devotion to teeth, clamshell, and flame in implacable rites of marathon sacrifice more highly developed than in Europe). The poem shows the unromantic state of nature in all its monstrosity, even if natural man there shows courage, fortitude, and charity to his own kind. This is certainly in keeping with Parkman; the difference lies in Parkman's assumption that the race could not profit from European civilization, his negative reaction to the idea of assimilados.

Margaret Atwood in Survival,[24] though from a different perspective, also tends to regard the Jesuit enterprise as a crime against nature. She suggests that Brébeuf might better have accepted the pristine wilderness and its inhabitants as is rather than try to impose his garrison mentality and a sterile European order. Here she speaks not so much as a Canadianist but as the voice of a recognizable zeitgeist of neo-primitivism. I shall, by way of a conclusion, present the poem's image and model of what might have been, remembering that historically the plan involved a mixed and intermarried community of Indians and French.

Book X of the poem is the moment of pastoral peace before the Iroquois storm breaks with its annihilating fury upon the western missions.

> Each year they felled the trees and burned the stumps
> Pushing the frontier back, clearing the land,
> Spading, hoeing. The stomach's noisy protest
> As sagamite and wild rice found a rest
> With bread from wheat, fresh cabbages and pease
> And squashes which when roasted had the taste
> Of Norman apples. Strawberries in July,
> October beechnuts, pepper roots for spice,
> And at the bottom of the spring that flowed
> Into a pond shaded by silver birches
> And ringed by marigolds was watercress
> In chilled abundance. So was this the West?
> The Wilderness?

The picture and the activities involved suggest not a hatred of nature, but, rather, a desire to perfect it.

One must grant that there were certainly other forces in the movement West, and here we may recall one of Parkman's sardonic episodes (Vol. I, XVII) in which Brébeuf, the captive of a Huguenot privateer, protests that the Jesuits came purely for the glory of God, exposing themselves to every danger to convert the Indians. The angry Protestant, aware that they worked together with French material interests, angrily retorts "You mean to convert the beaver!" The imperial, mercantilist dream was that Sainte Marie, fort and mission, might be the western citadel, bastion of one half of the continent, perhaps the gateway to the fabled Cathay. The priests, however,

> ...were breathless with another space
> Beyond the measure of the astrolabe –
> A different empire built upon the pulses,
> Where even the sun and moon and stars revolved
> Around a Life and a redemptive Death.

Theirs was a noble vision without parallel in the Westering movement in North America; and Pratt, by a radical act of imagination, claimed it for all of Canada, the country allegedly without a mythology. Through his achievement the Jesuit enterprise became available to the world community of Anglophones as one of the great human adventures of the Americas. It does seem appropriate that this story of the Canadian wilderness should have been given its definitive form by someone who had emerged into the twentieth century from the cultural experience of the embattled Newfoundland outports, who came from an Atlantic community itself a significant stage in that westering movement across the northern latitudes which constitutes the distinctive history of Canada.

Western Washington University

NOTES

[1] O Canada (New York, 1965), pp. 36-37.

[2] Wilson, p. 48. Carole Gerson, a doctoral candidate at the University of British Columbia specializing in nineteenth century Canadian fiction has pointed out to me that Parkman's history was received with enthusiasm by contemporary English-Canadian reviewers. A characteristic notice: The Canadian Monthly and National Review II (May 1877), p. 564, rated Parkman as "our best chronicler."

[3] Eli Mandel, ed. Contexts of Canadian Criticism (London and Chicago, 1971) pp. 48-70.

[4] Carl F. Klinck and Reginald E. Watters, Canadian Anthology, 3rd ed. (Toronto, 1974) p. 317.

[5] Canada has had, in addition to its hunter and trader West, its miner West, rancher West, and farmer West as in Frederick Jackson Turner's North

American historiography; but history and geography have combined to make the frontier of the hunter and trader the formative one in Canada.

[6] Contexts, pp. 58-64.

[7] David Levin, History as Romantic Art (Palo Alto, 1959), gives, in his opening chapter, an excellent account of the New England school and its postulates.

[8] Ernest Cassirer, An Essay on Man (New Haven and London, 1944) p. 189.

[9] Levin, pp. 27-36.

[10] Pelham Edgar, The Romance of Canadian History (Toronto, 1902).

[11] Fred Cogswell, "E. J. Pratt's Literary Reputation," Canadian Literature, 19 (Winter, 1964), pp. 6-12.

[12] Sandra Djwa, E. J. Pratt: The Evolutionary Vision (Toronto and Montreal, 1974), p. 2.

[13] Cogswell, p. 7. What appears to be involved is a dislike for such archaic and objective poetry in our self-conscious age of anxiety.

[14] Djwa, p. 100.

[15] E. K. Brown, On Canadian Poetry (Toronto, 1943), pp. 132-152. Reprinted David G. Pitt (ed.), E. J. Pratt (Toronto, 1969) pp. 28-38.

[16] Pitt, p. 33.

[17] Even when the critic is sympathetic, as is Djwa, the impulse is to find a problematic hero in harmony with dominant conventions of our time. Pratt's poem, naive in Schiller's sense, has to be the expression of a unified philosophic view, rendered fit for modernist explication.

[18] Desmond Pacey, Ten Canadian Poets (Toronto, 1958) p. 187.

[19] I have not attempted a structural analysis, but these binary oppositions stand out. Most are explicit in Bk. II where Brébeuf, returned to Normandy after his first wilderness venture, feels that he is a man of two worlds.

[20] See, in particular, Frank Davey, "E. J. Pratt, Apostle of Corporate Man," Canadian Literature 43 (Winter, 1970) p. 55; and "E. J. Pratt: Rationalist Technician," Canadian Literature 61 (Summer, 1974) p. 77. Peter Buitenhuis, who settles for "reverent agnostic," rehearses some of the theological readings and misreadings in his Introduction to Selected Poems of E. J. Pratt (Toronto, 1968) pp. xiv-xviii.

[21] Dwja, p. 101.

[22] Frank Birbalsingh, "The Tension of His Time," Canadian Literature 64 (Summer, 1974) pp. 75-82.

[23] The Indians, in their turn, respected the material civilization and technology of the 17th century French; but they were disgusted with French standards

of personal hygiene, thought French hairiness repulsive, and believed their own doctors far superior. See Cornelius J. Jaenen, "Amerindian Views of French Culture in the Seventeenth Century," Canadian Historical Review, LV (Sept. 1974), pp. 261-287.

[24]Survival (Toronto, 1972), p. 93.

EXPLORER/SETTLER/POET

by Peter Stevens

In his survey "Explorers by Land to 1860" in the Literary History of Canada, Victor G. Hopwood makes a distinction between the European consciousness "which goes back directly to ritual and myth" and Canadian consciousness which "was born literate and historical." Canadian literature faces the "problem of creating from the record according to a sense of history." Hopwood concludes that the "proto-form of our still largely unwritten foundation literature is the record of our explorers, fur traders and pioneers."

Increasingly in recent years Canadian writers, and in particular the poets, have turned to these early figures as a basis for some mythic ground to construct a sense of a Canadian poetic or literary consciousness. E. J. Pratt attempted this in Brébeuf and his Brethren and Towards the Last Spike but these poems are more in the nature of historical recreations in poetic form than an investigation of the psyche of the country through the figures of explorers and settlers. Contemporary poets are trying to discover a sense of themselves as Canadian poets through the figures of explorers and settlers in such a way as to use these historical figures as part of the poet's own persona, as if these people are part of the shadow-play of the poet's own consciousness. The very language of those historical figures, famous or ordinary, is becoming part of the contemporary poet's concern. If Canadian consciousness "was born literate and historical," as Hopwood suggests, then that literateness contained in documents, records, spoken narratives will be the natural basis for a contemporary poetry, not only for the narrative line but also for the language in which the poem is expressed. A recent issue of the journal Sound Heritage includes examples of poems by various contemporary Canadian poets based on spoken records, transmuted into poems but remaining true to the language of the original telling. Analysis is being left behind as exploration and settlement have become metaphors for ritual and myth which is at the root of European consciousness. The contemporary poet delves into the lives of the pioneers and explorers in their own accounts in order to discover himself and his poetic consciousness.

John Newlove is a case in point. His most often-quoted poem in this connection is "The Pride" in which his investigation of the Indian past leads him to find the roots of poetry in the land itself: "the grand poem / of our land, / ... sought for, and found / in a line of running verse," until "the sunlit brilliant image suddenly floods us / with understanding."

But Newlove's poetry often has the tone of offhand speech, pared down to essentials, so that even when he deals with the explorer Samuel Hearne, he deliberately refuses to make him a literary hero on an epic scale. He wants the real man in the poem, placed in the context of the poet's own reality. The

189

explorer is simply doing a job, however hazardous his life is. This is of course true to Hearne's own report of his journeys, for his journal is admirably straight-forward in its language, though it carries enough resonance to give substance to the travels and to the man himself. Newlove accomplishes the same thing in his sparse poem, "Samuel Hearne in Wintertime." The poet avoids the romantic image of exploration: "your camp must have smelled / like hell whenever you settled down / for a few days of rest and journal work." And the poet moves into an expression of his own difficulties in trying to write poetry, for his non-heroic domesticities cause problems for him:

> One child is back from the doctor's while
> the other wanders about in dirty pants
> and I think of Samuel Hearne and the land.

Thus the poet and the explorer become one: historical and contemporary, lit-erate and literary, the proto-form and the poetic form, the explorer and the poet.

In other poems Newlove explores the history of the country but is vague about the details. He does not elevate his heroes to the stature of mythic he-roes. Like Hearne, they represent to him people he admires who approach the country as a poet must approach his poetry. His poem about Louis Riel is in fact more a poem about making a poem. The Riel rebellion and the white man's inroads into Indian culture serve Newlove as the basis for a discursive sermon on limitation. A poem for Newlove must be something more than just a way of filling up a page. It must generate its own truth, as these men he mentions did, "the men you admire. / And cannot understand." Too fixed a form will destroy their images by defining them, and definitions are a limitation stopping motion and openness:

> Politics must have its way.
> The way of noise. To fill up.
> The definitions bullets make,
> And field guns.

This use of proto-forms as a basis for poetry is not simply part of an interest in Canada's past; it is also a part of a search for a viable literary tra-dition to fit the contemporary poet's need for a form to suit his linguistic con-cerns. Thus, the search for roots within the continent by settlers is seen as a search for the roots of a true Canadian poetry, divorced from an alien past, ready to settle into indigenous patterns out of which might spring the material for ritual and myth.

The pioneer attempts to carve out for himself a settled space. As David Sinclair points out in his Introduction to Nineteenth Century Narrative Poems, pioneering, a theme central to the narrative poems he includes in his anthology, simply means "the breaking and settling of the land and the imposition of man's works on the new surroundings"[1] and "man introduces culture in its dual senses of agriculture and the arts."[2] This means that in most nineteenth century poems in Canada, the landscape is subjected to a language and an idea derived from other literature, mainly English.

But the contemporary poet is now doing a different kind of pioneering. Instead of breaking the land, he is breaking down those civilzed walls; he is beginning to explore the whole in order to find his real roots, and this in turn will mean turning his back on the structures of older civilization, avoiding the older, traditional structures and materials of poetry. He will need to turn to the older records of his country, that is, the proto-forms.

Margaret Atwood makes use of a settler, Susanna Moodie, in her sequence of poems, The Journals of Susanna Moodie. Although Susanna Moodie did not venture to the west in the accepted sense of that region, she fits admirably into the theme of explorers and settlers as embodiments of the search for poetic language to express Canadian myth, for she was a cultured lady who came to Canada in the 1830s and tried to establish herself eventually as a writer. She and her husband, however, also tried to settle a portion of land and farm it, though they had little experience of farming. Their experiences are recounted in her book, Roughing It In The Bush, which has been described as "an unpretentious, highly literate account of an heroic if not always intelligent struggle against a hostile environment."[3] She closes her book by warning other people who were in her situation against coming to Canada on the assumption that it was a promised land. But in a sense, that warning is a paradox, for in writing the book Mrs. Moodie seems to come to terms with her life in Canada. She accepts it, and it may have been the writing of the book that enabled her to accept it. Indeed, Clara Thomas suggests that she overcame the culture shock of her first years until she experienced "the timeless reality of a contained world of the imagination."[4] Such a figure would obviously be an attractive persona for the poet Margaret Atwood who sees her as an example of the Canadian national sickness, paranoid schizophrenia:

> The country is too big to inhabit completely, and in the parts
> unknown to us we move in fear, exiles and invaders. This
> country is something that must be chosen--it is so easy to
> leave--and if we do choose we are still choosing a violent
> duality.[5]

In the very first poem of the sequence Susanna feels herself to be totally out of place in the new landscape, for it does not reveal anything to her about herself. She is obviously expecting the new country to expand her sense of herself but "The moving water will not show me / my reflection." Susanna feels herself to be "a word / in a foreign language." As the sequence progresses, Susanna (the persona of a writer within the country) pursues the topic of the necessity to discover ways of expressing the country. What attitudes are essential? She resolves "to be both tentative and hard to startle." She does not know what will happen, for she does not have the literary means to take a clear view. Still, she does not want to be thrown completely off balance, even though

191

she has not yet won through to the right method of expressing herself in relation to the country:

> my damaged
> knowing of the language means
> prediction is forever impossible.

Towards the end of Journal I she describes herself in these terms: "my skin thickened / with bark and the white hairs of roots" and "fingers / brittle with twigs." But she also feels that the new land has stripped away the veneer of civilization she has brought with her: her heirloom face is now "a crushed eggshell" so that what she now sees is her essential self: "you find only / the shape you already are." Thus this mirror-poem of Susanna's and Margaret Atwood's is also a poem about the poet making herself available as writer to that outer landscape in order to allow the design, and the way to express the design, move through her. In fact, she feels her "mouth cracking / open like a rock in fire / trying to say." But she is still tentative, for when she leaves the bush for the relative security of Belleville and the clearings, she feels only that she has almost been taught something, but that she "came away not having learned." But she has made herself available to the new country. In a sense, the continent reflects and is reflected by the inner continent: "my mind is a wide pink map." She is moving into a Canadian consciousness, so that even when there are stirrings of her old English patriotism at the time of the rebellion of 1837, she sees deep into her mind to discover what that English background is:

> those tiny ancestral figures
> flickering dull white through the back of your skull,
> confused, anxious, not sure any more
> what they are doing there.

The shapes of her former self, though not finally obliterated, are reduced in importance. When she is told about a charivari, she recognizes that more primitive responses lie within and must be faced, just as the poet must be open to the outer wilderness to be able to release the new language, the basic frame for poetry in a new land:

> take care
> to look behind, within
> where the skeleton face beneath
>
> the face puts on its feather mask, the arm
> within the arm lifts up the spear.

Yet this poem ends ambiguously. The message is not to surrender to those impulses but merely to recognize them. One is not to become primitive but rather to "become human."

192

Through the course of the sequence Susanna discovers that she has a kind of double expression: a mannered and cultured voice and another voice which comes from direct experience of her new life. The first is romantic, seeing old myths and rituals, whereas the other voice is realistic, seeing death but also seeing life flourishing within the realism of her vision:

> a dead dog
> jubilant with maggots
> half-buried among the sweet peas.

The last section of the sequence deals with Susanna in her old age and after her death, where she comes to reject her old ideas of art and literature. She begins to see herself as a spirit embedded within the land, haunting all those who follow. At the end she speaks from the grave. She admits that her mind remains split, and the language she uses partakes of that doubleness, the double bind of the poet in the new world:

> I began to forget myself
> in the middle
> of sentences. Events
> were split apart
>
> I fought. I constructed
> desperate paragraphs of praise.

This same poem reiterates the notion that all previous responses are of no value in the world, even when some semblance of civilization begins to grow: "it is still no place for an english gentleman."

She finally becomes one with the land by dying into it, but her death does not silence her voice. Her spirit will be resurrected, for the last two poems suggest the idea of resurrection, perhaps the reality of a real Canadian consciousness passed on to us within the landscape:

> those who have become the stone
> voices of the land
> shift also and say
>
> god is not
> the voice in the whirlwind
>
> god is the whirlwind
>
> at the last
> judgement we will all be trees.

And at the end of the sequence Susanna is still with us, riding on the bus through a "wilderness of wires" in Toronto. The persona of Susanna rides ghostly with us till we discover, as Margaret Atwood discovers, the right kind of voice to express our kind of vision.

Margaret Atwood uses Susanna Moodie's two books as proto-forms, that is, as a basis for her own concerns as a poet. In an Afterword she relates how when she read the books, she was disappointed in them: "The prose was discursive and ornamental and the books had little shape." But she found beneath the surface of the prose another "voice running like a counterpoint," and it is this other voice that speaks in the poems, so that Susanna Moodie is a persona not only of Margaret Atwood herself but of all those writers who have tried to find the right language to deal with the Canadian experience, to explore their own responses and to settle them into a literary work. Thus, these proto-forms serve not only as historical record but as a text on which the Canadian voice can base its own language.

Al Purdy is another poet who hears the voices of ancestors in the pioneering past of Ontario. His ancestors seem almost to be physically embodied in him, for in the 1950s the poet re-enacted the idea of settlement by building his own house in the area his forebears came to as United Empire Loyalists. He recounts his building of the house, his sense of the surrounding land, his reactions to the present inhabitants and the ghosts of the past, all in relation to his own personal trials and domesticities. The proto-forms for him are town records, the feel of the place itself, his own place in it, as well as his place as a poet in Canadian poetry.

His long poem In Search of Owen Roblin starts with the poet looking at the photographs of his long-dead ancestors. He wants to hear their voices from the past just as he can hear them buzzing within the party-line telephones. It is the voice of his grandfather which first transports him to the past, a voice he tries to transcribe accurately in his poems, for it has the effect of bringing the real past into solid reality.

Purdy's settlement by Roblin Lake in Ameliasburg, which was his way of "trying to get out / from under the town pavement" parallels his own discovery of his real poetic voice. Purdy has rejected all his poetry written before the 1960s as being too self-consciously literary, too much a part of an alien tradition. His poetry from 1960 on is looser, more colloquial, more of a release of a voice with roots in rural Ontario, and this can be attributed to his interest, perhaps cursory at first, in Owen Roblin, the man who owned the original grist mill in Ameliasburg. Purdy started a search for information about his life but found little. What he did find, however, was enough for him to conjure up Roblin in one poem. After that, he began to dig into different records, documents, history books, to discover the real Roblin. He connects this with his own pursuit of a poetic voice, of a place for himself as poet, for he keeps the autobiographical framework clear, writing in the midst of his "own despair and failure." He uses the facts but also invents incidents which seem characteristic of the sort of man Roblin was, seeing this act of creation as a collaboration, even as something in which he as poet is the secondary figure:

194

> First my grandfather, then Owen Roblin
> me hanging on their coattails
> gaining strength from them.

He uses this same phrase earlier about his failure as a writer, so the link is made again between the search for a poetic voice and the search for Owen Roblin. It is as if the poet is suggesting that if he can rescue these settlers from oblivion, present them on paper in real language, then he will rescue himself as poet from oblivion, though in the process he loses that self-conscious pose and feels himself to be simple settler:

> as if I too had hacked at monster trees
> sowed between stumps the first grain
> and once stood with them in spring
> when the quivering air changed direction
> from north to warm south wind
> the time when seeds leaped under the earth
> and green leaves unfurled like sudden flags...
> and felt what I couldn't say
> except somehow they gave me the words.

He has become part of these settlers, so that he now has more confidence as a poet, so much so that he now no longer has to rely on the historical fact. He can conjure up his own characters in his own terms.

Eventually, as the poem moves to its close, Purdy again takes up his feelings about being a poet. This whole era he has researched and invented and formed into a poem is "really a backward extension of myself. . . . For it wasn't only Owen Roblin I was looking for/but myself thru him always myself." The poet finds himself "embedded in all I've written about / a fly speck in history / dust mote cruising the galaxies." In this place he senses them; in his poem he has caged them, their "meanings and reachings and fragments"; even though to others they may be forgotten, he has raised them up, released their ghosts, given them bodily presence within his poetry which is an extension of himself:

> they had their being once
> and left a place to stand on.

Florence McNeil approaches the problem of her relation to the settler as poet in a different way. The place to stand on for the pioneers she records is more elusive. The place is Walhachin by the Thompson River in British Columbia. The settlers came in 1907 and although this region is a dry belt, by irrigation they managed to grow fruit trees. But the 1914 War was instrumental in destroying their new prosperity, for most of the men returned to Europe to fight. A storm destroyed most of the flumes and those people remaining were refused governmental aid to restore their venture, so the project was abandoned. The poet concludes her brief prose note which introduces the poetic sequence by

195

describing what Walhachin now is:

> In time, the sage reclaimed the land. But even in the
> present day, one can see glimpses of the dead, gnarled
> trees in the midst of what is now a wilderness.

Walhachin's history, this proto-form, is transmuted into a sequence of twenty-two poems, twenty-one of which are monologues spoken by an imagined Englishwoman in the settlement. But in many ways the woman is also the poet who is trying to come to terms with her own inhospitable terrain of Canadian poetry. The sequence of poems expresses a gradual movement away from that provincial refined Englishness--the poet often uses references to speech, messages and prayers to elucidate it, till the woman feels as free as the river, and the poetry emerges naturally from the landscape:

>   fruit is
> breathtaking
> these small poems
> baring themselves to the
> August heat
> are here at their own request
> allowing us to read them.

To begin with, the narrator defines the landscape as "incomprehensible" as opposed to the English countryside she left with its "predictable bloom of churches." The signs of nature here make no sense to her, but the water used for the irrigation flumes is free, uncivilized, democratic, devoid of any hierarchical value, so the settlers' history is now wedded to its flow, just as the poet finds that she too has to accept the new, unfettered flow of language. It is as if the poet is saying that the question of language and poetry here in relation to English roots is not simply one of a change from a civilized tongue to a primitive one, for the landscape is full of "the tense movement / of complicated things."

From incomprehension the narrator / poet moves into uncertainty. The settlers still hang on to "the essential propriety of our lives," but the woman speaking to her lover breaks down those proprieties: "there are barbarities / in our lineage too," linking this notion to her view of the Indians, of whom she uses the phrase "their civilized lineage." Right at the centre of the sequence is another love poem, in which the woman discovers her other selves lying beneath that proper surface she cultivated as an Englishwoman. The presence within the landscape makes itself felt:

> if there are gods in
> these hills
> I understand their silence.

Obviously, in terms of the poet as settler, she has reached only a new awareness, not a way to express that awareness, and when winter comes, she re-
treats. The hard landscape seems to have no connection with her or with her
attempts to grasp it in language: "the snow speaks coherently / only to the
others."

The turning point in the poet's attempt to be at one with the landscape and
with language comes in Poem XIV, for in it, while she is still failing ("dry rivers in my mouth," sitting "uselessly / sewing misty patterns / into no defined
clarity"), she also becomes a priestess, a prophetess perhaps, trying to bap-
tise the trees, to take them into her own consciousness like a new Eve: "I
anoint the trees with drops of wet dust / and give them names for my own protection." In the following love poem this new world is full of "strange content,"
so strange that their previous love might be considered inadequate in this new
land:

> where meaningless lines catch fire
> where we walk on volcanoes
> for the chance of reading
> the official statement of a row of trees.

The settlement has grown for them, and the narrator / poet sees clearly
the new expression forming:

> from these lines
> have radiated white orchards spreading softly
> through the hills
> orchestrating for us a larger
> symphony
> filling our lives with the softness
> of their delivering.

This is followed immediately by the section quoted earlier in which poetry
reaches its fruition, but the sequence ends quickly after this. Everything begins to collapse. A brief letter to England seems almost to presage war, which
erupts in the last poem, dated August, 1914. The whole sequence closes with
two lines that epitomise the turning away from the new back to the old destructive, threatened civilization the narrator / poet felt she had finally sloughed:
"the small grass bayonets my shoes / there are dreadnoughts at anchor in the
Thompson."

Walhachin illustrates the questions about literary tradition in relation to
settlement, for the poet, in the guise of the narrator, is on a voyage of exploration to find an adequate language to respond to the landscape; Florence McNeil's
latest volume of poetry is titled significantly Ghost Towns and in the poem
"Ghost Towns" she summarizes her feelings toward those earlier settlements
which have died. They become for her symbols of that past life we have ignored,
but she insists that in spite of their deaths they have a life beyond our meagre

modernity. The strength of those pioneers is beyond ours, and we are only tourists taking snapshots of the trappings of their lives, not of their integral, essential meanings. That meaningful life, in fact, continues, even though modern civilization thinks it has erased that early settlement from its knowledge. The poem ends on a paradox: the poet maintains these pioneers defy immortality and refuse to be called up, yet in writing the poem she has called them up, presented them to the reader in the context of his own modern and civilized consciousness, which photographs only the "rebuilt salons," "the barber shops the gilded dance halls." These are only "plaster replicas" whereas the pioneers here are wedded to the landscape:

> with legs of stone   mountainous
> in your temples   the flumes
> pouring endlessly like blood.

Their lives are the proto-forms of our lives; their records are the proto-forms of our poetry. We are beginning to come to terms with the question of a literary tradition through our use of those proto-forms, protoplasms from our past. Earle Birney expressed the problem in a different way. In his poem "can lit" he maintains Canadians were too busy settling the country to respond to the mythic qualities of the landscape. According to Birney, our country has no quintessential poet to give us a sense of ourselves: our civil war is "a bloody civil bore" and we have no Whitman to sing the praises of the fight to establish Canadianism or to mourn the slaughter of Canadians in that fight. None of this kind of feeling for the country has emerged: "it's only by our lack of ghosts / we're haunted." But now the ghosts are beginning to rise in more palpable forms in contemporary poetry. More and more, the land and man's relation to it, the sense of exploration and settlement, figure in Canadian literature. The ghosts are the proto-forms and these are being exorcised into poetry by means of which our settlers and explorers are being transformed into our poets.

University of Windsor

NOTES

[1] p. vii.

[2] p. viii.

[3] Edward McCourt, "Roughing it with the Moodies," in A. J. M. Smith, ed. Masks of Fiction, p. 90.

[4] "Journeys to Freedom," Canadian Literature, No. 51, Winter, 1972, p. 18.

[5] Afterword, The Journals of Susanna Moodie, p. 62.

RALPH CONNOR AND THE TAMED WEST

by Susan Wood

The major difference between the Canadian West and the American West, it seems, is not geographical or historical; it is cultural. Canadians have little or no "Wild West" mythology. In fact, our social ideal is that of a tamed West, our "national dream" the collective effort of building the transcontinental railroad, taming vast distances and rugged mountains to bring eastern civilization to the frontier. The Canadian pattern of western settlement involved sending missionaries to build churches, surveyors to divide up the land into homestead sections, Mounties to maintain order, and troops to tidy away the Indians and Métis, all before the would-be pioneers entered the country. These settlers, initially from eastern Canada and Britain, in turn brought with them attitudes to the West, and to pioneer life, established in the East by popular writers. Despite some attempts to transplant the wild West adventure novel into a Canadian setting, most writers presented an ideal of civilization moving westward to the frontier. The archetypal scene south of the border might show the lone hero confronting his foes at high noon; but a typical scene in western Canadian fiction shows the American desperado surrendering his six-shooter at the quiet, firm command of a Canadian Mountie. [1]

The most famous and influential of the Canadian myth-makers was "Ralph Connor," the internationally acclaimed author of twenty-five bestselling novels including Black Rock: A Tale of the Selkirks (1898), The Sky Pilot: A Tale of the Foothills (1899); The Man From Glengarry: A Tale of the Ottawa (1901); The Doctor: A Tale of the Rockies (1906); and The Foreigner: A Tale of Saskatchewan (1909). His presentation of the Canadian West, both the prairies and the British Columbia mountains, in these novels provides a fascinating view of a social mythology in development.

Connor was, in fact, the Rev. Charles Gordon, a Presbyterian minister and son of a Presbyterian minister, born in 1860 in what was then the frontier settlement of Glengarry County, Canada West. After completing his education at the University of Toronto, he became a missionary, riding the Alberta foothills on a bronco to bring Christianity and civilization to hardworking, often hard-living settlers. He became the most famous Canadian novelist of his day almost by accident. While in Ontario to raise funds for the western missions, he was asked to write down some of his experiences for the Presbyterian magazine Westminster Review. These sketches became the basis of Black Rock, a national bestseller with a first edition of an unprecedented 5,000 copies. Connor later wrote in his autobiography, Postscript to Adventure (1938), that his sole aim was to awaken my church in Eastern Canada to the splendour of the mighty religious adventure being attempted by the missionary pioneers in the Canada beyond the Great Lakes by writing a brief sketch of the things...I had come to know by personal experience.[2]

His preface to Black Rock indicates his views both of fiction, and of pioneer life:

> The story of the book is true, and chief of the failures in the making of the book is this, that it is not all the truth. The light is not bright enough, the shadow is not black enough to give a true picture of that bit of Western life of which the writer was some small part. The men of this book are still there in the mines and lumber camps of the mountains, fighting out that eternal fight for manhood, strong, clean, God-conquered. And, when the west winds blow, to the open ear the sounds of battle come, telling the fortunes of the fight.
>
> Because a man's life is all he has, and because the only hope of the brave young West lies in its men, this story is told. It may be that the tragic pity of a broken life may move some to pray, and that the divine power there is in a single brave heart to summon forth hope and courage may move some to fight. If so, the tale is not told in vain.[3]

Connor's novels set forth a Christian version of the Victorian myth of progress. He equates the pioneer spirit, the drive to transform the wilderness, with missionary zeal, the desire to tame lives and emotions into a new godliness. His church militant regarded the West as a sacred trust, its land and people given to them to civilize. "God is calling on us to go in and possess the land," wrote James Robertson, Superintendent of the Presbyterian home missions and Connor's mentor.[4] Connor's autobiography echoes this tone, with its sense of participating in a mighty fight to establish the western missions.

As Connor's novels gained a vast readership throughout North America and Europe, so they influenced popular attitudes to the Canadian West through a com ination of several ideas: religion, as a simple evangelical creed based on faith in Divine love; pioneering as a "great adventure" which included the spread of religion and culture; and the fictionalized "personal experience" which, though highly sentimentalized, created vivid scenes of frontier life. His bestsellers summed up a providential vision of the new land.

It is significant that Connor's attitudes to the land do not change, though he deals with such diverse physical and social situations as the vanished frontier of the Scots settlements in Glengarry, the new Doukhobor settlements in Saskatchewan, and the mining camps in the Rockies. His natural setting is, first, a beautiful, awe-inspiring backdrop for human actions. The description of the sunset in The Sky Pilot would be echoed by innumerable prairie romances in the following decades:

Before us lay the hills, softly curving like the shoulders of great
sleeping monsters, their tops still bright, but the separating valleys full of shadow. And there, far beyond them, up against the
sky, was the line of the mountains--blue, purple and gold, according as the light fell upon them. The sun had taken his plunge, but
he had left behind him his robes of saffron and gold. We stood
long without a word or movement, filling our hearts with the silence
and the beauty, till the gold in the west began to grow dim. High
above all the night was stretching her star-pierced, blue canopy,
and drawing slowly up from the east and over the sleeping hills the
soft folds of a purple haze. [5]

Descriptions such as the following of the "wealth of loveliness" found in
the British Columbia forest by moonlight seem cliché-ridden and romantic:

The dark pine masses stood silent in breathless adoration; the daz-
zling snow lay like a garment over all the open spaces in soft waving
folds, and crowned every stump with a quaintly shaped nightcap.
Above the camps the smoke curled up from the camp-fires, standing
like pillars of cloud that kept watch while men slept. And high over
all the deep blue night sky, with its star jewels, sprang like the roof
of a great cathedral from range to range, covering us in its kindly
shelter (BR, p. 140).

While vague and idealized, this passage nevertheless indicates an attempt to
humanize nature, to see it as "homelike and safe," so that even "the lone cry
of the wolf from the deep forest" seems "like the voice of a comrade." Moreover, the sense of religious awe ("breathless adoration") and the Biblical references ("pillars of cloud") reinforce the ideal of nature as a "great cathedral"
within which men learn to worship the Creator (BR, p. 140). When human settlements create despair, the "ministry of the woods" brings Divine peace to a
troubled soul (BR, p. 255); the grandeur of mountains, sunsets and starry skies
evokes awe as it suggests the glory of Heaven. In The Sky Pilot, in one of his
most famous passages, Connor has his missionary hero describe a flower-
filled foothills canyon to illustrate a parable of human pain and spiritual growth
(SP, pp. 176-79). Nature, then, is made by God for humanity's use and inspir-
ation--an attitude common in nineteenth century Canadian literature.

The Canadian West, in this view, would call forth human greatness to
shape it. The Foreigner depicts the process of settlement in Saskatchewan:
"Those great empty spaces of rolling prairie, swept by viewless winds, were
to be filled up now with the abodes of men." [6] The heroine, Marjorie Harris,
on learning that the Doukhobors have become Canadian farmers, exclaims:
"How wonderful the power of this country of yours to transform men!...It is a
fine thing to have a country to be made, and it is fine to be a man and have a
part in the making of it" (F, p. 378). Pioneering offers the European settlers
the opportunity to forget old world feuds and become "good Christians and good
Canadians, which is the same thing" (F, p. 253).

Yet untamed nature can also appeal to untamed men; and Connor's novels reveal a deep suspicion of both. In The Foreigner, the prairie freedom which is to redeem the young Doukhobor Kalman Kalmar is also seen as an absence of civilized restraints and spiritual aspirations (represented by Margaret French, a Connor Good Woman), which has left Jack French a drunken wastrel barely capable of managing his prosperous ranch. The cowboys of The Sky Pilot, in a similarly inspiring natural environment, forsake religion for the debauches of "Permit Days" during which they drink to blot out hardships and loneliness. The church services provided by the missionary or "sky pilot" represent "the advance wave of the great ocean of civilization which many of them had been glad to leave behind" (SP, p. 38). Nevertheless, this "limitation of freedom" represented by obedience to God is necessary to the individual; as the Sky Pilot preaches, "Men can't live without Him and be men!" (SP, p. 64). The restraints of civilization, too, are necessary to the developing country, as eastern values such as hard work, co-operation, self-discipline and charity shape the western frontier, and are in turn tested and confirmed by it.

The action of a Connor novel typically involves a representative of civilization, a dedicated missionary or a saintly woman from an eastern city, struggling to subdue the frontier's wildness in a human heart, while at the same time preserving the "manly" and heroic qualities which that frontier has called forth. Black Rock, set in the Selkirk mountains in the 1880's, illustrates this process clearly. A Presbyterian missionary, Craig, and a saintly young widow, Mrs. Mavor, work to save the souls of miners and lumberjacks in "a devil's camp-ground" where "whisky is about the only excitement they have" (BR, p. 97). Their work to replace Slavin's saloon, with its gambling and drunken dances with "Kalifornia Female Kickers," with a Total Abstinence, a coffee-club and church services is a "fight...to the death" against evil (BR, p. 206). Their "Waterloo" is won in part when the narrator helps fight off Slavin's men and break countless whisky bottles, in part when various hard characters, including Slavin, accept God and kneel to pray. The equation of drink and damnation, in observations like "He could not drink whisky and kiss his baby," now seems naive (BR, p. 85). Under the pulpit rhetoric, however, there does emerge a sense of the monotony and hardship of frontier life, as well as of the excitement Connor felt at its human potential. Craig, speaking of the natural resources which will ensure a "great future for British Columbia," makes no distinction between economic and spiritual concerns. Regarding the province with "the eye of a general," he notes "the strategic points which the Church must seize upon.... The Church must be in with the railway; she must have a hand in the shaping of the country. If society crystallizes without her influence, the country is lost, and British Columbia will be another trap-door to the bottomless pit" (BR, p. 131). Several later novels echo this view, notably The Doctor, which shows a missionary, a nurse, and a doctor fighting to rescue a railway camp in the Kootenays from the influence of gamblers, prostitutes, and saloon-keepers.

Connor best expresses his Christian version of the ideal of progress, and his vision of frontier life in the Canadian West, in his most popular novel, The

Man From Glengarry. The narrative is a powerful one, and the values, though outdated, still suggest the power they held for Connor, his characters, and the many readers who agreed with him that "not wealth, not enterprise, not energy can build a nation into sure greatness, but men, and only men with the fear of God in their hearts, and with no other."[7]

The novel opens in the 1850's, in the frontier settlements in Glengarry, where the children of dispossessed Highlanders continue their parents' "heroic struggle with stern nature" to "hew from the solid forest, homes for themselves and their children that none might take from them" (MG, p. 15). As they transform the forest, so the civilizing influence of the Presbyterian minister, Mr. Murray, and especially of his good and cultured wife, transforms them. Their chief enjoyment, drunken sprees climaxing in massive brawls with rival shanty gangs of French and Irish Catholics, is replaced by the emotional release of the Great Revival, an evangelical movement which softens doctrinaire Presbyterianism with a broader Christian charity and simple trust in God, and thus transforms an ordinary frontier community into a city of God on earth. The novel's hero, Ranald Macdonald, struggles personally, with Mrs. Murray's aid, to subdue a primitive passion for revenge through a Christian ethic of forgiveness. He thus becomes a true man, one whose innate strength is controlled by obedience to God. In Connor's simple creed of "muscular Christianity," this ideal is illustrated equally well by Ranald's prowess in a ploughing match or football game, his work with slum children, and his honesty in refusing to cheat an American lumber magnate. Hired by this American as the manager of a British Columbia lumber camp, he proceeds to clean up the operation by throwing out the chief troublemakers--with the same righteous zeal shown by Bronco Bill of The Sky Pilot, who converts an outspoken atheist by beating him up. Ranald then introduces such innovations as fair wages, sanitation, and reading rooms for the workers, since a company must take care of its employees, both body and soul. He extends operations, and climaxes his achievements when he persuades the "British-American Coal and Lumber Company" to extend its investments in British Columbia, and convinces Sir John A. Macdonald to begin the promised railroad: both developments which will aid easterners to exploit the province's seemingly limitless resources. Ranald, in sum, represents the idealized Glengarry men to whom the book is dedicated, "who in patience, in courage and in the fear of God are helping to build the empire of the Canadian West."

Connor himself attributed his success to the synthesis of social and religious values with adventurous plots and colourful descriptions of western life. In his novels, he wrote, religion is

> set forth in its true light as a synonym of all that is virile, straight,
> honourable and withal tender and gentle in true men and women. And
> it was this religious motif that startled that vast host of religious
> folk who up to this time had regarded novel-reading as a doubtful in-
> dulgence for Christian people. I have received hundreds of letters
> expressing gratitude for a novel that presented a quality of religious
> life that "red-blooded" men could read and enjoy (PA, p. 150).

Moreover, he felt, novels such as <u>Black Rock</u> and <u>The Sky Pilot</u> were enthusiastically received in Britain and the United States, as well as in Canada, because they

> gave an authentic picture of life in the great and wonderful new country in Western Canada, rich in colour, and alive with movement, the stamping ground of the buffalo and his hunters, the land of the trapper, the Mounted Police and that virile race of men and women, the first pioneers who turned the wild wilderness into civilization. Then, the pictures were from personal experience. I knew the country. I had ridden the ranges. I had pushed through the mountain passes. I had swum my bronco across its rivers. I had met the men--Hi Kendall and Bronco Bill and the rest were friends of mine (<u>PA</u>, p. 150).

Canadian readers mistrusted and condemned literary "realism" but welcomed an appearance of "real life." Connor was careful to win acceptance for his ideas by pointing to the factual basis of his work. The "pictures from personal experience"--the ploughing match in <u>The Man From Glengarry</u>, the sale of Gwen's pony in <u>The Sky Pilot</u>--combined with the authenticity of the shantymen's and cowboys' speech and with the simplicity of Connor's morality to ensure the novels' popularity. Ironically, such scenes help to overcome the preaching to maintain readers' interest now. Certainly, the combination set a pattern for Canadian novels of rural life for several decades.[8]

Most important, "real life" novels such as these defined an image of frontier Canada. Connor's readers made him a national spokesman, summing up and, by his extraordinary popularity, helping to spread a set of materially progressive, socially conservative values associated with pioneer life, and with the control of individual ambitions to the progress of established society. In particular, he popularized a view of the Canadian land as a source of great majesty where "the mountains rose grandly on every side, throwing up their great peaks into the sky" (<u>BR</u>, p. 12); of great inspiration, where "the mountains...in all the glory of their varying robes of blues and purples, stood calmly, solemnly about us, uplifting our souls into regions of rest" (<u>BR</u>, p. 247); and of great challenge, a new land of infinite resources where the task of building civilization is "worth a man's life" (<u>BR</u>, p. 297). These novels, which sold millions of copies, helped to foster an ideal of material progress sanctified by association with fundamental Protestantism. The missionaries would work with the eastern entrepreneurs to build the nation; indeed, there seems to be little distinction, as Leslie Graeme of <u>Black Rock</u>, Ranald Macdonald of <u>The Man From Glengarry</u>, and Barney Boyle of <u>The Doctor</u> speak of building railroads, running lumber camps, and "lending a hand to fellows on the rocks" through prayer and example, with the same evangelical tones (<u>BR</u>, p. 305). The CPR, the lumber interests, and the Presbyterian church would unite to build the future of "the great Dominion reaching from ocean to ocean, knit together by ties of common interest, and a common loyalty" (<u>MG</u>, p. 445). Though later generations would call this process "exploitation," in Connor's novels these interests all represented civilization, as it moved from the East to accomplish the noble task of taming the Canadian West.

University of British Columbia

NOTES

[1]See Ralph Connor's Black Rock and Robert J. C. Stead's The Bail Jumper for examples.

> This self-image of Canada, defined as a peaceful, ordered society by contrast with the United States, was widely held. Sir Wilfrid Laurier, in the famous House of Commons speech in which he declared "that as the nineteenth century had been the century of the United States, so the twentieth century would be the century of Canada," went on to contrast western growth in the two countries. In the United States, he said, "frontier civilization was...a byword for lawlessness." In Canada, however, "Our institutions in our own Northwest have been developed by gradual stages, so as to ensure at all times among these new communities law and order, and the restraints and safeguards of the highest civilization" (House of Commons Debates, Feb. 21, 1905, p. 1422).

[2]"Ralph Connor," Postscript to Adventure (New York: Farrar and Rinehart, 1938), p. 148.

[3]"Ralph Connor," Black Rock: A Tale of the Selkirks (Toronto: Westminster, 1898), p. 7.

[4]Charles W. Gordon, The Life of James Robertson, D.D. (London: Hodder and Stoughton, 1908), p. 223.

[5]"Ralph Connor," The Sky Pilot: A Tale of the Foothills (Toronto: Westminster, 1899), p. 50.

[6]"Ralph Connor," The Foreigner: A Tale of Saskatchewan (New York: Doran, 1909), p. 286.

[7]"Ralph Connor," The Man From Glengarry: A Tale of the Ottawa (Toronto: Revell, 1901), preface.

[8]A different picture is given in M. Allerdale Grainger's contemporary account, Woodsmen of the West (London: Edward Arnold, 1908). Refusing to idealize life in the British Columbia coastal lumber camps, Grainger (who became Chief Forester of the province) depicts "the boys" as "free of the West"-- roaring drunk, swearing, perpetually broke, and surviving. He comments:

> The logger cannot stand a missionary. It must be a rather dreadful thing to be a convinced missionary and to have to mix with your fellowmen, not frankly (you and the others, just human beings together), but as a man exploiting the forms and even the spirit of friendliness for a more or less secret purpose of your own..." (p. 27).

WESTERING AND THE CHICANO LITERARY TRADITION

by Carlota Cárdenas de Dwyer

The Mexican American or Chicano literary tradition of the Southwest has been developing since before the Spanish Conquistadores first traveled across what is now considered the American Southwest. In 1598, several years before the first boatload of English immigrants landed on the coast of Massachusetts, a form of Spanish religious drama was enacted on the shores of the Rio Grande by the followers of Don Juan de Oñate. This group eventually settled in New Mexico and established the foundation of a Hispanic culture that was to grow and flourish in the isolation of the spectacular New Mexican landscape.

Not alone in his drive nor in his success, Oñate was one of numerous Spanish settlers who sowed the seeds of Spanish culture and tradition throughout the area north and west of central Mexico. The names, if not the early history of such sites, are all fairly familiar to most of us--San Antonio, El Paso, Santa Fe, Los Angeles, San Francisco, and so on. These places testify to a westering impulse initially experienced by the Hispanic colonizers of the New World.

It is into this basically Hispanic, frontier civilization provided by Spanish expeditions that the Anglo American explorers and settlers marched. They did not, as many would have us believe, encounter a cultural vacuum.

The Mexican American or Chicano literary tradition itself is a long one--from before 1598 to the present--and is too complex to condense in a few simplistic generalizations. What is important to remember is that the contemporary Chicano reveals the efforts of two westering experiences--the Hispanic and the Anglo. Together these two powerful forces exert a significant influence on the development of the contemporary literature.

An examination of the Mexican American literary tradition, from its early, purely Hispanic period to the more recent Chicano phase, suggests that the effects of the Anglo westering phenomenon and the concomitant progress of the twentieth century had at least three basic influences on the evolution of Mexican American literature:

1) The usual mode of expression changes from one of only Spanish to a combination of Spanish and English, or English alone. The use of Spanish is, however, not abandoned.

2) Traditional forms, such as <u>cuentos</u>, <u>corridos</u>, and <u>pastorelas</u> are supplemented by more modernistic and experimental forms, such as free verse in poetry and the improvisational <u>actos</u> of Luis Valdez in drama.

3) Much of the rather elevated diction and subject matter of the nineteenth century are replaced by a modern preference for the "common man" situated within a realistic frame of reference.

Rather than embark on an exhaustive--and exhausting--survey of these elements in the literature, focus here will be concentrated on a few selected works which illustrate certain important trends and that are also major examples of the Chicano literary tradition itself.

And so, following the example of my colleagues in the Anglo American literary tradition who begin with the writings of John Smith and William Bradford, I begin with those of someone who might be considered John Smith's counterpart, Don Juan de Oñate. I will start here, not because of compelled imitation, but because the writing of the original colonizers yields clues to the attitudes, ideas, and ideals shared by all of those early emissaries of European civilizations.

In Aztlan: An Anthology of Mexican American Literature[1] it is said that Don Juan de Oñate was often called "the first Spanish settler" of New Mexico. Oñate was born in Mexico, an Espagnol mexicano, and married the great-granddaughter of the Emperor Motecuhzoma.[2] In a proclamation which he nailed to a tree with a cross before crossing the Rio Grande into New Mexico, Oñate expresses the grandiose sense of purpose that marks almost all colonizers:

> Be it known, therefore, that in the name of the most Christian king, Don Philip, our lord, the defender and protector of the holy church, and its true son, and in the name of the crown of Castile, and of the kings that from its glorious progeny may reign therein, and for my said government, I take possession, once, twice, and thrice, and all the times I can and must, of the actual jurisdiction, civil as well as criminal, of the lands of the said Rio del Norte, without exception whatsoever, with all its meadows and pasture grounds and passes. And this possession is to include all other lands, pueblos, cities, villas, of whatsoever nature now founded in the kingdom and province of New Mexico, and all the neighboring and adjoining lands thereto, with all its mountains, valleys, passes, and all its native Indians who are now included therein.

> From A History of New Mexico by Gaspar Perez de Villagre, "How Oñate Took Possession of the Newly Discovered Land"[3]

Gradually the Spanish-speaking settlers developed a New World civilization and culture which was as dense and varied as it was extensive. Of Spanish language newspapers alone, a total of three hundred and eighty are reported to have existed by researcher Herminio Rios. In the Summer 1970 issue of El Grito, Herminio Rios and Lupe Castillo printed Part I of "Toward a True Chicano Bibliography,"[4] a listing of one hundred and ninety-five Mexican American newspapers published between 1848 and 1942. In the summer 1972 volume, Rios added one hundred and eighty-five Mexican American newspapers published between 1881 and 1958.[5] One has only to look at the spate of publications which appeared in the post 1965 era to perceive that this literary tradition is still formidable.

In addition to the printed legacy, there is the oral tradition that is perhaps best known and loved by the Chicanos themselves. From the strongly Mexican epoch of the late nineteenth-century is the <u>corredo</u> or ballad. In "<u>With His Pistol in His Hand</u>": <u>A Border Ballad and Its Hero</u>[6] folklorist Américo Paredes documents and records a classic example of the Mexican American <u>corrido</u> tradition, "The Ballad of Gregorio Cortez." Students of the European ballad will recognize many of the stock characteristics of this form--the refrain, the running narrative, the use of concrete detail, etc. What is most interesting to note here is the degree to which the protagonist of this <u>corrido</u> approaches the heroic dimensions of another familiar narrative type--the epic hero. Gregorio Cortez, truly a traditional epic hero, exhibits not a miscellaneous mix of undistinguished traits but, in fact, displays and personifies a crucial selection of particular qualities valued in the traditional Mexican culture prevalent in Texas and much of the Spanish-speaking Southwest.

In recording the wonder of Gregorio Cortez's deeds, the legend's narrator is careful to note that in addition to his courage and daring, Gregorio Cortez was a man of certain virtue:

> For Gregorio Cortez was not one of your noisy, hell-raising
> type. That was not his way. He always spoke low, and he was
> always polite, whosoever he was speaking to. And when he
> spoke to men older than himself, he took off his hat and held it
> over his heart. A man who never raised his voice to parent or
> elder brother, and never disobeyed. That was Gregorio Cortez,
> and that was the way men were in this country along the river.
> That was the way they were before these modern times came, and
> God went away.[7]

This excerpt from the legend of Gregorio Cortez elaborates on the special epic qualities Cortez embodied. The Spanish or possibly Roman Catholic virtue of humility that Cortez reflects here would forever be misinterpreted as cowardly or obtuse timidity by alien observers.

In direct contrast to the dignified and heroic tone of the border ballads are the numerous poems of the more recent era. The virtuous epic heroes of the frontier <u>corridos</u> have been replaced to a great extent by the anti-heroes of modern, urban barrios. These individuals are young Mexican Americans belonging to street gangs and known among the Spanish-speaking people as pachucos. During the forties, their flamboyant uniforms of pegged-legged pants and wide-shouldered jackets were called "zoot suits." The sporadic and uncoordinated conflicts which punctuated Anglo American and Mexican American relations in the Southwest achieved national awareness in 1943 with a series of violent confrontations publicized in the press as "the zoot suit riots." The so-called "riots" were actually a series of street battles between a few scattered pachucos and literally hordes of sailors from nearby bases. However, regardless of the substantial and thorough analyses of these events and their causes by writers like Carey McWilliams in North from Mexico,[8] disagreement still exists about whether the pachuco is a hero or hoodlum.

Most of the pachucos or vatos (dudes) as they called themselves of the World War II period lived and died unacknowledged by their contemporary Mexican Americans. However, within the last several years, with the surge of Chicano consciousness and a new wave of poetry appearing in Chicano publications, the pachuco has emerged as a twentieth-century hero. So accepted, if not endeared has this figure become to many Chicanos, that the pachuco's argot of Spanish and English is generally acknowledged as a major source of the modern Chicano's blend of Spanish and English.[9] In addition, many ascribe early impulses of the modern Chicano movement to the inchoate rebellion of the pachuco.

Like the vatos themselves, pachuco poetry usually displays an intriguing combination of distinctive characteristics. These elements vividly reflect some of the major changes in the literature since the second westering phenomenon of the Anglo American and the advent of modernism:

1) Language is often a blend of Spanish and English. Usually, the pachuco dialect, sometimes called caló, is incorporated into the text of the poem.

2) Modern in form, standard patterns of rhythm and rhyme and many poetic conventions are abandoned.

3) The pachuco himself or some aspect of his existence serves as subject. While he is often recalled with affection and respect, he rarely escapes the role of tragic victim.

A study of a few "pachuco poems" will introduce the truly new and dynamic poetics devised by contemporary Chicano writers. "Los Vatos"[10] by Jose Montoya, and "Pachuco Remembered"[11] and "Aquellos Vatos"[12] by Tino Villanueva are among the most popular of all pachuco poems with readers of Chicano literature.

One of the best known poems by a Chicano poet is "Los Vatos," which appeared in one of the first collections of Chicano literature, the anthology El Espejo (1969). "Los Vatos" offers a revealing and incisive portrait of the pachuco and his code of behavior, in a narrative that recounts the fatal results when a pachuco, Benny, falls into disfavor with his fellow gang members:

(The vatos always carried guitars and drove
around in low chevies with bad metallic paint
jobs.)

Two got down soothing long sleek hair,
Hidden eyes squinting behind green tinted tea-timers.
In cat-like motions, bored and casual, they sauntered
Then settled heavily on the car. (14-19)

Benny, summoned by his former friends, does not shirk the encounter although
he realizes that he goes to meet his death. A vague reference to something at
last night's dance is all the poet furnishes for justification of Benny's violent
death that closes the poem. While Benny's "brave deathwalk" is commendable
in its fidelity to the pachuco code, there is pathos rather than tragedy in the dis-
proportion between the surmised offense and the ultimate penalty.

Still, "Los Vatos" is noteworthy for its skilled rendering of the complex
character of this enigmatic figure. While Montoya includes numerous details of
the pachuco's appearance and life style, these alone might have produced nothing
more than an exercise in local color of the southwestern barrio. But the major
proportion of the poem is devoted to the ill-fated Benny and his varied responses
to the death he accepts as inevitable. Yet in spite of the author's sensitive portrayal of a variety of emotions, Benny remains a pathetic victim, meriting the
reader's pity rather than the admiration evoked by the epic hero Gregorio Cortez or an historical hero like Emiliano Zapata.

While "Los Vatos" is thoroughly enmeshed in the pachuco culture, English
is the almost exclusive mode of expression. Use of the pachuco dialect or Spanish is restricted to a few words and phrases. Yet in form "Los Vatos" shows a
marked departure from traditional poetic patterns. This is not to say that poetic
devices are absent, but merely that they appear in something other than the conventional forms of previous eras. Innovations in technique are not what distinguish "Los Vatos" most significantly.

What is most remarkable about the poem in relation to the early evolution
of contemporary Chicano literature is this appearance of the pachuco as a central figure. While such lofty personalities as Gregorio Cortez, Joaquin Muri-
eta, Pancho Villa, and Emiliano Zapata endure as traditional heroes, the pachuco quickly became a new hero for the Chicano artistic community. Seemingly downtrodden and defeated in pragmatic terms, the pachuco offered a gen-
uinely Chicano experience and identity with which readers and writers could
identify immediately. The pachuco became in effect the "common man" of the
modern Chicano sensibility. Response to poems like "Los Vatos" was so enthu-
siastic that succeeding poems became increasingly "pachuco" in form as well
as content.

Following Montoya's initiative and direction, numerous Chicano poets begun publishing poems about pachucos during the years following 1969. In two
poems from his collection Hay Otra Voz Poems (1973), Tino Villanueva flavors
his lines with liberal portions of caló. Like Montoya's "Los Vatos," Villanueva's poems focus on aspects of the pachuco and his role as valiant victim.
While Villanueva's two poems, "Pachuco Remembered" and "Aquellos Vatos"
(those dudes) contrast in mood and tone, they both feature the use of caló as an
inventive and vivid poetic language.

In "Pachuco Remembered" caló is juxtaposed with standard English. The poem's narrator directly addresses this figure from the past in a familiar and personal tone with terms and expressions taken from the pachuco's own dialect:

!Ese!
Within your will-to-be culture,
incisive,
aguzado
clutching the accurate click &
fist-warm slash of your filero
(hardened equalizer gave you life,
opened up counter-cultures U.S.A.). (1-8)

Later, the narrator calls the pachuco a "vato loco alivenado" (a cool dude) and comments on his calcos (shoes in caló), lisa (shirt), and la jura (the police). The narrator goes on to describe the pachuco as an early prophet of the current Chicano ideology of ethnic pride and assertion of cultural differentness. The pachuco is called accordingly a "precursor" and "a juvenile la causa."

In "Aquellos Vatos" identification with the pachuco is complete as the dramatic voice is that of a pachuco himself recalling the various vatos from his youth. One of the very few light-hearted poems in this category, "Aquellos Vatos" weaves colloquial Spanish, caló, and English. Apparently responding to inquiries about his former associates, the pachuco speaker makes telling comments about each one in their common dialect:

Then there was la Polla de San Anto--lived
across the creek y tenia un ranfle sentao
pa' tras, me entiendes? (8-10)

Here, he begins in English but quickly reverts to Spanish with the nickname "la Polla" (the chicken) for his friend and their abbreviation for San Antonio, "San Anto" pronounced with a soft, Spanish intonation. "Ranfle" is another caló term and is used for car, especially the hot rod or low rider of the pachucos. This one is slung low in the rear and described in a clipped Spanish vernacular; "Sentao pa' tras" is the audible rendering of sentado para atras (set toward the rear). Because of the continuous flow and blend of the languages, there is little distance between the poet or audience and the subject or speaker. Except for a few vocabulary items, it is almost impossible to differentiate between contemporary Chicano Spanish and the pachuco's caló. Similarly the pachuco as a mythic or literary figure has become internalized into an immediate and personal frame of reference. Rather than the distant figures addressed in earlier works, the pachuco and his language have become extensions of self and participants in a common experience for the Chicano audience.

In conclusion, while it would be incorrect to state that the pachuco antihero has replaced the frontier epic hero in the Chicano literary imagination, there is no doubt that to a certain degree the advent of the twentieth century,

211

the Anglo American westering experience and all that it precipitated did make a decisive mark on the evolution of Chicano literature. Perhaps it would be most accurate to state that to the ranks of such morally unequivocal and culturally pure, frontier heroes are added the morally ambiguous and culturally divided, urban heroes of the American barrios--the pachuco.

University of Texas at Austin

NOTES

[1] Luis Valdez and Stan Steiner, Aztlan: An Anthology of Mexican American Literature (New York: Vintage Books, 1972).

[2] Valdez and Steiner, p. 42.

[3] Valdez and Steiner, pp. 43-44.

[4] Herminio Rios and Lupe Castillo, "Toward a True Chicano Bibliography," El Grito, 3, No. 4 (1970), 17-24.

[5] Herminio Rios, "Toward A True Chicano Bibliography--Part II," El Grito, 5, No. 4 (1972), 40-47.

[6] Américo Paredes, "With His Pistol in His Hand": A Border Ballad and Its Hero (Austin: University of Texas Press, 1958).

[7] Paredes, pp. 35-36.

[8] Carey McWilliams, "The Pattern of Violence" and "Blood on the Pavements," in North from Mexico (1949; rpt. New York: Greenwood, 1968), pp. 227-58; Octavio Paz, "The Pachuco and Other Extremes," in The Labyrinth of Solitude, trans. Lysander Kemp (New York: Evergreen, 1961), pp. 9-28; and George I. Sanchez, "Pachucos in the Making," Common Ground, 4 (1943), rpt. in Wayne Moquin and Mark Van Doren, eds., A Documentary History of the Mexican Americans (New York: Bantam, 1971), pp. 409-15.

[9] Beatrice Griffith, "The Pachuco Patois," Common Ground, 7 (Summer 1947), 77-84; George Carpenter Barker, Pachuco: An American-Spanish Argot and Its Social Functions in Tucson, Arizona (Tucson: Univ. of Arizona Press, 1950); and Arturo Madrid-Barela, "In Search of the Authentic Pachuco," Aztlan, 4, No. 1 (1973), 31-60.

[10] Jose Montoya, "Los Vatos," in El Espejo--The Mirror: Selected Mexican-American Literature, ed. Octavio I. Romano-V. (Berkeley: Quinto Sol, 1969), pp. 186-87.

[11] Tino Villanueva, Hay Otra Voz Poems (Staten Island: Editorial Mensaje: 1973), pp. 40-41.

[12] Villanueva, pp. 42-43.

"DIRECTIONALITY": THE COMPASS IN THE HEART

by John Ditsky

North, South, East and especially West: we are all too ready to reduce the literary--or, more generally, the cultural--significances of the compass points to concepts no less brief and simple than their names themselves: West, East, South, North. And if we live and write and read in terms of such associations, our actions in themselves affirm the value for us of such reductionist thinking. I would not challenge the validity of our racial compass--myths, the propriety with which we use our cultural directional signals, with any expectation of success. How could I, and to what ends? My point is otherwise; that the very automatic quality of our responses to notions of cardinal direction-points can often obscure the subtlety with which some writers attempt to reorder our assumptions, or undercut them through ironic usage.

I am interested in the geographic implications of works whose authors possess the requisite knowledge and sensitivity for creating extra dimensions for readers themselves possessed of similar attributes. For example, there is the way the daughters' marriages in King Lear graph onto the map of Britain not so much the fragmentation of an old man's kingdom as the psychic sundering of Lear himself--and the way those marriages even computer-project, by their triangulation, just which English husband Cordelia might have had had her play been comedy. Or take the way Edward Albee's Zoo Story shows that the only way that Jerry could bridge the gap between his West Side and Peter's East is by a sacrificial journey that draws something not unlike a cross upon Manhattan's map.

But if these examples suggest that an approach premised on mere ingenuity is about to be outlined here, let me correct that impression. I will be concerned less with the drawing of maps than with their mental presences--and with, especially, the way our culture (in "life" and literature both) responds to notions of specific directional movements. In other words, I am attempting to speak to the matter of the mental set that accompanies the words with which I began: North, South, East, and West: with directionality, to choose a word. What is the psychological adjustment that accompanies commitment to movement in a specific direction--whether that adjustment be logical or imaginative, far-fetched or even mistaken? Such a discussion, I need hardly maintain, will be necessarily premised on an arbitrary selection of materials, and just as necessarily tentative in the validity of its conclusions.

One culture thinks in terms of the East, and takes its emblem from the rising sun; content with this organically perpetual assurance of renewal, the Japanese were characterized for centuries by stasis--until a rude Prince Charming's kiss destroyed their presuppositions and made them race the sun

215

in an orgy first of violent territorial expansion followed by a no less wrenching economic aggrandisement.   Particle displaces particle; and though each one pursues its own conceived-of goals, the issue remains one of directionality. And on the other side of the Pacific, in 1976, the followers of Ronald Reagan seemed to think of the Panama Canal as the westward extension of Orange County; and in terms of time and cultural orientation, they were perfectly right. Again, the matter concerns directionality.

As we know quite well, North American culture is characterized by a singular commitment to the westering experience. Yet it is also by now a cultural truism to note that one great segment of that society, the Canadian, has developed not by holding to the American view of a moving frontier rather like a battlefront maintained against a stubborn but eventually succumging enemy, but instead by possessing the notion of being a series of pockets of civilization surrounded by hostile wilderness.   Hence, and not surprisingly, a siege mentality develops which Willa Cather rightly traces to the national foundation: a citadel, a Rock, Québec. The ancestral home of the French-Canadian imagination is a cabin around which snow swirls constantly--even if the cabin is in fact a moving sleigh or a house in town. One is surrounded by enemies of one's imaginings; and if all the nasty threatening foreigners turn out to be Canadians themselves, as they do in Margaret Atwood's Surfacing, that fact but demonstrates directionality as paranoia's source.

Small wonder that in so many contemporary Canadian books and films, the emphasis is on movement--any movement away--and on getting that ponderous solitude of self going down the road (there is usually only one road, and it leads Away From Here), such movement generally accompanied by sexual initiation of a prolonged and emphatic sort. One necessarily exaggerates in generalizing for the sake of an artificial clarity, I admit; and there are Winesburgs and Altamonts galore in the literature of the United States that exist mainly for the leaving. Yet I wonder whether the common American paradox that you can't go home again because you can't ever really leave operates with quite the desperate urgency it seems to assume in Canadian works, or even--as Joan Didion and others have inquired--whether going home again is any longer a relevant principle of American life. More generally, it is amusing to note that whereas once we sought to kill our bears (from Boone to Faulkner and Mailer), they now seek to enter our beds (Engel and Elkin); perhaps that change is the ultimate commentary on North American marriage, and the reason Huck sought to keep his honey on the raft.

But let me turn fully to the literature I am more competent to distort in the name of a unifying approach. If in Canadian writing the notion of the road, any road, as escape matches geography--a culture linear as a beaded string-- then in U.S. writing directionality, not extent of travel, assumes importance, and the linear journey itself may often evolve an unsatisfying sense of incompleteness.   Faulkner's Lena Grove has come a "fur piece, " but her journey westward has an interior, organic necessity to it; its motivation is not intellectually imposed. Steinbeck's Travels with Charley, on the other hand, represents the attempts to give circularity, and hence a sense of perfection, to both a journey and the career they are meant to epitomize; when the book loses heart in mid-course, its author scurries for home, for relative creative silence, and for death. Consistently in American writing, the journey of importance involves a linear directionality and a single goal. We do not follow the Bundrens "home" again, for what they knew no longer exists; we leave them their further motion can be posited from what has happened earlier, as we do the Joads. In other words, we see them last at the point of a crucial reorientation to life, as we do the protagonists of Bellow's Seize the Day and Ellison's Invisible Man. We may leave others, one must note, at the point of death, if that is the only course open to them.

Nor is the idea of the frontier itself quite the constant spur to westering we often take it for. The "Territory" that Huck Finn would light out for is a place of diminished responsibility to a corrupt social structure; while for the heroine of True Grit the Territory is a lawless place that wants, but seldom gets, a man of courage to establish Order. Huck's manhood is therefore in search of Territory the way a specimen requires a bell jar, for preservation's sake; while Portis's Mattie Ross ironically achieves a life-distorting sort of manhood there. Both Territories happen to be the West, but "frontier" can be anywhere; for James's Christopher Newman, it is the East of a settled Europe, while for the real-life Howells, it is the Eastern shore of the United States-- Boston and New York. For Mailer's D. J., it is the Alaskan North; while for the Civil Rights workers of the early Sixties, it was a violent South. "Frontier" is where you think it is, in time and space: the past, perhaps, or the Moon; it is wherever you externalize the challenge you define within you as the threshold of fuller existence. The westering experience is ultimately internal, then--like a spring-wound tape measure taking up its own extended length.

...Whence come those lovely ironies that are the glory of American writing. Take Melville's sea, as neutral a dish of culture in the biology lab, or as that wilderness around the Canadian community we spoke of earlier. That sea so peopled with leviathans is life, is death, is self-attainment: is the amniotic fluid to our post-Freudian mind. What does one's choice of "course," of route, then ultimately matter? For these are merely absurd reductions of a three- (or four-) dimensional sphere to a simplistic and deceptively straight line on a map.

Yet course, directionality, is relatively meaningful, once men imbue it with importance. It is, as Gatsby said in another context, only personal, but that is enough to make it worth studying. Take Huck Finn yet another time. Society and Tom turn eastward, toward repression in the name of legal order; Huck yearns westwardly to keep his law-defying selfhood whole. Between the two the River flows: time, event, and change. Jim the runaway would flee, of course, to freedom in the North--like the cast of Stowe's thriller--but life conspires to send him southward, "down the River," where history and Pudd'n- head Wilson tells us wait the worst of servitudes; yet irony of ironies, it is there he drops his chains at last. Of course, he has been free all along, but how else could Jim's narrative end relatively comically? For the potentially tragic implications of directionality in Huck Finn are terrifying to consider, and only the imposition of artifice rescues the novel from social horror.

In the symbolic melodrama on the same themes that is Ken Kesey's One
Flew Over the Cuckoo's Nest, on the other hand, refuge is the Canadian border
--if you are an Indian, a Type completing a national purpose of directionality
already delayed the better part of a century.   Presumably, if you are a white
man, your country of sanctuary is Death.   The theme of madness and sanity is
here reduced to the issue of necessary coercion to Order. and what was possible
to a Huck Finn or to a Jeffersonian Huck-of-a-nation in the previous century
now begins to appear as a bit of simplistic Peter Pan-fantasizing.   In all of
these instances, the mind is set on purposes which take on geographic import
and features; and what the soil and water do finally affirm in their configura-
tion is the alignment of the inner self.   The soul of the individual American
harkens after its private West like a needle charged and hanging from a thread ,
or like the leg of that other sort of compass Donne described.

But the lessons of our journeying are fraught with ironical discovery, as
they were for Columbus--who tested his round-world credo by empirical means
only to come to doubt its validity.   Such pioneers in the mythologizing of westering as R. W. B. Lewis and Leslie Fiedler hint at the conclusions available
from both classic and popular literatures: that we search for the Eden we have
been excluded from only to find that we have never left it, or it had never been.
As Herr C. says in Kleist's "On the Puppet Theatre," "But Paradise is barred
and the angel stands behind us; we have to go all the way around the world and
see if it might not be open again somewhere in the back."   Though East and
West are only apparently dichotomies, we identify our attainments as recover-
ies to justify the guilts inherent in our motivations.

When Steinbeck's The Red Pony acquired its fourth or westering chapter,
it became an adult novel as surely as if it had climbed aboard a raft; his Joads
seek Eden along the national lifeline, Route 66, and in their quickening of the
pioneer spirit demonstrate the defects of the American dream even as they
stand poised on the edge of discovering the revolutionary consciousness which
is its essence.   Directionality is fundamentally a reworking of that old cliché,
the Road of Life, in terms that are at least apparently acceptably logical and
reassuring of purpose. Therefore we hold to the notion that westering is futur-
ity, is promise, even though the sunset land--as Nathaniel West has shown us--
is in fact the next room to death and the western shore littered with the carcasses of hopes and populated with embittered old.   There is a century of bitter
experience and "achievement" between Thoreau's decision to do his traveling
in Concord and Jeffers' vigil for the end of urban man. Though such writers as
Ellen Glasgow occasionally use "westering" to mean the declining, deathward
years (In This Our Life, Avon. ed., p. 116), we ignore her logic and insist on
the quest for renewal and youth--keeping the Spanish explorer's commitment
alive with hormone shots of deliberate re-infancy, with one Disney empire for
Florida and another for California, thus chaining the children to the practically-
dead.

Thus we generalize about the Whitman of "Passage to India" and "A Broad-
way Pageant, "full of the optimism and attainment of westering, but conUni ently ignore the plaintive wondering evident in "Facing West from California's

Shores"--where the poet asks why he has not found what he set out for even though he has done what he wanted to do, gone where he wished. (Directionality can be a lemming-impulse as mindless as an electric locomotive grinding toy wheels against an obstacle; needless to say we usually mistake the activity for the purpose.) We are as perplexed as Carraway when, on behalf of his circle of westerners, he faces tragedy for daring to buck destiny by coming east, a boat against the current. Because the green breast of the New World, in Fitzgerald's image, constantly recedes before us as we move to possess it, we take our frustrated westering as absolute of virtuous activity, and thus identify its opposite as failure. Drive eastward along the Oregon Trail as I did a few months ago and you feel somehow unAmerican for moving against the tide, even as you gain the sense of time being wound upon its reel like fishing line. What else could the cyclists of Easy Rider do, once they had blown their chances, but ride to the East through the South to their deaths.

We kill the dreaming in the dream's pursuit; in wilderness, we seek Dominion--and get Condominium instead. We joke about the madness of "Lotusland," but do not like to think too much along the lines of the narrator of Wallace Stegner's new The Spectator Bird (pp. 109-10), who calls California "the western or suicide edge of the New World,"and asks what the westering experience was worth "if we end in confusion and purposelessness on the far Pacific shore of America, or come creeping back to our origins looking for something we have lost and can't name?" The paradox of our directionality in life is that it ends in mere extension; in art, that we devote ourselves because of it to finding words to fit an emptiness, and thus we end in silence. Or we arrive at an apparent form by means of Art, but does it satisfy?

If not, perhaps it is because we have created this our culture almost exclusively out of the matter of male intellectuality, a raw and rugged assertion of will like the firearm over the fireplace. Directionality's rough thrust is hardly adequate to base a culture on. That would require a harmonizing of East and West, male and female, and not a flight from the East's influence. John Steinbeck, who more than any other writer institutionalized the concept of "westering," wrote in The Grapes of Wrath of a westward quest that, seen simply as movement in a given direction, amounts to loss and failure, yet even as the remnants of the Joads are seen at last in a Sinai-state of disoriented wandering, they approach the recognition that a new social order is possible, a revolutionary realignment of potentialities and resources whose metaphor is Rose of Sharon's offered breast. Grandpa is buried in the sterile land back home, and Grandma lies in California soil; in their deaths, a kind of marriage of soils and natures takes place that is signified by a shuffling of sexual roles. Mere westering leads nowhere, but harmony and reconciliation are both the justification and the reward of their attaining. Like Steinbeck himself late in life, we can find our West buried in our own East.

Well, we are not likely to surrender the pleasures of the road that easily. We are not yet old enough to see that Oz, Omega=Zed, the End of the Road, is where we have always been; we are not yet ready to see Kansas as anything more than geographical dead center: the map of stasis, black-and-white. We long for tornados of spirit to whirl us skyward in our adolescence; that is our name, that storm, for we are Dorothy Gale. And there we will be heroes, slaying the Witch of the East at once, and in a most urban fashion (for that is how you slay your eastern witches: mugging them by dropping a house on them, while midgets cheer; killing western witches takes manipulating of natural forces, fatiguing travel, and much peril). And we would follow the road of gold with our friends, the harnessed powers of the animal, vegetable, and mineral kingdoms--conquering en route the poppy fields of unambition and surviving the San Simeon/Xanadu/San Clemente of sheer frightful, misused power. Then on to the heavenly city green as Daisy's voice, where we'll learn doubt and self-reliance as technology runs off with providence. And at the end we will come back to Kansas, Zen-content.

But that is a fairy tale. Now, still, there is "reality"--the literary prairie girlhood Willa Cather painted, where somewhere on the high plateau the wheel ruts confirm the myth of westering and beckon, and command.

University of Windsor

CONTRIBUTORS' NOTES

GEORGE M. ARMSTRONG, instructor in English at Washington State University, is interested in 20th century Western American history and literature, wrote his dissertation on H. L. Davis (University of California, Berkeley), has published several articles on Davis, and is presently writing a book on Loren Eiseley.

ANTHONY ARTHUR, who received his Ph. D. from SUNY, Stony Brook, has published articles on 19th century British poetry and fiction, on children's literature, and on teaching. He recently completed two papers on Frederick Manfred's Conquering Horse and Scarlet Plume.

ROBERT M. BENTON is Professor of English at Central Washington University. His journal publications include American Literature, Early American Literature, Bulletin of the New York Public Library, and Steinbeck Quarterly; his essays are included in four books of Steinbeck criticism and in American Literature, 1764-1789, The Revolutionary Years. Benton is currently working on the frontier hero and, for Summer, 1977, was a NEH Fellow at UC, Davis.

JACK BRENNER teaches in the English Department at the University of Washington. His book on Western fiction, The Life of Significant Soil, will be published shortly.

MARTIN BUCCO is Professor of English at Colorado State University. His books include The Voluntary Tongue, Frank Waters, Wilbur Daniel Steele, and E. W. Howe. At present he is working on a second book for Twayne, René Wellek.

RICHARD COLE has taught English at the University of California, where he has been a graduate student. He is working on his first collection of poems. The poem "North American Primer" first appeared in Concerning Poetry.

JACK L. DAVIS, an Associate Professor of American Studies at the University of Idaho, has published numerous articles and reviews in such journals as New England Quarterly, Western American Literature, American Indian Quarterly, South Dakota Review, ESQ, and others. His principal interest is the impact of the American Indian upon our national culture and literature, and he is currently working up a book, The Clash of Cultures, on that subject.

221

ROBERT GLEN DEAMER is an Assistant Professor of English at Thiel College. His main interest is in American myths of region as they are dramatized in the lives and writings of American authors. He has written on "Stephen Crane and the Western Myth" (Summer, 1972, Western American Literature).

JOHN DITSKY is Professor of English at the University of Windsor, Ontario, where he teaches American Literature and Modern Drama. He has written some forty critical articles for such journals as Georgia Review and Queen's Quarterly, and is a Steinbeck specialist. His poems have been widely published.

CARLOTA CÁRDENAS DE DWYER is an Assistant Professor in the Department of English at the University of Texas at Austin. She has published an anthology of Chicano literature. As a recent recipient of a post-doctoral fellowship, she is completing her manuscript, Contemporary Chicano Literature: The Flowering of the Southwest, a critical study.

WAYNE FRANKLIN is Associate Professor of English at the University of Iowa, where he teaches American literature of the colonial and early periods. He has published several articles on writers and topics in those fields, and is completing three books at the present time: one on the early American travel narrative, one on the frontier in James Fenimore Cooper, and one on the historian John Lothrop Motley for the Twayne U. S. Authors Series.

ROBERT F. GISH is an associate professor of English at the University of Northern Iowa where he teaches British and American literature. His writing has appeared in such journals as Modern Fiction Studies, English Literature in Transition, and the Virginia Woolf Quarterly. He reviews occasionally for the North American Review and The Christian Science Monitor. His Hamlin Garland: the Far West is number 24 in Boise State University's Western Writers Series.

DICK HARRISON was born in Alberta and has spent most of his life in the West. After a Ph.D. at the University of Western Ontario, he came West to the University of Alberta where he been teaching Canadian Literature for ten years. He has published in various journals on the subject, and has a book entitled Unnamed Country: The Struggle for a Canadian Prairie Fiction in press with the University of Alberta Press.

KENNETH INNISS is an Associate Professor of English at Western Washington University, Bellingham. The author of D. H. Lawrence's Bestiary: A Study of His Use of Animal Trope and Symbol (The Hague, 1971), his interests include Canadian and Commonwealth Literature. He is presently engaged in a study of fables of identity in the literature of his native West Indies.

WILLIAM LOCKWOOD, who recently spent a sabbatical year living in New Mexico, is an Associate Professor of English at the University of Michigan

--Flint. He is at work on a book on contemporary American poets entitled A Landscape of New World Poets.

KENNETH A. REQUA, Assistant Professor of English at the University of Washington, has published several essays on American literature and is currently at work on a study of seventeenth and early eighteenth century American poetry.

JAMIE ROBERTSON is a Ph.D. candidate in American Studies at the University of New Mexico. His dissertation is "The Dream of Westering and the Vision of Place: Studies in the Literature and Art of the American West." Forthcoming in Western American Literature is "Stephen Crane, Eastern Outsider in the West and Mexico," and in New America: A Review, "Photography in the Southwest to 1912: An Annotated Bibliography." He is a Fulbright Junior Lecturer in American Studies at the University of Barcelona, Spain for 1977-78.

FRANK SADLER's article on Edward Dorn was first printed in Concerning Poetry. He has also published articles on Stephen Crane (American Literature) and "Relativity and the Universe of Fiction" (West Georgia College Review); his poems have appeared in various journals.

PETER STEVENS, Professor of English at the University of Windsor, Ontario, has published many articles on Canadian literature in various journals and books, including Literature of the World in English (Routledge, Kegan Paul) and Supplement to the Oxford Companion to Canadian History and Literature (O. U. P.). He has edited collections of and about Canadian literature including The McGill Movement (McGraw Hill--Ryerson), Forum (University of Toronto Press) and Raymond Knister: The First Day of Spring (University of Toronto Press). He has published nine volumes of his own poetry, the last of which is The Bogman Pavese Tactics (Fiddlehead Books).

DON D. WALKER, Professor of English at the University of Utah, has published innumerable essays on western literature, western history, and western historiography over the past twenty years as well as short stories using western motifs. One of his most recent essays is "Criticism of the Cowboy Novel: Retrospect and Reflections," in Western American Literature, XI (Feb. 1977).

MAX WESTBROOK teaches English at the University of Texas. Publications include essays on Stephen Crane, Ernest Hemingway, criticism, and Western American literature. He is the author of Walter Van Tilburg Clark and editor (with William J. Handy) of Twentieth Century Criticism.

ANDREW WIGET completed his doctorate in June, 1977, at the University of Utah where he was both a Teaching Fellow in the English Department

223

and a Research Assistant at the American West Center working on a traditional Navajo history. His primary research and teaching interests are Native American oral literature and the literature of culture contact. He has published reviews and articles in _Folklore Forum_, _Quarterly West_, and _American Indian Quarterly_.

SUSAN WOOD is an assistant professor of English at the University of British Columbia, where she teaches Canadian literature and, sometimes, science fiction and fantasy. She even managed to combine both interests in a paper, "The Martian Point of View," on the poetry of Margaret Atwood. In her dissertation on English and French Canadian fiction for the University of Toronto, an introduction to Robert Stead's _The Homesteaders_, and other publications, she examines the relationship between literature and the society which produced it.

Merrill Lewis, professor of English and Director of American Studies at Western Washington University, is co-author of *Wallace Stegner* (BSU Western Writers Series). He has published essays on George Bancroft, Frederick Jackson Turner, and Theodore Roosevelt as well as on western fiction and criticism.

L.L. Lee, professor of English at Western Washington University, is the author of *Vladimir Nabokov* (Twayne) and *Walter Van Tilburg Clark* (BSU Western Writers Series). He is also editor of *Concerning Poetry*.

$4.95